Contrasting Decades:
The 1920's and 1930's

Inquiries into American History

Our Colonial Heritage: Plymouth and Jamestown
by William Gee White

The Middle Colonies: New York, New Jersey, Pennsylvania
by James I. Clark

The American Revolution
by D. Duane Cummins and William Gee White

The Federal Period: 1790–1800
by Lloyd K. Musselman

Andrew Jackson's America
by Thomas Koberna and Stanley Garfinkel

The American Frontier
by D. Duane Cummins and William Gee White

The Origins of the Civil War
by D. Duane Cummins and William Gee White

Reconstruction: 1865–1877
by James I. Clark

Industrialism: The American Experience
by James E. Bruner, Jr.

American Foreign Policy: 1789–1980
by Thomas A. Fitzgerald, Jr.

Contrasting Decades: The 1920's and 1930's
by D. Duane Cummins and William Gee White

Combat and Consensus: The 1940's and 1950's
by D. Duane Cummins and William Gee White

Conflict and Compromise: The 1960's and 1970's
by D. Duane Cummins

America at War: World War I and World War II
by Douglas Waitley

America at War: Korea and Vietnam
by Douglas Waitley

Women in American History
by William Jay Jacobs

Contrasting Decades: The 1920's and 1930's

D. Duane Cummins
William Gee White

Glencoe Publishing Company
Encino, California

REVISED EDITION

Copyright © 1980 by Glencoe Publishing Company, a division of Macmillan, Inc.
Copyright © 1972 by Benziger, Inc.

Glencoe Publishing Company
17337 Ventura Boulevard
Encino, California 91316

Library of Congress Catalog Card Number: 72-81696

Printed in the United States of America

ISBN 0-02-652900-9

3 4 5 6 7 8 9   88 87 86 85

To
VIRGINIA

CONTENTS

INTRODUCTION

In one sense, the 1920's and 1930's were significantly different decades in U.S. history. The years 1920 to 1929 are generally considered to be economically prosperous, politically placid, and socially kinky in a harmless sort of way. In the political sphere at least, a parallel is often drawn between the twenties and the Eisenhower fifties: both periods, it is said, were characterized by modest, popular, easy-going, and conservative presidents. We shall see, however, that despite "prosperity" and the Harding "normalcy," the 1920's had their share of political passion, if not hysteria. It will be seen that such twentyish problems as Red scares, prohibition, and monkey trials had features that have by no means disappeared from the American scene.

The thirties are, on the other hand, frequently characterized as an "action" decade—great problems were faced head-on by a vigorous, reform-minded president, the nation was lifted out of confusion and despair, and the political, economic, and social scaffolding of the United States was remade and left more resilient and stable than ever before. We shall see that this view is also subject to some modification or at least challenge.

Needless to say, a great deal was going on in the 1920's and 1930's—both in America and in the world—that has no place in the main story this book has chosen to tell. For this reason, it might be useful to try to place the American

The photograph on the opposite page shows Fifth Avenue in New York City, about 1920.

9

twenties and thirties in a broader historical perspective. If we do this, we soon run into what many observers have considered the central and most bitter paradox of our age.

Governmentally, the twentieth century has been a disaster. Governments have, as a matter of policy, engaged in widescale destruction of lives and property. The twentieth century has seen many such acts of destruction—among others, the Soviet government deliberately starving to death millions of its people to pay for heavy industry, the Nazi extermination policy, the Allied fire-bombing of civilian populations in Europe and Asia, the atomic bombing of Hiroshima and Nagasaki. And although the effects of the more than ten years of American military activity in Indochina have yet to be assessed, future historians will probably regard them as among the most destructive of the century. One commentator, looking around him at what was left of Europe after World War II, said that the twentieth century would be known as the century of rubble.

And yet, in roughly the same period, from 1905 to 1945, a magnificent work of *construction* was also taking place. There was a fabulous outpouring in the arts and sciences, an outpouring so immense and varied that its true dimensions have yet to be accurately measured. It is likely that the European Renaissance of the fourteenth, fifteenth, and sixteenth centuries will ultimately pale in comparison with the renaissance brought forth by the first half of the twentieth.

In 1905, while the Russians and Japanese were killing each other over Manchuria, a German-born clerk in the Swiss Patent Office published some of the most important and exciting contributions ever made to human thought. The clerk's name was Albert Einstein. In 1918, as hundreds of thousands of corpses rotted along the Marne, Marcel Proust published the second volume of what was to become one of the grandest works in all of imaginative literature—*Remembrance of Things Past.* In 1939, as the German government turned for the moment from savaging its own people and began its beastly tour through Poland, the greatest English poet since William Shakespeare did his last work and died. The physical remains of William

In 1905, Albert Einstein published four brief journal articles, three of which rocked the world of theoretical physics.

Butler Yeats could not be moved from a small town in France to their final resting place at Drumcliffe, county Sligo, Ireland, until World War II had finished stamping on the decent works and lives of men; but while this war will in time become a despicable curiosity, some of the Yeats poems will be praised as long as men read.

And so it went, in the dance, in psychology, in philosophy, in music, in architecture, in literature, in physics, in medicine, in painting, in history, in sports, in astronomy, in sculpture—in every field of worthy human endeavor there was greatness. Not since the Elizabethan dramatists had a popular form of entertainment produced so many great works of art as did the movie industry during the first forty-five years of its life. The films of D. W. Griffith, Chaplin, Keaton, the Marx brothers, Eisenstein, Jean Renoir, Carl Dreyer, Orson Welles, John Huston, John Ford—these films will be consulted as long as the filmic art is practiced. The great\actors and actresses who worked in these films will be studied and admired just as intensely as the lives and utterances of the world leaders who were their contemporaries. Out of the twenties and thirties also came a great popular music-making—jazz, the blues,

MUSEUM OF MODERN ART, FILM STILLS ARCHIVE

Charlie Chaplin in his 1925 silent film, *The Gold Rush*.

Edna St. Vincent Millay.

swing, tin-pan alley. The music—and the artists who created or performed it—still give pleasure.

American artists, scientists, and men of letters contributed significantly to the twentieth-century renaissance. In the realm of high culture, America produced at least four poets of world stature—Wallace Stevens, Ezra Pound, Robert Frost, and T. S. Eliot—as well as a host of such fine though narrower talents as William Carlos Williams, Hart Crane, e. e. cummings, Langston Hughes, Edna St. Vincent Millay, and John Crowe Ransom. Major novelists active in the twenties and thirties included William Faulkner, F. Scott Fitzgerald, and Ernest Hemingway; during the same period, good books came from Horace McCoy (*They Shoot Horses, Don't They?*), Pearl Buck, Nathanael West, Sherwood Anderson, James T. Farrell, Theodore Dreiser, Sinclair Lewis, John Steinbeck, Richard Wright, John Dos Passos, Willa Cather, John O'Hara, Thomas Wolfe, George Santayana (*The Last Puritan*), and Margaret Mitchell (*Gone With the Wind*).

It was also a rich time for dramatic and musical theater —from Eugene O'Neill, Clifford Odets, Thornton Wilder, Lillian Hellman, and Maxwell Anderson to the marvelous comedies of Moss Hart and George S. Kaufman, Jerome Kern's *Showboat*, Rogers and Hammerstein's *Oklahoma!*, and Cole Porter's *Anything Goes*.

American painters active in the 1920's and 1930's included Thomas Hart Benton, Edward Hopper, Georgia O'Keeffe, Reginald Marsh, Ben Shahn, Grant Wood, Andrew Wyeth, and Lyonel Feininger. In the thirties under the sheltering wing of WPA-funded artists' projects, painters who later would become world-renowned began their apprenticeships—Jackson Pollock, Willem de Kooning, and Ad Reinhardt, among others.

Among the popular artists and performers who enriched American life in the twenties and thirties, many are still deeply cherished. Billie Holiday, Bessie Smith, Duke Ellington, Fletcher Henderson, Louis Armstrong, Bix Biederbecke, Jack Teagarden, Ma Rainey, Frank Sinatra, Hoagy Carmichael, Artie Shaw, Joe Oliver, Ethel Merman, Ella Fitzgerald, Gene Krupa, Harry James, Benny

Goodman, Ethel Waters, Tommy Dorsey, Jelly Roll Morton, Fats Waller, Bing Crosby, Eddy Duchin, Count Basie —these are but a few great names in a veritable galaxy of talent. To these names there should perhaps be added that of Marian Anderson, whose magnificent contralto voice went begging in this country during the twenties and thirties. Such a voice had not been heard since Madame Schumann-Heink in her prime at the turn of the century, and its true home was the operatic stage. But she had to go to Europe for that, where people listened to the voice and cared less about the color of her skin. Even in 1939, the Daughters of the American Revolution refused to let her sing at their Constitution Hall in Washington, D.C. Secretary of the Interior Harold Ickes, with the full public support of Eleanor Roosevelt, arranged for an open-air concert on the steps of the Lincoln Memorial. Seventy-five thousand people came to hear Marian Anderson sing. She was fifty-three years old before she appeared on the stage of the Metropolitan Opera in New York City—by then her voice, though still lovely, was no longer in its prime.

Marian Anderson. Her recital performances, especially of Negro spirituals and German lieder, will not be forgotten by those who heard them.

It is likely that an accurate social portrait of the twenties and thirties can be reconstructed from the popular media entertainments—from radio, movies, and mass magazines and their advertisements. But it will inevitably be a complex and composite portrait. In the thirties, for example, radio came of age, and brought with it a gaggle of soap operas, many of which are still going strong today. The "soaps," then and now, have an intimate connection with the quality of people's lives, and represent a huge and largely untapped resource in the sociological sense. Orson Welles' first major job in radio was as the voice of Lamont Cranston, "The Shadow"; his radio career came to a temporary halt in 1938 when his Mercury Theater of the Air presented a dramatization of H. G. Wells' *War of the Worlds*. It was a broadcast that panicked thousands of listeners, who believed that they were hearing about an actual invasion by Martians; some had to be prevented from killing themselves before the Martians got them, and

Radio comedians Freeman Gosden and Charles Correll broadcasting their "Amos 'n' Andy" show.

Rudolph Valentino.

W. C. Fields.

others set fire to their homes in the belief that the fires would stop the advancing Martians.

Radio brought into American homes Amos 'n' Andy, Fibber McGee and Molly, Edgar Bergen and Charlie McCarthy, Kate Smith, Jack Benny, and the Lone Ranger; at the same time, as many as ten million families also listened to the Saturday matinee broadcasts of the Metropolitan Opera and to NBC's Symphony of the Air, with Arturo Toscanini conducting. Every year Lionel Barrymore would read Dickens' *A Christmas Carol*, and listening to it was a Christmas ritual in countless American homes. Beginning in the late thirties, competent reporters like Edward R. Murrow and William Shirer began to broadcast their stories.

In the silent-screen twenties, stars like Rudolph Valentino, Greta Garbo, Lillian Gish, John Barrymore, Douglas Fairbanks, Ramon Navarro, Clara Bow, Mary Pickford, Tom Mix, Lon Chaney, Charlie Chaplin, Buster Keaton, and Harold Lloyd caused audiences to swoon, shudder, or laugh. Cecil B. De Mille produced spectaculars like *The Ten Commandments*, D. W. Griffith made *Orphans of the Storm*, King Vidor did *Big Parade*, and Eric von Stroheim made *Greed*.

In the talking thirties, stars like Clark Gable, Leslie Howard, Paul Muni, Edward G. Robinson, William Powell, James Stewart, John Wayne, Errol Flynn, Gary Cooper, Humphrey Bogart, Spencer Tracy, Henry Fonda, James Cagney, Vivien Leigh, Greta Garbo, Joan Crawford, Bette Davis, Katharine Hepburn, and Claudette Colbert played in all sorts of films—romantic melodramas, grimly serious works like *I Am a Fugitive from a Chain Gang*, gangster flicks, and swashbucklers. Some of these films were awful, and some of them were very good indeed. There were the sophisticated adult comedies of Ernst Lubitsch and Frank Capra; there were the broader comedies featuring W. C. Fields and Mae West, the Marx brothers, and Laurel and Hardy. There were the classic horror flicks with Bela Lugosi as Count Dracula and Boris Karloff as Frankenstein; there was *King Kong*, in 1932. There were pasty "singing" Westerns with Gene Autry, but there was also

John Ford's *Stagecoach*. There were spectacular musicals by Busby Berkeley, and other musicals built around the song-and-dance team of Fred Astaire and Ginger Rogers; there was Shirley Temple, the top box office draw from 1935 to 1938, replaced in 1939 and 1940 by Mickey Rooney as "Andy Hardy"; there was the 1920's swimming star Johnny Weissmuller grunting the classic camp line "Me Tarzan, You Jane," and there was also *Petrified Forest*, *The Informer*, and Chaplin's *Modern Times* and *City Lights*. In the last two years of the decade, as the world went downhill, there was Walt Disney's *Snow White and the Seven Dwarfs, Goodbye, Mr. Chips, The Wizard of Oz*, and *Gone With the Wind*.

Johnny Weissmuller, Olympic gold medalist who was never beaten in any free-style race, went on to be one of the more durable of the screen Tarzans.

The rich and varied movie fare of the thirties has often been called "escapist," as well it might be. But before we wave away this "escapist" corpus, we should perhaps ask what the wielders of economic and political power—the industrialists, the newspaper owners, the bankers, the congressmen, the presidents—had provided in *their* line of work. Apart from their role in creating or perpetuating conditions that anybody would want to escape from, one of their direct contributions to the film industry was a philistine clamor that resulted in the vigorous enforcement in 1934 of a Production Code, a censorship package that cut off large areas of the American life from realistic treatment, and drove some of the most perceptive and talented film-makers into comedy and musicals.

Films like *Snow White* and *The Wizard of Oz* may not seem very substantial contributions to American culture. But these films were joyful, sane artifacts. They appealed to their audiences in terms of what people shared—a sense of humor, sentiment, delight in form or color; to achieve their effects, such films did not call upon the passions and interests that divided people. These films not only built upon but also richly rewarded the human capacity for warmth and laughter. It remains to be seen if the same things can be said of their historical time.

Ray Bolger, Judy Garland, and Bert Lahr in the 1939 film, *The Wizard of Oz*.

The new prosperity held certain perils, as this 1922 traffic jam on Michigan Avenue in Chicago demonstrates.

CHAPTER ONE

PROSPERITY

The chief business of the American people is business.

CALVIN COOLIDGE

The end of World War I brought certain economic problems with which the nation was ill-prepared to deal. When peace came abruptly in November, 1918, nine million people were employed in war-related industries, four million men were in the armed forces, and no serious thought had been given to the problems of demobilization and reconversion to a peacetime economy. Responding to the demands of a public sickened by war and all things military, the government of Woodrow Wilson demobilized nearly all of the four million servicemen within a year, even though no adequate means for absorbing these men into the economic life of the country had been provided. In the same way, the government simply cancelled all war contracts outright, leaving the nation's industrial complex to survive on its own. The effects of these policies, on an economy already inflated by war, were not long in coming—spiraling prices, tightened credit, a rash of bankruptcies, and rising unemployment. By 1919, the cost of living was ninety-nine percent higher than it had been five years before. Employment held up fairly well until 1920, then took a dive. When Warren G. Harding assumed the presidency in 1921, the number of unemployed workers was 4.5 million, three times what it had been at the end of the war.

17

The Technological Revolution

By 1922, the country had begun to recover from the postwar depression. Then, with the results of half a century of industrial progress and invention to build on, the nation proceeded to achieve an unprecedented level of prosperity that was maintained until the autumn of 1929. This prosperity, in the opinion of economists, was brought about by the explosive growth of manufacturing that occurred during the period. Underlying the enormous increase in industrial output was a revolution in industrial management and technology, as the historian Arthur Link has pointed out:

> Of all the causes of America's industrial development in the twentieth century, the technological revolution was the most basic and therefore most significant, for the mass production age could never have come without the techniques it afforded.[1]

The automobile industry provided a dramatic example of the efficiency resulting from scientific management and the use of new technology on the production line. In 1913, it took fourteen hours to assemble an automobile. One year later, after the introduction of the moving assembly line, the time had been reduced to ninety-three minutes. By 1929, most major industries had converted to electricity. The machine, the factory, and standardized production came into their own in the 1920's.

The effects of the technological revolution were far-reaching. Although the physical output of American industry nearly doubled during the decade, there was no expansion in the labor force. By 1929, fifty-one workers could produce as much as eighty-four workers ten years earlier. Manufacturing offered the same number of jobs in 1929 as it had in 1919. In addition, work loads were lightened. United States Steel introduced the eight-hour work day, a radical departure from the traditional twelve-

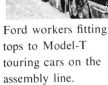

Ford workers fitting tops to Model-T touring cars on the assembly line.

UNITED PRESS INTERNATIONAL

---

[1] Arthur S. Link, *American Epoch: A History of the United States Since the 1890's*, 3 vols. (New York: Alfred A. Knopf, 1967), 2:258.

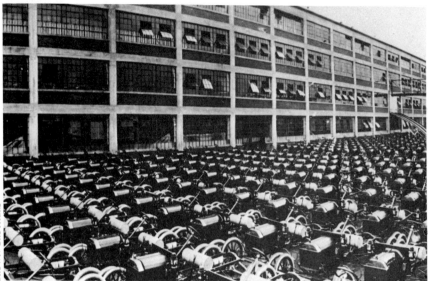

BROWN BROTHERS

Arrayed about the Ford factory at Highland Park, Michigan, are one thousand Model-T chassis, a single day's output in 1913–1914. The Model-T was both rugged and inexpensive, characteristics which led to the joke that a Ford could go anywhere—except in society.

hour shift. Just as radical was Ford's five-day work week, and the most stunning innovation of all was International Harvester's two-week paid vacation.

The business boom had captured America and large portions of the general public were able to enjoy lower prices, higher wages, and more leisure time than ever before—as well as an astonishing variety of new products to make life easier and more interesting. Many people in the 1920's felt that they were living in an age of miracles, an age in which anything was possible. The technological revolution generated not only material prosperity but also an unbounded faith in the future as described by the economic historians Charles and Mary Beard:

> The most common note of assurance was belief in unlimited
> progress . . . a faith in the efficacy of that new and
> mysterious instrument of the modern mind, "the invention
> of invention," moving from one technological triumph to

another, overcoming the exhaustion of crude natural resources and energies, effecting an even wider distribution of the blessings of civilization—health, security, material goods, knowledge, leisure, and aesthetic appreciation. . . .[2]

The Age of the Flivver

Before and after pictures showing the same road in 1914 and 1915.

The historian William Leuchtenburg has remarked that without the automobile industry the prosperity of the Roaring Twenties would scarcely have been possible. The "horseless carriage" stimulated enormous growth in the rubber, nickel, lead, petroleum, and steel industries. After automobiles were enclosed with permanent windows and better tops and doors, similar growth occurred in the glass, leather, and textile industries. Equally important, automobile production put pressure on government at all levels to begin extensive programs of road construction. By 1928, a driver could travel paved roads from New York to Kansas. Along these highways were hot-dog stands, garages, filling stations, tourist shops, guest houses, billboards—all new industries sparked by the automobile. The increased mobility afforded by the motor car helped to produce a suburban housing boom. Altogether, more money was spent and more men were employed in road and building construction than in any other single private industry, and the principal reason for that construction was the automobile. Accompanying these economic changes were profound changes in the living habits and social attitudes of millions of people. The automobile was one of the primary causes of the social revolution that happened in the United States during the 1920's.

At first, the motor car made more enemies than friends —it was too noisy and too fast for a generation geared to the easy pace of the horse. Keith Sward, in *The Legend of Henry Ford*, described the hostility encountered by the earliest "gasoline buggies":

... The first American cars, built entirely by hand, were so expensive they were beyond the reach of the average

[2] Charles A. and Mary R. Beard, *The Rise of American Civilization*, rev. ed. (New York: Macmillan Co., 1933), p. 800.

BROWN BROTHERS

citizen. Thus for a decade the automobile failed to displace the horse because, as Duryea [a pioneer automobile manufacturer] once put it, "Oats were too cheap." Furthermore, the early models were utterly undependable. Breakdowns were the rule. . . .

The antagonisms toward America's first gasoline buggies are reflected in the laws and journals of the period. In 1899 the town of San Rafael, California, had an ordinance which required the driver of an automobile to come to a dead stop within three hundred feet of every passing horse. A year later Vermont was enforcing a statute which compelled every motorist in motion to employ "a person of mature age" to walk ahead of him one-eighth of a mile, bearing a red flag in his hand. The speed limit within the city limits of Savannah, Cincinnati and San Francisco in 1902 was eight miles per hour. By act of city council, motorists at this time were barred from the parkways of most of the country's larger cities. An "automobileer" who defied such an ordinance in Chicago in 1902 was arrested for "riot, disturbance and breach of the peace."[3]

Garages and billboards. Apartment houses did not have underground parking, so garages were built on nearby lots.

The twin concepts of interchangeable parts and mass production, introduced to the auto industry by Ransom E. Olds and expertly applied by Henry Ford, increased production rates at a fantastic pace. This made more cars available and brought prices down. In 1919, only one of every sixteen people owned an automobile. By 1929, with the industry producing 4,800,000 cars a year, one person of every five was a car owner. The automobile entered into the everyday life of the country, strengthening the growing addiction to comfort, leisure, and what the sociologist Thorstein Veblen called "conspicuous consumption." It was a favorite topic of idle conversation, and the man who couldn't distinguish a Model-A from a Pierce-Arrow was considered eccentric. During the 1920's, the automobile became the symbol of the American standard of living. In *Only Yesterday*, Frederick Lewis Allen remarked:

[3] Keith Sward, *The Legend of Henry Ford* (New York: Atheneum, 1968), pp. 5–6. Copyright 1948 by Keith Sward. Reprinted by permission of Holt, Rinehart and Winston, Inc.

A gas station before 1920, in Newark, New Jersey.

In 1919 there had been 6,771,000 passenger cars in service in the United States; by 1929 there were no less than 23,121,000. There you have possibly the most potent statistic of Coolidge Prosperity. As a footnote to it I suggest the following. Even as early as the end of 1923 there were two cars for every three families in "Middletown," a typical American city. The Lynds and their [sociological] investigators interviewed 123 working-class families of "Middletown" and found that 60 of them had cars. Of these 60, 26 lived in such shabby-looking houses that the investigators thought to ask whether they had bathtubs, and discovered that as many as 21 of the 26 had none. The automobile came even before the tub![4]

TEXACO ARCHIVE, INC.

In that same year, 1923, one of every 43 persons owned a car in Britain, one of 325 in Italy, and one of 7,000 in Russia.

The basic technology and raw materials necessary for the manufacture of automobiles had been developed long before the automobile itself, and when the demand came the nation's industries were ready to meet it. Keith Sward wrote of the 1890's:

A later gas station, with self-measuring pumps instead of cans for dispensing gas.

The land was rich in steel and oil. Rockefeller's work was all but finished. Ten years earlier, S. F. Bowser had invented a self-measuring oil pump, the forerunner of the modern filling station. By 1890 the United States was producing more than one-third of the world's annual tonnage of iron and steel. The 90's brought Andrew Carnegie's career to a close. Likewise in this decade the pioneers of the American automobile could draw on the experience of a mature rubber industry. Goodyear had vulcanized rubber twenty years before the Civil War. Hard rubber tires had been used on horse-drawn vehicles since the 50's. And the principle of the pneumatic valve, which made possible the air-filled tire of the American bicycle of the 90's, had been conceived by August

BROWN BROTHERS

[4] Frederick Lewis Allen, *Only Yesterday* (New York: Harper & Row, Perennial Library, 1964), p. 136. Copyright 1931 by Frederick Lewis Allen, 1959 by Agnes Rogers Allen. By permission of Harper & Row, Publishers.

Schroeder half a century before the invention of the automobile. . . . Most of the fundamental factory appliances like the jig and the crane, and most of the basic machine tools—the pneumatic drill, the air-hammer, the turret lathe and other power machinery for molding and milling and grinding—had become standard equipment. . . . Among the assets which made America of all the semi-industrialized nations best suited for the development of the automobile was the most extensive railroad system in the world, the largest self-contained population—hence, the largest body of potential users of the automobile and the greatest reaches of sheer space.[5]

Henry Ford in the first car he built, his "quadricycle."

Chief architect of the automobile industry's success was Henry Ford. He built his first automobile in the 1890's, founded the Ford Motor Company in 1903, and created the famous Model-T in 1909. Sometimes called the "Flivver King," he was one of the most respected personalities in America, and to many people a folk hero. One group of college students voted him the third greatest figure of all time, surpassed only by Napoleon Bonaparte and Jesus Christ. A British tourist remarked, "Just as in Rome one goes to the Vatican and endeavors to get audience of the Pope, so in Detroit one goes to the Ford Works and endeavors to see Henry Ford." Early in 1923, both major parties boomed "Ford for President," and in a poll conducted by *Collier's Weekly* he ranked ahead of President Harding by eight to five, leading Harding even in the president's home state of Ohio. So great was the nation's confidence in Henry Ford that when the Model-A was announced in 1928, half a million people made down payments without seeing the car or knowing the price.

Why did Henry Ford inspire such admiration? It was partly because he brought the automobile to the masses. The car that cost $950 in 1909, when the average annual income of a factory worker was $518, had been reduced to $360 by 1916. In 1914, Ford began to pay his employees five dollars a day, then an unheard-of wage and

[5] Sward, *Henry Ford*, pp. 4–5.

UNITED PRESS INTERNATIONAL

Women workers sorting parts for use on the assembly line at a Ford plant.

one that allowed a worker to buy the product he assembled. Ford's policy of high wages, low prices, and technological efficiency made him a symbol of the promise of material abundance.

People were also impressed by Ford's Horatio Alger success story—from lowly mechanic to captain of industry. His stature as an individualist was reinforced by his independent financing and his denunciations of "Wall Street bankers." One historian called him "the last Populist." The facts that his business was family-owned, that he distrusted and constantly opposed labor unions, that he hated Jews, Catholics, and tobacco, that he collected McGuffey readers, were approved by many people and contributed to his popularity in a Puritan-capitalist society. But these qualities did not endear him to everybody, and they may have had their darker side, as William Greenleaf has suggested:

By 1925, . . . there was substantial evidence of a disparity between the public image of Ford as a machine-age innovator, far-seeing benefactor, folk hero, and culture symbol, and, on the other side, the comparatively unfamiliar reality of Ford as an industrial despot and a pathetically ill-informed bigot in many fields outside his immediate interests.[6]

Henry Ford was the last great example of the self-made man, the personal ruler of an industrial empire. He gave the nation a cheap, reliable car. But he ruthlessly applied the speed-up on his assembly lines. He played off suppliers and dealers against each other and condoned the use of dictatorial tactics to keep them in line. As rumors of these practices began to circulate, Ford's popularity declined. In 1927, *Harper's Monthly Magazine* published an article entitled "Confessions of a Ford Dealer." It revealed some interesting things about how Ford automobiles were sold:

A 1927 cartoon showing the Ford hen about to hatch her new model— the Model-A.

. . . When Mr. Ford says business cannot control or force the demand I can't quite think he means it. Or maybe it's his little joke. You *can* force demand if you ride people hard enough. And, believe me, you have only to get on the inside of a Ford agency to learn how.

. . . When I first took the agency I was my own boss like any other business man, selling as many cars as I could and buying more when I needed them. I didn't have to make many sales on installments, because people who wanted cars usually saved up in advance and had the cash in hand when they got ready to buy. Occasionally some man that I knew would want a little time, in which case I just charged it the same as if it was a bill of dry goods or groceries, and when the account fell due he paid me. There was no such thing then as putting a mortgage on the car and taking it away from him if he didn't pay up. If I didn't believe a man was honest I simply didn't give him credit.

I did a pretty good business this way and by 1916 was selling an average of about ten cars a month. Then one day a representative of the company came to see me. . . .

---

[6] In ibid., preface. Preface copyright © 1968 by William Greenleaf. Reprinted by permission of Atheneum Publishers.

This man that I call Benson came into my place at the time I speak of and said that ten cars a month was not enough for a dealer like me to sell. It seems the Company had made a survey of my territory and decided that the sales possibilities were much greater. Benson said my quota had been fixed at twenty cars a month, and from then on that number would be shipped to me. . . .

By [1920] I had agreed to take thirty Fords a month, which was a pretty heavy job to get away with in good times, to say nothing of the sort of a situation we were going through. These cars came in each month, regular as clock work, and I had stretched my credit at the bank about as far as it would go in paying for them as they arrived. The bank kept hounding me all the time to cut down my loan, which I couldn't do with my expenses running on all the time and hardly any business going on. From September to January that year I sold exactly four cars.

REGISTERED
MOTOR VEHICLE
No. 5
MICHIGAN MOTOR
VEHICLE LAW

SMITHSONIAN INSTITUTION

Altogether I had more than one hundred and forty new cars on hand, besides a lot of trade-ins, and no immediate prospect of selling any. Then all of a sudden came notice that a shipment of fifteen Fords was on the way to me, and that I would be expected to pay for them on arrival. I thought there must be some mistake, and got the branch manager in the city on the long distance. . . .

"What's the meaning of these fifteen cars that are being shipped me?" I asked. "I've already taken my quota for the month. . . ."

I tried to explain to him that I was in no position to get hold of the cash for such a purchase, and even if I was I wanted to know the whys and wherefores.

"You know as much about it as I do," he snapped. "Those are my orders, and my advice to you is to pay for those cars when they arrive."

Of course I sensed the reason later on, when it came out in the newspapers about Mr. Ford's little tilt with the money sharks down in New York, how they tried to get a hold on his business and how he fooled them by getting the cash without their help and then told them to go chase themselves. . . .

Among other things I had to do was to keep a card file of people in the territory who had not bought cars, and usually on these cards we wrote items like "says maybe will be in market this fall," or "not ready to buy yet." Burke [Ford Motor Company's district sales representative] was always raising Cain because we didn't make people give more explicit reasons for not buying. I remember once he laid me out because a card said only "Can't sell him." The man was a poor devil of a renter seven or eight miles out of town who never had enough cash ahead to buy a wheelbarrow, but Burke insisted that one of my salesmen go out there with him to try and land a sale. When they got there a couple of the children were down with whooping cough and a hailstorm had laid out his bean crop, but Burke came back and told me he would expect me to put over a Ford on the fellow before he came on his next trip.

A farm couple and their first Model-T.

You do a lot of things when someone is riding you all the time that you wouldn't do under ordinary circumstances. . . . Not being able to get my quota reduced, I had to take business wherever I could find it. . . . I had a talk with [an army] captain and at first was inclined not to sell him, especially when he said he only had fifty dollars to lay down as a first payment. We are supposed to get a third down on a new car, but of course when the branch manager is riding you all the time you sometimes make deals that are not strictly according to Hoyle, and with my quota of thirty cars coming every month and no farmer trade in sight I was inclined to take chances. The upshot was that I took the captain's fifty dollars and off he drove.

He had promised to bring in another hundred dollars when he got his salary check, but the first of the month rolled around and no captain. . . . I reported him to the army authorities as a deadbeat. I guess he was a little daffy anyhow . . . because it turned out he had been buying a lot of other things on installments. . . .

If Mr. Ford knew personally some of the things that

William C. Durant, founder of General Motors.

go on I am sure he would call a halt to his branch managers riding the local agents the way they do.[7]

Although he was its most dominant figure, Ford was not the only leader of the industry. William Durant founded General Motors Corporation, and Walter Chrysler, merging with the Dodge brothers, created the Chrysler Corporation. By 1929, the "big three" were producing eighty-three percent of all cars manufactured in the United States.

According to William Greenleaf, General Motors Corporation was able to overtake Ford Motor Company because its pattern of corporation management was superior to Ford's archaic method of one-man rule. Greenleaf has suggested that the removal of Ford Motor Company's most imaginative and pragmatic officers in the great management purge of 1919–1921 caused the vast innovative energies of the Ford enterprise to falter and run down:

> The negative example of Henry Ford as a company despot teaches us that his methods are inimical to the rational governance of big business and incompatible with the obligations of private economic power in a democratic society.[8]

Construction

Walter P. Chrysler.

Another significant stimulus to the prosperity of the 1920's was the phenomenal increase in building. Construction demands accounted for the rapid growth of the brick, lumber, cement, tile, plumbing supply, and hardware industries. Builders consumed a sizable portion of the nation's output of steel, glass, and electrical equipment. Railroads and other transportation businesses profited by hauling these materials from the points of production to the sites of construction. Enormous profits

[7] Jesse Rainsford Sprague, "Confessions of a Ford Dealer," *Harper's Monthly Magazine,* June 1927, pp. 26–31. Copyright © 1927, by the Minneapolis Star and Tribune Co., Inc.

[8] In Sward, *Henry Ford*, preface.

CULVER PICTURES, INC.

Above, construction is underway on the Empire State Building in New York City. Below, the building nears completion. It was the tallest building in the world.

BROWN BROTHERS

also accrued to the banking institutions which financed speculation in commercial building.

An unprecedented demand for housing began immediately after World War I as returning veterans, most of them forsaking rural home towns, swarmed into the cities. New suburbs developed around every sizable city in the nation, and existing suburbs were greatly expanded. For example, the borough of Queens, across the East River from Manhattan, doubled its population in the 1920's. Grosse Pointe Park near Detroit grew by more than 700 percent, and the movie colony in Beverly Hills increased its population by 2,500 percent. The total expenditure for all types of construction in 1929 was over $16 billion; of that amount, twice as much went into residential construction as was spent on industrial and commercial construction. However, as early as 1926 the rate of growth had begun to flatten out, and in retrospect this could be seen as a warning sign of economic trouble to come.

Although residential construction accounted for the biggest part of the building boom, enough was spent on commercial construction to change the skylines of many cities. The skyscraper became the symbol of urban maturity, and every city of consequence acquired at least one. The 102-story Empire State Building was erected during the 1920's; but anything over ten stories was considered a skyscraper, and such buildings went up in many small cities that were not at all cramped for space. Some people saw the new skylines as displays of American energy and optimism. Others condemned the skyscrapers for making concrete canyons of city streets and saw in them only a vulgar commercialism.

The Florida Frenzy

A vigorous construction industry, an active urge for speculation, and easily obtained financing combined to produce real estate booms in many parts of the country. The mania for land speculation reached its height in the early 1920's in Florida, where a large portion of the population was busily converting swampland into fashionable winter resorts and building lots.

The Florida boom did not occur overnight. The price of Florida real estate had been climbing since the turn of the century, the result of many years of careful promotion by such men as Henry Flagler and Carl Fisher. By 1923, Florida—particularly Miami—was well known as the playground of the nation's elite:

> In 1923 William H. Luden, the coughdrop king, arrived for the season at his home on the Drive, and William K. Vanderbilt came in his $3,000,000 yacht, *Alva.* Senator T. Coleman Du Pont of Delaware was staying at Flagler's Royal Palm Hotel, and Harvey S. Firestone came to visit and then to buy a great Georgian-style showplace. Other visitors of note that year included labor secretary James J. Davis, chain-store genius J. C. Penney, auto mogul William C. Durant, and the 1920 Democratic presidential candidate, James M. Cox, who purchased control of a Miami newspaper and transformed it into the Miami *Daily News.* . . . The climax of the 1923 season was the arrival at the Flamingo Hotel of President and Mrs. Warren Harding.[9]

By 1924, growing prosperity and the Model-T had made Florida accessible to thousands of people who were not among the very rich but who wanted to be. From all over the country they converged on Florida and feverishly bought up acres of overpriced land, land which they expected to be able to resell at enormous profits. Those who arrived without knowing the names of reputable real estate firms often fell victim to dishonest promoters. People were lured into handing over their life savings to complete strangers for property they had never seen. The sale of underwater lots was among the better-known frauds, yet customers stood in line for hours to buy lots on Davis Islands in Tampa Bay and Venetian Islands in Biscayne Bay before there was any land above the water.

Real estate companies used numerous devices to interest

FORD ARCHIVES

Miami Beach in
the 1920's.

BROWN BROTHERS

prospective buyers. A common scheme was to bring a busload of likely prospects to Florida for an all-expenses-paid weekend, with the simple stipulation that they look at several pieces of available real estate.

The prototype of the Florida subdivisions was Coral Gables, owned and promoted by George Merrick. Unlike the many fraudulent and second-rate real estate developments that imitated it, Coral Gables really did live up to the prospective buyer's dream. Yet its promotion was not without gimmicks:

> . . . To guarantee that prospective buyers would be in a receptive mood once they reached his heaven on the Atlantic, Merrick had band leaders Paul Whiteman and Jan Garber making sweet music at the Venetian Pool with "When the Moon Shines on Coral Gables." . . . In addition, from a platform in the pool itself, the champion of silver, William Jennings Bryan, earned a little gold by orating on the miracle of Miami. . . . Bryan received an annual salary of more than fifty thousand dollars. And just in case Bryan didn't do the trick, he was sometimes followed by the original "shimmy girl," Gilda Gray, who shook her chemise with such gusto that it took the viewers' minds off the prices quoted for lots by salesmen circulating through the audience.[10]

The Florida boom continued unabated throughout 1925. According to one estimate, the number of lots offered for sale reached twenty million. It was scarcely an exaggeration to say that everybody in Miami was in real estate in one way or another. The city was forced to pass an ordinance against making sales in the streets or on the sidewalks. Prices rose to fantastic heights. A strip of land in Palm Beach sold for $84,000 in 1915, for $240,000 in 1922, for $800,000 in 1923, for $1,500,000 in 1924, and was estimated to be worth nearly $5,000,000 in 1925. A New York bank clerk who went to Florida with $1,000 returned three weeks later with $375,000. A New York cab driver took a passenger all the way to

[10] Ibid., p. 109.

The Roxy Theater, a movie palace, in New York City, 1927.

Miami, stayed, and made a fortune speculating with the money he earned from driving his cab.

The bubble burst in 1926:

> ... By January, 1926, it was apparent that something had gone wrong; the visitors were not coming in the numbers expected, installment collections were beginning to fall off, new purchasers grew harder and harder to find. It was all over even before nature took a hand, but a vicious hurricane that struck the state on September 18, 1926, and turned the jerry-built developments into ruins, sobered up even the most ardent enthusiasts.[11]

New Industries and New Products

Several industries, in their infancies when the decade began, attained positions of economic importance during the 1920's. The radio industry is an example. The basic components of radio transmitters and receivers had been perfected before World War I, but it was not until 1919, when the government lifted its wartime ban on the private operation of sets, that the commercial possibilities of

[11] John D. Hicks, *Republican Ascendancy: 1921–1933* (New York: Harper & Row, 1960), p. 118. By permission of Harper & Row, Publishers.

A 1930 advertisement for a table model radio.

radio could be exploited. The Radio Corporation of America was organized in that year, and by 1922 it was manufacturing thousands of sets and parts. The radio industry grossed $60 million in 1922; by 1929, that figure had reached $852 million. By 1939, eighty percent of the nation's families owned radios.

It was not long before advertising slogans became as well known in most homes as nursery rhymes. Historian William Leuchtenburg has described the impact of the early radio programs:

> They introduced a whole new vocabulary and within
> a few months used the terms—"tune in," "network,"
> "airwaves"—so casually that the words lost their gloss
> of technological novelty. People clamped on earphones
> to hear Roxy and His Gang, the Clicquot Club Eskimos,
> the Ipana Troubadours or the A & P Gypsies. Grantland
> Rice broadcast the World Series, Floyd Gibbons narrated
> the news with a machine-gun staccato, and Rudy Vallee
> warbled the latest songs.[12]

Some programs became so popular that they were almost national obsessions. Thousands of people refused to be disturbed while "Amos 'n' Andy" was being broadcast, and in order to keep their patrons small-town movie theaters were forced to interrupt their own shows to tune in the program.

The motion picture industry offers another example of phenomenal growth. George Eastman began manufacturing film on rollers in the 1880's, and shortly afterwards Thomas Edison invented a projecting machine. The first "kinetoscope parlor" opened in New York in 1894. In 1905, a promoter in Pittsburgh rented a warehouse and projected movies on a screen, charging a nickel for admission. Within two years, there were some 5,000 "nickelodeons" throughout the country. It was during the 1920's, however, that movies began to reach huge audiences. By the end of the decade there were 23,000 movie theaters with a combined average attendance of a hundred million

[12] William E. Leuchtenburg, *The Perils of Prosperity: 1914–1932* (Chicago: University of Chicago Press, 1966), pp. 196–197.

people a week. Unlike the nickelodeons, the movie theaters built in the 1920's were elaborate structures, "palaces" with architectural themes ranging from Chinese to European baroque to Egyptian.

> Every respectable American town had its own movie
> palace. The movie houses became the temples of a secular
> society. In New York, Roxy's called itself "The Cathedral
> of the Motion Picture," the Capitol described itself as
> "The Theater with a Soul," and the Fifty-Fifth Street
> Theater advertised itself as "The Sanctuary of the
> Cinema."[13]

Although the motion pictures of the 1920's were silent, films like D. W. Griffith's *Orphans of the Storm* and Charlie Chaplin's comedies revealed the high levels of technical and artistic sophistication that had been achieved since the nickelodeon shows. The silent films of the twenties turned millions of people into habitual moviegoers. By the time "talkies" began to appear at the end of the decade, the role of the movie in American life was so great that not even the depression could affect the industry's growth.

Charlie Chaplin as "the little tramp."

During the years from 1900 to 1929, the electric power industry rose from comparative insignificance to become the second most important economic interest in the United States. Business consolidation had been a feature of the American economy before the war, but during the 1920's it gained new momentum, particularly in the field of public utilities. Nearly 4,000 utility companies were absorbed into mergers during the decade. By 1930, ten holding companies, among them American Superpower Corporation and Insull, controlled three-fourths of the nation's electric power.

Other new industries brought new products: refrigerators, electric stoves, vacuum cleaners, wristwatches, cigarette lighters, antifreeze, dry ice, and pyrex glass, to name a few. The latest products also included a wide range of synthetics. Consumers readily incorporated such words as

[13] Ibid., p. 196.

plastic, *rayon*, *bakelite*, *cellophane*, and *celanese* into their vocabularies, while the chemical companies that introduced them, like Dow and Du Pont, enjoyed an astronomical growth. Machines and mass-production techniques also increased the output of older industries. Mass-produced furniture, clothing, and shoes of reasonable quality became available at reasonable prices. The consumer could also choose from a seemingly infinite variety of canned goods, his diet no longer dictated by the season of the year or the part of the country in which he lived.

The Stock Market

The 1920's witnessed a number of speculative orgies on the stock market, but none compared with the big bull market that reached its climax in 1928 and 1929. One of the most startling aspects of the bull market was the suddenness with which it developed. No one has satisfactorily explained what caused a speculative surge in 1927. The average price of common stocks increased 300 percent, and the number of shares traded on the New York Stock Exchange doubled, as this table shows:

Year	Number of Shares Traded
1923	236,000,000
1925	454,000,000
1926	451,000,000
1927	577,000,000
1929	1,125,000,000

Calvin Coolidge.

Brokers' loans, which were used to finance the speculation, rose from $3.5 billion in 1926 to $8.5 billion in 1929.

Historian William Leuchtenburg has suggested that the increase in stock-market speculation prevented the depression from occurring sooner than it did:

If it had not been for the wave of speculation, the prosperity of the twenties might have ended much earlier than it did. Coolidge's deflationary policies had withdrawn government funds from the economy, consumers had cut spending for durable goods in 1927, and the market for housing had been glutted as early as 1926. But with the

BUREAU OF ENGRAVING AND PRINTING

economy sparked by fresh funds poured into speculation, a depression was avoided and the boom continued.[14]

The Cult of Business

"The man who builds a factory builds a temple; the man who works there worships there," said President Calvin Coolidge. Popular devotion to business standards and goals as guides to daily living assumed the proportions of a national religion during the 1920's. The chief index of a man's worth was his income, and critics who questioned the values of the business civilization were seen by many of their contemporaries as frustrated men who had been unable to succeed in the business world and who were simply blaming society for their own inadequacies. In 1925, *Nation's Business* identified the American businessman as "the most influential person in the nation," and one writer called him "the dictator of our destinies." The successful businessman was considered an authority on all subjects.

Like his product, the businessman's message was standardized: the principal function of business was to serve the people, and business should therefore remain free from any sort of governmental restriction or regulation. Once a week, throughout the country, business leaders came together for luncheons as Rotarians, Lions, or Kiwanians, always in the name of social service. Frederick Lewis Allen commented on the businessmen's service clubs in *Only Yesterday*:

A typical 1920's "message" from *The Rotarian* magazine.

> Rotary, the most famous of them, had been founded in 1905; by 1930 it had 150,000 members and boasted—as a sign of its international influence—as many as 3,000 clubs in 44 countries. The number of Kiwanis Clubs rose from 205 in 1920 to 1,800 in 1929; the Lions Clubs, of which the first was not formed until 1917, multiplied until at the end of the decade there were 1,200 of them. Nor did these clubs content themselves with singing songs and conducting social-service campaigns; they expressed the

[14] Ibid., pp. 242–243.

national faith in what one of their founders called "the redemptive and regenerative influence of business." The speakers before them pictured the business man as a builder, a doer of great things, yes, and a dreamer whose imagination was ever seeking out new ways of serving humanity. It was a popular note, for in hundreds of directors' rooms, around hundreds of conference tables, the American business men of the era of Coolidge Prosperity were seeing themselves as men of vision with eyes steadfastly fixed on the long future. At the end of the decade, a cartoon in the *New Yorker* represented an executive as saying to his heavy-jowled colleagues at one of these meetings: "We have ideas. Possibly we tilt at windmills—just seven Don Juans tilting at windmills." It was a perfect bit of satire on business sentimentality. The service club specialized in this sort of mysticism: was not a speaker before the Rotarians of Waterloo, Iowa, quoted by the *American Mercury* as declaring that "Rotary is a manifestation of the divine"?[15]

While business took on some of the qualities of a religion, religion itself adopted some of the techniques of the business world. One church offered "stock certificates in heaven" to everyone who contributed a hundred dollars or more to its building fund. Churches advertised their services in the newspapers to build up attendance, and ministers gave their sermons alluring titles like "Solomon, the Six-Cylinder Sport." One clergyman, preaching on the Trinity, called his sermon "Three-in-One Oil."

Business became a cult and religion became secularized as each used the values of the other to demonstrate its virtues. At times it was hard to tell where one began and the other left off. In the mid-twenties, a prosperous advertising executive, Bruce Barton, wrote a best-selling book called *The Man Nobody Knows*. In it, Barton described Jesus as a first-rate executive and praised his parables as the most powerful advertisements ever written. Jesus, claimed Barton, was the founder of modern business:

[15] Allen, *Only Yesterday*, pp. 147—148.

A physical weakling! Where did they get that idea? Jesus pushed a plane and swung an adze; he was a successful carpenter. He slept outdoors and spent his days walking around his favorite lake. His muscles were so strong that when he drove the moneychangers out, nobody dared to oppose him!

A kill-joy! He was the most popular dinner guest in Jerusalem! The criticism which proper people made was that he spent too much time with publicans and sinners (very good fellows on the whole, the man thought) and enjoyed society too much. They called him a "wine bibber and a gluttonous man."

A failure! He picked up twelve men from the bottom ranks of business and forged them into an organization that conquered the world. . . . [The story of Jesus is] the story of the founder of modern business.[16]

Frederick Lewis Allen wrote of the cult of business:

Millions of people wanted to be reassured that this religion was altogether right and proper, and that in the rules for making big money lay all the law and the prophets.

Was it strange that during the very years when the Barton Gospel was circulating most vigorously, selling and advertising campaigns were becoming more cynical and the American business world was refusing to exercise itself over the Teapot Dome disclosures and the sordid history of the Continental Trading Company? Perhaps; but it must be remembered that in all religions there is likely to be a gap between faith and works. The business man's halo did not always fit, but he wore it proudly.[17]

The Inequities of Prosperity

Prosperity in the twenties rested on a foundation much more shaky than most Americans knew. In the election campaign of 1928, the Republican slogan was "A Chicken

---

[16] Bruce Barton, *The Man Nobody Knows* (New York: Bobbs-Merrill, 1925), preface. Copyright 1925 by The Bobbs-Merrill Company, Inc., 1952 by Bruce Barton, reprinted by permission of the publishers.

[17] Allen, *Only Yesterday*, p. 150.

in Every Pot, a Car in Every Garage." Accepting the presidential nomination, Herbert Hoover said, "We are in America today nearer to the final triumph over poverty than ever before in the history of any land." "My God, How the Money Rolls In!" was a national theme song, and the ticker tape machines clattered, showing stock prices climbing steadily upward. In this mood of self-congratulation, the nation almost overlooked two groups whom prosperity had passed by–farmers and workers.

World War I had made soldiers of European farmers and battlefields of European farms. By 1915, England and France were requesting substantial food shipments from America, and food prices rose along with the demand. Anticipating large profits, American farmers planted every acre they owned, even mortgaging their farms to buy more land and equipment with which to increase productivity. The boom lasted until 1920, when European farms began to resume production. Food prices fell sharply, reaching a low in 1921 and then slowly rising again. A bushel of corn that sold for $1.36 in 1918 was worth 41¢ in 1921, 97¢ in 1924. But farm prosperity did not return with higher farm prices. In his biography of Claude Wickard, an Indiana corn and hog farmer who became secretary of agriculture in 1940, Dean Albertson described the "farm problem" of the 1920's:

> By 1924 Claude Wickard's income was far below what it had been during the war boom, and his purchasing power was only two-thirds that of the average city factory worker. There were so many fixed charges on Wickard's income which remained at boom year levels, that his money was spent as soon as he received it. The interest on his note to his father remained the same. His taxes were the same, if not higher. His freight and telephone bills were the same. In comparison with prewar levels, money which Wickard received for his crops lagged more than 20 percent behind prices the Wickards paid for food and clothing, fertilizer, tractor tires and parts, seed, and fence lumber. This price differential worked a doubly difficult burden on the Wickards, for they had been among those farm folk who demanded the same material comforts which magazines

advertised for residents of Indianapolis and Chicago. Their standard of living had increased. Their "belt" no longer would cinch up as tightly as had Claude's parents' [during the depression of 1893]. In the barn lot stood the basic tools of the modern farmer—tractor, drill, disc, and harrow—as well as a new Ford. . . . For the farmstead now there was plumbing and a Delco plant to give a minimal amount of wavering electricity for lighting. If good tools, a car, and running water were considered essential in Chicago, so they should be considered in Carrollton Township. The difficulty was that Chicago laborers' wages would pay for them; the income from Carroll County's crops would not.

Industrial prices, protected by the tariff, could be maintained during a depression by letting off a few workers and cutting production to meet demand. Farmers, one competing against another, could not limit production. Their only chance to make the money necessary to feed their families was to work ever harder, to plant more and more. The greater their production in the face of dead foreign markets, the larger grew the surpluses which depressed farm prices. Like the White Queen, farmers were running as hard as they could to stand still.[18]

By 1927, the purchasing power of factory workers, particularly those who did not belong to labor unions, had also begun to fall off. Although corporate profits increased sixty-two percent from 1923 to 1929, workers received only an eleven percent increase in wages over the same period. Near the end of the decade, assembly line workers found it difficult to purchase the products they produced. In many working-class families, wives and children were forced to take jobs in order to supplement the family income.

On the surface, the nation had never seemed so economically sound as in 1929. In reality, prosperity was unevenly and dangerously divided. Too large a portion of the national income was going to industrial and finan-

[18] Dean Albertson, *Roosevelt's Farmer: Claude Wickard in the New Deal* (New York: Columbia University Press, 1961), pp. 32–33. Reprinted by permission of the publisher.

cial institutions, too small a portion to the prospective buyers so necessary for the maintenance of rising prices and industrial growth. Frederick Lewis Allen described this "maladjustment of prosperity" in *The Big Change*:

> During . . . 1929, according to the subsequent estimates of the very careful and conservative Brookings Institution, only 2.3 per cent of American families had incomes over $10,000 a year. Only 8 per cent had incomes over $5,000. No less than 71 per cent had incomes of less than $2,500. Some 60 per cent had incomes of less than $2,000. More than 42 per cent had incomes of less than $1,500. And more than 21 per cent had incomes of less than $1,000 a year.
>
> "At 1929 prices," said the Brookings economists, "a family income of $2,000 may be regarded as sufficient to supply only basic necessities." One might reasonably interpret this statement to mean that any income below that level represented poverty. *Practically 60 per cent of American families were below it—in the golden year of 1929!*[19]

Still, the extent of the prosperity of the 1920's should not be underrated, as William Leuchtenburg has pointed out:

> . . . If one focuses exclusively on farm poverty or on depressed West Virginia coal towns, it is easy to get a distorted picture of life in the 1920's. As Henry May writes, "Sometimes even prosperity—an important fact despite its exceptions—is belittled almost out of existence." If prosperity was by no means as pervasive as Chamber of Commerce publicists claimed, it was still widespread enough to change markedly the life of millions of Americans. The change resulted less from a considerable increase in income for the average American . . . than from the fact that Americans could buy things with their paychecks that they had never been able to get before.[20]

[19] Frederick Lewis Allen, *The Big Change: America Transforms Herself, 1900–1950* (New York: Harper & Brothers, 1952), pp. 143–144.

[20] Leuchtenburg, *The Perils of Prosperity*, p. 194.

SUGGESTED READINGS

Allen, Frederick Lewis. *The Big Change: America Transforms Itself, 1900–1950*. Harper & Row, Perennial Library.

Barton, Bruce. *The Man Nobody Knows*. Bobbs-Merrill.

Dreiser, Theodore. *An American Tragedy*. New American Library, Signet Books.

Fitzgerald, F. Scott. *The Great Gatsby*. Charles Scribner's Sons.

Krutch, Joseph Wood. *The Modern Temper: A Study and a Confession*. Harcourt Brace Jovanovich, Harvest Books.

Leighton, Isabel. *The Aspirin Age: 1919–1941*. Simon & Schuster, Clarion Books.

Leuchtenburg, William E. *The Perils of Prosperity: 1914–1932*. University of Chicago Press.

Link, Arthur S. *The Impact of World War I*. Harper & Row.

Lynd, Robert S. and Helen M. *Middletown*. Harcourt Brace Jovanovich, Harvest Books.

Mowry, George E., ed. *The Twenties: Fords, Flappers, and Fanatics*. Prentice-Hall, Spectrum Books.

Soule, George. *Prosperity Decade*. Harper & Row, Torchbooks.

Sward, Keith. *The Legend of Henry Ford*. Atheneum.

Tarkington, Booth. *The Magnificent Ambersons*. New American Library, Signet Books.

This Fourth of July float, with children dressed in homemade patriotic costumes, might have been photographed on almost any main street in any small town in 1920. In fact, it was photographed in Washington, D.C., a world city that had not yet lost its small-town soul.

CHAPTER TWO

NORMALCY

[America's present need is] not heroics but healing, not
nostrums but normalcy, not revolution but restoration,
not agitation but adjustment, not surgery but serenity,
not the dramatic but the dispassionate, not experiment
but equipoise, not submergence in internationality but
sustainment in triumphant nationality.[1]

Although called "an alliterative quagmire" by some and
"typical Gamalielese" by others, this statement by Senator Warren Gamaliel Harding of Ohio correctly expressed
the political temper of the nation in May, 1920. Tired of
high idealism and weary of moral obligations, the people
of the country longed for release from the demands of
war and reform. The ugliness and horror of World War I,
bitter debate over the League of Nations, postwar inflation, and "Red hysteria" all contributed to the public
rebellion against the idealism of Woodrow Wilson.

The Republicans understood this shift in mood well—
indeed, they shared it. As keynote speaker and chairman

[1] Quoted in Samuel Hopkins Adams, *Incredible Era: The Life
and Times of Warren Gamaliel Harding* (Boston: Houghton Mifflin, 1939), p. 117. Copyright © 1939, by Samuel Hopkins Adams.
Copyright renewed, 1967 by Hester H. Adams. Reprinted by permission of Brandt & Brandt.

Henry Cabot Lodge represented Massachusetts in the Senate for thirty-two years, from 1893 until his death in 1924. His grandson, Henry Cabot Lodge II, held the same job for fourteen years before becoming ambassador to the United Nations in the 1950's.

of the party's national convention in 1916, Senator Harding had delivered a strong appeal for internationalism:

We must assume the responsibilities of influence and example, and accept the burdens of enlarged participation. The cloistered life is not possible to the potential man or the potential nation. Moreover, the Monroe Doctrine, stronger for a century's maintenance, fixes an obligation of new-world sponsorship and old-world relationship.[2]

By 1920, the party had entirely abandoned its internationalist theme. At the convention that year, Senator Henry Cabot Lodge, keynoter and chairman, described the new Republican posture:

Let us stand fast by the principles and policies of Washington and Monroe and against—utterly against— those of Mr. Wilson. We must be now and ever for Americanism and Nationalism, and against Internationalism. There is no safety for us, no hope that we can be of service to the world, if we do otherwise.[3]

"Normalcy" was what people wanted, and it was what they got during the Republican administrations of Harding and his successor, Calvin Coolidge—"normalcy" to the extent, at least, that nothing very dramatic in the way of leadership or legislation emerged from Washington in the years from 1921 to 1929. The relative pallor of government during the 1920's may be the reason that so many writers have emphasized the more bizarre aspects of American society during the period. Interpretations of these years as "golden," "roaring," or "an era of wonderful nonsense" make interesting reading, and are true enough as far as they go, but they ignore much that political historians regard as significant when they chronicle the history of an epoch.

[2] Quoted in Andrew Sinclair, *The Available Man: The Life Behind the Masks of Warren G. Harding* (New York: Macmillan Co., 1965), p. 68. Copyright © Andrew Sinclair 1965. Reprinted with permission of Macmillan Publishing Co., Inc.

[3] Quoted in ibid., p. 139.

Warren G. Harding—The Traditional View

The commonly accepted view of the twenties holds that the political bankruptcy of the decade was glaringly revealed in the proceedings of the Republican national convention of 1920 and in the character of the man the convention nominated for the presidency, Warren G. Harding. To a great extent, this view has been influenced by one book, Samuel Hopkins Adams's *Incredible Era: The Life and Times of Warren Gamaliel Harding*, which from its publication in 1939 until recently, was the only serious biography of Harding available. Accordingly, much of the material in this section of the chapter has been drawn from Adams's book.

Warren G. Harding.

In the traditional view, the proceedings of the Republican national convention were controlled by old-guard conservatives, "the Senate soviet," who were determined that their candidate should present a sharp contrast to the progressive idealism of Woodrow Wilson. And with a November victory all but assured, there was a mad scramble for the nomination. The reporter William Allen White later wrote that of all the conventions he had ever attended, he had never seen one so completely dominated by economic forces. Karl Schriftgiesser has described the scene in *This Was Normalcy*:

> Never in the political history of the United States had there been such an obscene spectacle as that which took place in Chicago in June, 1920. The Presidency was for sale. The city of Chicago, never averse to monetary indecencies, was jam-packed with frenzied bidders, their pockets bulging with money with which to buy the prize. The Coliseum became a market place, crowded with stock gamblers, oil promoters, mining magnates, munitions makers, sports promoters, and soap makers, all drooling with anticipation of success. The lobbies and rooms of the Loop hotels were in a turmoil as the potential buyers of office scurried about lining up their supporters, making their deals, issuing furtive orders, passing out secret funds.[4]

[4] Karl Schriftgiesser, *This Was Normalcy* (Boston: Little, Brown, 1948), p. 3. Reprinted by permission of the author.

Leonard Wood began his army career as a medical officer in the campaign against the Apache Geronimo. He helped Theodore Roosevelt organize the Rough Riders during the Spanish-American War and served as military governor in Cuba and the Philippines before becoming chief of staff in 1910.

A preconvention poll conducted by the *Literary Digest* identified eight leading Republican contenders. The figures represent a fairly reliable index of their popular support:

277,486	Leonard Wood	General, Army Chief of Staff
263,087	Hiram Johnson	Senator from California
240,468	Herbert Hoover	Wartime Food Administrator
120,391	Frank Lowden	Governor of Illinois
54,719	Charles Evans Hughes	Republican Candidate in 1916
36,795	Warren G. Harding	Senator from Ohio
33,621	Calvin Coolidge	Governor of Massachusetts
32,740	William Howard Taft	Former President of the United States, 1909–1913[5]

The name of Warren G. Harding appeared far down the list. The odds seemed overwhelmingly against him, yet his supporters were not discouraged. Indeed, four months before the convention his campaign manager, Harry Daugherty, had confidently predicted:

I don't expect Senator Harding to be nominated on the first, second, or third ballots, but I think we can afford to take chances that, about eleven minutes after two, Friday morning of the convention, when ten or twenty weary men are sitting around a table, someone will say, "Who will we nominate?" At that decisive time the friends of Harding will suggest him and can well afford to abide by the result.[6]

The convention closely followed Daugherty's script, and the story of Harding's nomination became a political classic. After four ballots, the delegates found themselves

---

[5] Quoted in Adams, *Incredible Era,* p. 129.

[6] Quoted in *The New York Times,* 21 February 1920. Copyright © 1920 by The New York Times Company. Reprinted by permission.

hopelessly divided among five candidates: Wood had 314½ votes, Lowden had 289½, Johnson had 140½, William C. Sproul (Pennsylvania's governor and favorite-son nominee) had 79, and Harding had 61½. Four hundred ninety-three votes were needed for the nomination. The convention, obviously stalemated, was adjourned by chairman Henry Cabot Lodge until the following day.

The "Senate ring"—which included Lodge and Murray Crane of Massachusetts, Boies Penrose and Philander Knox of Pennsylvania (both absent from the convention but in close touch with the proceedings), Reed Smoot of Utah, Frank Brandegee of Connecticut, James Watson and Harry New of Indiana, James Wadsworth and W. M. Calder of New York, and Charles Curtis of Kansas—had not yet decided on a candidate. Both frontrunners, Wood and Lowden, were conservative enough to present the desired contrast to Woodrow Wilson. But neither met the senators' primary requirement, that of absolute party loyalty. They wanted a man who would "listen," who could be trusted to "cooperate"—in other words, a man who would take orders.

Wood and Lowden had additional drawbacks. General Wood, despite his proven ability, high principles, sturdy intellect, and preconvention popularity, was losing ground with the delegates. As a military man, his opponents pointed out, he would lack appeal to a public fed up with war. A Senate investigation into his preconvention campaign finances, led by the incorruptible William E. Borah of Idaho, had damaged his reputation by revealing sizable contributions from "fat-cat" industrialists. Governor Lowden, a wealthy man with an aura of machine politics and unpopular with labor, had also been affected by the investigation. A convention rumor that he was buying delegates further limited his chances of taking the nomination.

All of this was satisfactory enough to the senators. But they liked the third-place nominee, Hiram Johnson, even less than Wood or Lowden. The strong-minded California senator had split from the Republican party in 1912 to join Theodore Roosevelt on the Bull Moose

As governor of California from 1911 to 1917, Hiram Johnson supported such progressive causes as women's suffrage, the initiative, referendum, and recall, and the regulation of railroads and other monopolies. He remained a controversial figure throughout his long Senate career, from 1917 to 1945.

Herbert Hoover, a mining engineer, had successfully managed several large companies before entering public service in 1914 as director of Belgian relief efforts.

UNITED PRESS INTERNATIONAL

ticket, had failed to support Hughes' campaign against Wilson in 1916, and had identified himself with a number of progressive causes. He was, furthermore, an "irreconcilable" isolationist. Herbert Hoover was another Californian with widespread popular support. Indeed, Samuel Hopkins Adams believed that he might well have been the nominee had the issue been left to the mass of voters. But the senators were doubtful of his party allegiance. Fortunately for them, he had no effective political organization to back him up at the convention.

The deadlock opened the way for a "dark horse," a candidate upon whom the convention's many factions could agree to compromise. *And* for a candidate who met the requirements of the party elders:

> The situation called for a candidate who had opposed the League of Nations, but one who would favor a league with some "American reservations," in order to keep that great body of Republican voters who wanted "some kind of a league." This candidate must also be a Republican who had remained loyal in 1912, but who was not too much of a reactionary who by his record might fail to win the confidence of the liberal element of the party. The nominee must, by temperament, record, and personality, be the complete antithesis of Wilson. He must be democratic and genial, not aristocratic and intellectual; he must be of that persuasion that the Senate would be able to assert its constitutional position; and he must be safe in that the Senators could trust him to listen to the reasonings of the leaders.[7]

The political bosses consulted with each other throughout the night. Word came from the sickbed of Senator Penrose: "Throw it to Harding." Penrose controlled the seventy-nine votes of the Pennsylvania delegation that had gone to Governor Sproul in the previous balloting, and his influence extended well beyond his own state. During the early morning hours, in a smoke-filled room at the

[7] H. F. Alderfer, quoted in Adams, *Incredible Era*, p. 152.

Blackstone Hotel, Daugherty's prediction came true. Several hours later, Senator Smoot confidently told newspaper reporters that Harding would be the nominee. The convention duly ratified the party leaders' choice on the tenth ballot. Gratified by the outcome, Senator Brandegee generously commented, "This year we had a lot of second-raters. Harding's no world-beater. But he's the best of the second-raters."[8]

The vice-presidential nomination was expected to be an anticlimax, but it proved to be the most surprising and spontaneous event of the entire convention. The party elders had hastily agreed on the more liberal Senator Irvine Lenroot of Wisconsin as a satisfactory running mate for Harding. Although they neglected to inform Senator Lenroot of their decision, his name was placed in nomination. Amid the flurry of seconding speeches, a delegate from Oregon managed to be recognized and, to the amazement of everyone, nominated the conservative Calvin Coolidge. The response was startling, and the Massachusetts governor was rousingly nominated on the first ballot. According to Karl Schriftgiesser,

> It was not that they wanted Coolidge so much as it was
> that they were determined to demonstrate their belated
> independence. In many ways it was an exhilarating spectacle,
> the turmoil in the Coliseum; in another it was comic. To
> witness a hallful of hot and angry Republicans rising in
> revolt against their political masters and lining solidly up
> behind the silent, uninspiring Calvin Coolidge—the only
> time in his life that he caused anyone to deviate from
> normalcy—was something no one, an hour ago, would have
> believed possible.[9]

Samuel Hopkins Adams characterized the Republican nominees: "So it was Harding and Coolidge, a curiously assorted pair. The hard-bitten New England Yankee and the soft, easy-going Ohioan; the hedonist and the Puritan."[10]

---

[8] Quoted in ibid., p. 163.
[9] Schriftgiesser, *This Was Normalcy*, p. 18.
[10] Adams, *Incredible Era*, p. 167.

CULVER PICTURES, INC.

Mr. and Mrs. Harding, left, with Mr. and Mrs. Coolidge.

Warren G. Harding never entertained ambitions of becoming president. He would have been perfectly content to remain in his position as editor of the Marion, Ohio, *Star* for the rest of his life. He achieved success with little effort and less ambition under the leadership of characters stronger than himself—his wife, Harry Daugherty, his party leaders. Reluctant each step of the way, he went from the state senate to the lieutenant governorship of Ohio, then on to the United States Senate. With his genuine liking for people, all kinds of people, and his ever-present desire to "harmonize" the differences among them, "W.G." was popular with his fellow legislators of both parties. He was not in politics for reasons of power, principle, or personal profit, although he enjoyed the prestige. On being in the United States Senate, he said simply, "I like the fraternity of this body." Harding held no illusions about his own abilities. He was often candidly, even pathetically, honest. He evaluated himself as a man of limited talents from a small town. "Oftentimes as I sit here," he remarked after his election, "I don't seem to grasp that I am President."

A public address often reveals much about the man who makes it. Harding developed and projected a distinctive style. He once told a friend that he loved to go out into the country and "bloviate." The old Ohio word is perhaps the best description that could be given his attempts to express himself. William McAdoo, secretary of the treasury under Woodrow Wilson and a contender for the Democratic presidential nomination in 1920 and 1924, offered the following evaluation of Harding's oratorical style:

> His speeches leave the impression of an army of pompous phrases moving over the landscape in search of an idea; sometimes these meandering words would actually capture a straggling thought and bear it triumphantly, a prisoner in their midst, until it died of servitude and overwork.[11]

If McAdoo's judgment seems harsh, consider that of H. L. Mencken, America's relentless critic-at-large during the 1920's:

> I rise to pay my small tribute to Dr. Harding. Setting aside a college professor or two and half a dozen dipsomaniacal newspaper reporters, he takes first place in my Valhalla of literati. That is to say, he writes the worst English that I have ever encountered. It reminds me of a string of wet sponges; it reminds me of tattered washing on the line; it reminds me of stale bean-soup, of college yells, of dogs barking idiotically through endless nights. It is so bad that a sort of grandeur creeps into it. It drags itself out of the dark abysm (I was about to write abcess!) of pish, and crawls insanely up the topmost pinnacle of posh. It is rumble and bumble. It is flap and doodle. It is balder and dash. . . . Almost I long for the sweeter song, the rubber-stamps of the more familiar design, the gentler and more seemly bosh of the late Woodrow.[12]

A few excerpts from Harding's speeches will illustrate the style that so irritated McAdoo and Mencken:

[11] Quoted in ibid., pp. 115–116.
[12] Quoted in ibid., p. 115.

Progression is not proclamation nor palaver. It is not
pretense nor play on prejudice. It is not of personal pronouns,
nor perennial pronouncement. It is not the perturbation
of a people passion-wrought, nor a promise proposed.
Progression is everlastingly lifting the standards that marked
the end of the world's march yesterday and planting them on
new and advanced heights to-day. Tested by such a standard,
President Taft is the greatest *progressive* of the age. [13]

Since freedom impelled and independence inspired and
nationality exalted, a world supergovernment is contrary
to everything we cherish and can have no sanction by our
Republic. This is not selfishness, it is sanctity. . . .

We have not only wrought the most of liberty and
opportunity for ourselves at home, but the firmament of
the earth, occident and orient, is aglow with shining suns
of new republics, sped to the orbs of human progress by
our example. . . .

We have mistaken unpreparedness to embrace it to be a
challenge of the realities, and due concern for making
all citizens fit for participation will give added strength
of citizenship and magnify our achievement. [14]

Criticism of Harding's "bloviations" was not lost on the
party leaders. Senator Penrose advised a "front-porch"
campaign: "Keep Warren at home. Don't let him make
any speeches. If he goes out on a tour, somebody's sure
to ask him questions, and Warren's just the sort of damn
fool that'll try to answer them." [15] The candidate was to
be a "modest, simple, sagacious, home-loving, home-
staying statesman," issuing Republican orthodoxies from
"the Mecca of Marion." [16] Calvin Coolidge, with his dry,
twangy, flavorless platitudes, was sent out on tour instead.
He aroused singularly little enthusiasm.

[13] Nominating speech for William Howard Taft, 1912, quoted in
Sinclair, *The Available Man*, p. 50.
[14] Inaugural Address, 1920, quoted in Adams, *Incredible Era*,
p. 116.
[15] Quoted in ibid., p. 170.
[16] Ibid.

But campaign tactics really didn't matter. The Democrats, apparently operating on the theory that the best way to beat an Ohio newspaperman was with another one, nominated James M. Cox, a Dayton editor and three-time governor of the state. President Wilson had announced that the election would serve as a "great and solemn referendum" on American participation in the League of Nations. Cox kicked off the campaign by making a pilgrimage to Washington to visit the ailing president and by unequivocally endorsing Wilson's position on the League. He and his running mate, Franklin D. Roosevelt, campaigned vigorously. Cox covered eighteen states in less than a month while Harding basked on the front porch in Marion, hedging on the issues. Harding won by a landslide, a plurality of seven million votes. According to Samuel Hopkins Adams,

Woodrow Wilson and his wife Edith, who made many of his decisions for him in the fall of 1919, when he was almost wholly incapacitated by arteriosclerosis and a thrombosis that paralyzed his left side. This 1920 photograph was the first taken of him after his illness.

> The overwhelming verdict was a mandate rather than a tribute to Harding. The country had made its choice, not that it loved Harding more, but Wilson less. Cox had manfully accepted the Wilson tradition; he was made the scapegoat. Insensate hatred for the broken man in the White House piled up in those ballots.[17]

Adams went on to ask, "What manner of man is this whom the American electorate has so impatiently chosen for its leader?"

> No President had ever been elected of whom so little was known. His career in state politics had been insignificant. His record in the Senate was less than mediocre; it was negative. Not one measure of any importance, not a speech of any influence derived from him. . . .
>   . . . Harding as incoming President is the same minor and well-meaning politician who made himself useful in hack-work at Columbus; who served a carefree, easy-going, inconspicuous term in the Senate; whose modest ambition it was to return to Marion and run his successful newspaper. He is uneducated, without precision or discipline of mind or power of analysis. In any broad sense he is unread.

[17] Ibid., pp. 185–186.

UNITED PRESS INTERNATIONAL

What little schooling he had is unsupplemented by his
contacts with life which are essentially superficial. His
experience of men and cities is wide but shallow. Travel
has not enriched him. . . . Intellectually he has never
traversed the boundaries of his own state, hardly those of
his home town. His is a parochial mind. He is unprepared
for the duties of statemanship. There is no subject, national
or international, among the many which enlist the anxious
thought of leaders, which he can confront with the authority
of the specialist or the interest of the student. In one of
[his] rare bookish allusions . . . , he personifies himself as
"Main Street come to Washington." Pride, not deprecation,
inspired the utterance. Marion's Main Street was, for him,
the epitome of success, soundness, enterprise, orthodoxy,
every worthy quality which he had in mind when he rolled
out his unctuous encomiums of Americanism.

Harding's patriotism and partisanship were equally
fervent. To his hazy and naive conceptions, Americanism
and Republicanism were one and inseparable. . . . It was
his misfortune to grow up in the faith at a time when the
party leadership was at its flood in power and its ebb in
principle.

Doctor H. F. Alderfer . . . regards him as an attractive
and pliant lay-figure for his party, raised to unexpected
authority, as if "a clothing store model, after years of
faithful service in displaying choice garments in the front
window, should suddenly find itself manager of the store."

For Harding the problems of the day were two-
dimensional. His vision could not penetrate the plane to
which his intellectual excursions were limited. To estimate
the effect of evil politics in terms of injustice, crime,
suffering, degradation of public and private standards and
morals, calls for imagination. Harding lacked that quality.
He could not project his mind beyond the immediate and
concrete. He was unfailingly sympathetic to the individual.
He loved humanity in detail, but had no conception of it
as a whole, the reverse of Wilson who could be a martyr
for the mass, but disliked most people.

Harding's conception of public service was to give a

friend a job. It made the seeker happy. It enlisted a
supporter in the party ranks. That the effect of the bestowal
might, if the recipient were unworthy, involve wrong,
oppression, injustice to ten thousand other men would be
quite beyond his vision. Implications other than the most
obvious did not occur to him. He never tried to see around
a corner.[18]

Aware of his own limitations and worried by them,
Harding determined to surround himself with men of good
judgment and good faith to provide the guidance he so
much needed. "The Best Minds would set the course. He
need only sift the advice of the leaders, select the best,
and go ahead."[19] Most of the men he chose for his cabinet
were in fact well qualified, both by character and ability,
for their positions: Secretary of State Charles Evans
Hughes, Secretary of Commerce Herbert Hoover, Secretary of the Treasury Andrew Mellon, Secretary of Agriculture Henry C. Wallace. As it later turned out, however,
he also selected one man of unusual incompetence, Secretary of the Navy Edwin Denby, and two men of bad faith,
Attorney General Harry Micajah Daugherty and Secretary
of the Interior Albert Fall. Daugherty and Fall were Harding's intimate friends, his only ones in the cabinet; but it
was from "Mr. Hughes," "Mr. Hoover," and "Mr. Mellon," as he deferentially addressed them, that Harding
took his official tone:

Andrew Mellon,
member of a wealthy
banking family,
served as secretary
of the treasury under
Harding, Coolidge,
and Hoover. He was
unpopular with lib-
erals in both parties
because his policies
consistently favored
big business, and in
1932 an unsuccess-
ful attempt was
made to impeach
him.

> In his official capacity the new President bore himself with
> dignity and gravity. Members of his Cabinet were struck
> with his seriousness; he seemed to them to be approaching
> his heavy task with a full appreciation of its import. He
> was eager to win and hold the respect of men whom he
> recognized as his mental superiors.[20]

Harding expected to find more "best minds" among the
Republican party leaders of the Senate and House of Rep-

[18] Ibid., pp. 187–189.
[19] Ibid., p. 192.
[20] Ibid., p. 224.

resentatives. Like his model, President McKinley, he was both temperamentally and philosophically inclined to subordinate the presidency to Congress. He believed that legislation was the business of Congress, administration the concern of department secretaries, and policy the affair of the political party. The president was simply the presiding officer who kept the governmental machinery running smoothly by "harmonizing" its various parts. The president should reflect, not influence, public attitudes. Shortly after the midterm elections of 1918, which restored Republican congressional control, Harding had observed, "The people have looked with apprehension on the executive assumption of power, and feel that safety for popular government lies in Congress asserting itself."[21] Later, when his support for American membership in the World Court was solicited in 1923, he would announce:

> I shall not attempt to coerce the Senate of the United States.
> I shall make no demand upon the people. I shall not try
> to impose my will upon any body or anybody. I shall
> embark on no crusade.[22]

But, unfortunately for Harding, the times were not suited to a presidency run on the McKinley model. Now that the Senate leaders had found a man who would listen, they had nothing valuable to say to him. They were growing old and weak; their authority was slipping. Knox and Penrose were dead before the end of Harding's first year in office. A group of western Republican senators, led by Robert M. La Follette of Wisconsin, had formed a bloc hostile to the old-guard easterners and powerful enough to obstruct them on almost every major issue. Intraparty squabbles also beset the House. On the three most important issues of the day, taxation, tariffs, and treaties, the "best minds" did not agree. Harding was left to struggle with problems beyond his comprehension.

[21] Quoted in ibid., p. 95.
[22] Quoted in Sidney Warren, *The President As World Leader* (Philadelphia: J. B. Lippincott, 1967), p. 145.

A remark to one of his secretaries, reported by William Allen White, revealed his confusion:

> "I can't make a damn thing out of this tax problem," he complained. "I listen to one side and they seem right, and then—God!—I talk to the other side and they seem just as right, and here I am where I started. I know somewhere there is a book that will give me the truth, but hell! I couldn't read the book."[23]

Nevertheless, Harding was determined to live up to the expectations of the people whose votes had overwhelmingly endorsed him. He worked diligently at the job that proved to be so much more difficult than the one he bargained for. And, on the whole, the people approved of his efforts. But, by early 1923, the strains of the presidency were evident in Harding's declining health. At the same time, his worries about the lack of "teamwork" in his administration sharply increased: it now appeared that he would have to deal with dishonesty and possible disgrace as well as dissension.

Like other incoming presidents, Harding had been besieged by hundreds of friends and acquaintances, social and political, old and new, wanting jobs. In his appointments he was probably more generous and trusting than most presidents; certainly he was more unlucky. Several of the men he selected (including his brother-in-law, the superintendent of federal prisons) had already been found unworthy for reasons of incompetence or worse. Of these affairs, the most serious involved Charles Forbes, director of the Veterans' Bureau and one of Harding's most intimate friends.

More than 300,000 wounded or disabled veterans, many of them suffering from nervous and mental disorders, returned from World War I to find that there was no governmental agency capable of providing the help they needed and very little public interest in their problems. Harding, however, was interested; he combined a number of disparate and overlapping functions to form a

---

[23] Quoted in Adams, *Incredible Era*, p. 222.

President Warren G. Harding with the members of his cabinet, the "best minds" he trusted to set his administration on the right course.

single, well-funded agency, the Veterans' Bureau. Unfortunately, it was Forbes, not the veterans, who profited from the bureau's first two years of operation. With the assistance of his legal advisor, Charles Cramer, Forbes promised hospital building contracts, without competitive bidding and for a $5,000 cash advance on "future transactions," to a St. Louis firm represented by his good friend Elias Mortimer. He sold "surplus and practically worthless" government-owned hospital supplies and equipment, in staggering quantities and again without competitive bidding, to a Boston company. Actually, most of these supplies—bandages, drugs, soap, bedding, pyjamas—were brand-new and desperately needed in hospitals across the country. Samuel Hopkins Adams estimated that about $3,000,000 worth of usable merchandise was disposed of in this way, at a total cost to the Boston firm of about $600,000. The official, day-to-day operations of the bureau had been bogged down in graft and inefficiency from the beginning. Harding loyally defended his friend against rumors of misconduct until those rumors were unequivocally confirmed in evidence gathered by Surgeon-General Charles Sawyer, Harding's personal physician and a member of the bureau's staff. Harding quietly obtained Forbes' resignation and sent him off to Europe on "official business." But the matter had gone too far to remain quiet for long. Forbes' replacement would have to be announced, and a Senate investigation was inevitable.

At the same time, Harding was defending two other intimate friends against rumors and congressional investigation. Secretary of the Interior Fall had been able to head off, temporarily, a Senate investigation into his handling of certain oil leases by hinting darkly at preparations for a possibly necessary war with Japan. Attorney General Daugherty had run into trouble in the House of Representatives. Congressman Oscar Keller of Minnesota filed a list of charges with the Judiciary Committee which alleged that

Albert Fall.

> Daugherty or his subordinates had failed to enforce the
> anti-trust laws, had refused to prosecute war profiteers
> and bootleggers, had obtained pardons for favored
> criminals, had secured the Chicago injunction against
> [railroad] strikers by undue influence on the local judge,
> had employed corrupt people in the Department of Justice,
> had set federal agents to shadow critics in Congress, had
> diverted funds to illegal uses, and had failed to prosecute
> the Standard Oil Company for trespassing on government
> oil lands.[24]

But Congressman Keller commanded little respect among his colleagues, and the Judiciary Committee refused to act on his motion to initiate impeachment proceedings.

[24] Quoted in Sinclair, *The Available Man*, p. 260.

This was lucky for Daugherty because, as it later turned out, Keller's allegations were substantially true.

Daugherty, too, had rewarded his friends and supporters from Ohio. Many of them found official employment in the Department of Justice—notably Alien Property Custodian Thomas W. Miller and Director of the Federal Bureau of Investigation William J. Burns, who in turn employed on special jobs an agent of highly dubious character, Gaston B. Means. Three others, Howard Mannington, F. E. Caskey, and Jesse Smith, found less official but most profitable employment in the "Little Green House" on K Street:

> The place became quite a social centre. Senators, Congressmen, and Cabinet members dropped in to have a drink from supplies obligingly furnished by Government officials who diverted confiscated wet goods thither [the Eighteenth Amendment prohibiting the manufacture and sale of alcoholic beverages had been in effect since January, 1920], and to play in the sky-limit poker game. Thomas W. Miller, who came to grief by trying to make too much money as Alien Property Custodian, was a frequent caller. . . . Gaston B. Means, Department of Justice operative and the most plausible confidence man of his day, used it for business purposes. Charlie Forbes drank and gambled there, as did his Nemesis, Elias H. Mortimer, the unofficial White House bootlegger [supplier of illegal alcohol]. It was a port of call for big liquor operators, office-buyers, jobbers in bribery, and all the sorry, furtive drift of the political underworld. There is contradictory evidence as to whether the President was ever in the house. In any case, he was not one of the regulars. He played his poker elsewhere.
>
> The Ohio Gang traded in liquor withdrawal permits, protection to bootleggers, appointments to office, illegal concessions, immunity from prosecution, pardons, paroles, privileges, and general graft. Howard Mannington ran the headquarters. He put out a shingle. He purported to be a lawyer, which he was not. His partner, Caskey, was. Caskey did the work and Mannington handled the loot,

while Jesse Smith skimmed the profits. They soon became the best if not the most favorably known triumvirate in the city.[25]

Jesse Smith supplied the Ohio Gang with that most necessary commodity, credibility. The son of a wealthy Ohio merchant, Smith was a foolish, vain little man—he was described as "a symphony in gray and lavender" on his last public appearance—who adored being known as the intimate friend of men in high office. And, as a result of his unfailing good humor, respectful flattery, and constant willingness to be helpful, he was in fact the close companion and confidant of both the attorney general and the president. Daugherty, whose wife was an incurable invalid unable to leave Ohio, shared his house on H Street with Smith, who was divorced. Smith became his right-hand man, a kind of combination chief butler, private secretary, business manager, and political fixer. (The house, incidentally, was lent to them by another wealthy and foolish Ohio businessman, Edward McLean, who owned the *Washington Post* and who entertained the Hardings and other political luminaries frequently and lavishly at his Virginia estate.) Although Smith had no official standing whatever, he occupied his own office in the Department of Justice, dictated letters—which went out on stationery bearing the department's letterhead—to a secretary whose salary was paid by the department, and had free access to the department's highly confidential files.

Jesse Smith.

Did a prospective contributor-under-pressure to the graft fund express doubt of the gang's ability to deliver?
Mannington or Caskey or Means was in a position to say:
    "So you think we're giving you the runaround, huh? Well, you meet me tomorrow evening at seven back of the Shoreham."
    Watching at the rendezvous, they would see Jesse Smith drive up in the Attorney General's car and enter with his latchkey.

[25] Adams, *Incredible Era*, p. 235.

"Do you know whose house that is?" . . . "Well, that's
Daugherty's. And Jess Smith lives there with him. He and
Harry Daugherty are just like that," with fingers entwined
in illustration. "But that ain't the half of it."

Presently the White House car would appear, guarded
by the ever-present secret service men. Out would step the
President and Mrs. Harding. Perhaps as the door opened,
there would be a glimpse of the Attorney General in
evening dress. Or the Postmaster General might follow,
or a pair of Cabinet officers or a group of Senators.

He was, indeed, a hard-boiled sceptic who would not
accept such evidence as warranty of the gang's ability
to deliver.

More simply the doubter might be invited to examine
a newspaper photograph, picturing that ardent fan, the
President, about to throw out the first ball of the season
at Griffith Park, with Jesse Smith seated in the place of
honor on his right, while Cabinet members bowed their
diminished heads in the background.[26]

Daugherty's later protests that he knew nothing about
Smith's involvement in the affairs of Mannington, Caskey
& Co. were unconvincing, to say the least. Samuel Hopkins
Adams believed, however, that Harding really did not
know:

There is something grimly ironic in the fact that Harding,
himself free of the taint of corruption, should have served
as guaranty for the most flagrant group of bandits known
to Washington since the days of Ulysses S. Grant. There
is no doubt that he was for a long time ignorant of those
Ohio operations already becoming notorious among the
cogniscenti. So many things go on in Washington that the
White House never hears, or, if it does hear, only long
after the fact. . . . Any president is bound to be the worst
informed man in Washington, because there are so many
people interested in keeping information from him.[27]

[26] Ibid., p. 239.
[27] Ibid., pp. 239–240.

As for Jesse Smith, probably it never occurred to him that his activities might bring disgrace to his good friend the president; possibly it never even occurred to him that he was doing anything dishonest. He seems to have had very few brains, and less moral sense than a peacock.

Evidently, believable rumors had reached Harding by May, 1923. Already worried by the impending Senate investigation of the Veterans' Bureau, and deeply shocked by the suicide of the bureau's attorney, Charles Cramer, Harding decided to escape the tensions of Washington for a while by making a speaking tour through the western states. The tour, he thought, would improve his faltering health and would also give him a chance to raise some early support for the following year's presidential campaign. The names Smith and Daugherty were not included on the official list of persons to accompany the president. The implications of this omission were unmistakable, and on May 29 Jesse Smith shot himself through the head. Washington was thick with ugly rumors, even dark hints of murder (these mostly the work of Gaston Means), when a profoundly depressed Harding boarded his special presidential train on June 20. In St. Louis, Harding was visited by the distraught wife of Albert Fall, who had resigned as secretary of the interior to go into the oil business. Their conversation was private, but shortly afterwards Harding was moved to remark to William Allen White:

> My God, this is a hell of a job! I have no trouble with my
> enemies. . . . But my damned friends, my God-damn
> friends, White, they're the ones that keep me walking
> the floor nights![28]

On July 26, in Seattle, Harding suffered severe pains which Surgeon-General Sawyer attributed to acute indigestion or possibly food poisoning, although a specialist declared that the president had had a heart attack. The party went on to San Francisco, where more specialists

---

[28] Quoted in William E. Leuchtenburg, *The Perils of Prosperity: 1914–1932* (Chicago: University of Chicago Press, 1966), p. 92.

UNITED PRESS INTERNATIONAL

Three million people lined the railroad tracks three thousand miles across the nation as the funeral train carried the dead president back to Washington.

were consulted. They confirmed the diagnosis of heart disease. On August 3, when a blood clot reached his brain, President Warren G. Harding died.

The American people, as yet unaware of the scandals to come, were genuinely grieved by his death:

> The feeling of the man in the street was one of personal loss. Harding himself was an ordinary man. He was one of the people, a prototype of the average as no other President within memory had been. His way of life, so far as it was known to the public, was typically American. In him the common man saw not only his type-representative, but, in a sense, himself. He was "just folks." Not only did the nation mourn him as a leader; the people mourned him as a comrade. There were dirges for the President; there were tears for the man.[29]

[29] Adams, *Incredible Era*, p. 384.

Three million people lined the railroad tracks, from the Pacific to the Atlantic, to catch a glimpse of the funeral train. "It is believed," said *The New York Times,* "to be the most remarkable demonstration in American history of affection, respect, and reverence for the dead."[30]

But the scandals could not be hushed up for long. The Senate investigation into the Veterans' Bureau affair came first. Then a Senate committee headed by Thomas Walsh of Montana revealed Albert Fall's sordid performance as secretary of the interior. By taking advantage of Edwin Denby's laziness and general incompetence, Fall had managed to get control of several government oil reserves transferred from the Department of the Navy to the Department of the Interior. Without calling for competitive bids, Fall leased the reserves at Elk Hills, California, to Edward Doheny, president of Pan-American Petroleum, in return for a small black satchel containing $100,000 in cash. Then, also without competitive bidding, Fall leased the oil reserves at Teapot Dome, Wyoming, to the Continental Trading Company, Ltd., a corporation registered in Canada. Actually, the Continental Trading Company was made up of Harry Sinclair of the Sinclair Oil Company, H. M. Blackmer of the Midwest Oil Company, Robert Stewart of the Standard Oil Company of Indiana, and James E. O'Neil of the Prairie Oil Company. In an ingenious and illegal operation, these men bought government oil at $1.50 a barrel and sold it, through the Continental Trading Company, to their own legitimate companies at $1.75 a barrel. In return for his cooperation, Fall received $265,000 in Liberty bonds from the Continental Trading Company, as well as $85,000 in cash and some fine blooded stock for his ranch in New Mexico from Harry Sinclair. Fall was able to pay nine years' back taxes on his ranch, put the dilapidated property in prime condition, and acquire adjoining land at a

President Harding's body lying in state in a flower-filled room in the White House.

---

[30] Quoted in Frederick Lewis Allen, *Only Yesterday* (New York: Harper & Row, Perennial Library, 1964), p. 111. Copyright 1931 by Frederick Lewis Allen, 1959 by Agnes Rogers Allen. By permission of Harper & Row, Publishers.

Oil tycoon Harry
Sinclair served a
three-month prison
term for his part in
the Teapot Dome
affair.

CULVER PICTURES, INC.

cost of $125,000. A cabinet officer's salary was $12,000 annually. Fall desperately attempted to convince the committee that his sudden prosperity had come about as a result of generous loans from friends—and even persuaded the gullible Edward McLean to testify that he had lent much of the money—but the evidence of bribery was overwhelming.

Harry Daugherty and his Justice Department also came under investigation. By shifting as much blame as he could on to his subordinates and on to his superior, the dead president, and by invoking the Fifth Amendment and various legal obstructions when the blame seemed to rest squarely on him, the attorney general was able to save himself from conviction on criminal charges. He was, however, forced to resign his cabinet position.

Few members of the Ohio Gang or their associates escaped exposure during the investigations, and those who, like Daugherty, lost only their jobs and reputations were lucky. Here is what happened to some of them:

Charles Forbes	jail
Albert Fall	jail
Thomas W. Miller	jail
Gaston B. Means	jail
Harry Sinclair	jail
Charles Cramer	suicide
Jesse Smith	suicide
Elias Mortimer	suicide
Frank Brandegee	suicide
Edward McLean	mental institution

At least a dozen more were fired or forced to resign, and several—including two of Sinclair's confederates in the Continental Trading Company—left the country in order to avoid facing criminal prosecution.

At first, the public greeted these revelations with incredulity, even indignation, as Frederick Lewis Allen observed:

... The harshest condemnation on the part of the press
and the public was reserved, not for those who had
defrauded the Government, but for those who insisted

on bringing the facts to light. Senator Walsh, who led
the investigation of the oil scandals, and Senator Wheeler,
who investigated the Department of Justice, were called
by the *New York Tribune* "the Montana scandalmongers."
The *New York Evening Post* called them "mud-gunners."
The *New York Times*, despite its Democratic leanings,
called them "assassins of character." In these and other
newspapers throughout the country one read of the
"Democratic lynching-bee" and "poison-tongued
partisanship, pure malice, and twittering hysteria," and
the inquiries were called "in plain words, contemptible
and disgusting."[31]

But Harding's ghost could not stand forever white
alongside such blackened companions, and within a few
years scandal had soiled the president's memory, too. In
1927, after failing to obtain financial support from the
Harding family for herself and her illegitimate child, a
young woman named Nan Britton published a book, *The
President's Daughter,* in which she described her role as
Harding's mistress. In 1930, following his release from
the federal penitentiary at Atlanta, Gaston B. Means published a book, *The Strange Death of President Harding,*
in which he "proved" that Harding did not die of a heart
attack as the public had been led to believe. Instead,
Means claimed, Harding was poisoned by his wife, who
was insanely jealous of Miss Britton. Means went so far
as to suggest that Mrs. Harding also poisoned her husband's physician, Dr. Sawyer, because he suspected her
guilt. And according to Means, Charles Cramer, Jesse
Smith, and several others were murdered, too, although
not necessarily by Mrs. Harding. Perhaps fortunately,
Florence Harding had died in 1924 and so was spared
the pain of knowing that such things were being whispered about her and her husband in homes across the
country.

These new rumors were accompanied by an older
rumor, a rumor that was revived and strengthened when
it was learned that in 1922 Harry Daugherty had used

[31] Ibid., p. 128.

the FBI to locate and destroy every copy of a book published that year by an obscure college professor, William Estabrook Chancellor. The book purported to prove that Harding had "African ancestry." For several generations it had been rumored around Blooming Grove, Ohio, that there was Negro blood in the Harding family, and the rumor accounted to some extent for the family's ill-defined social standing there and later in Marion. The rumor had first been used against Harding himself in the 1890's, when he was still a struggling young newspaper proprietor, and it resurfaced regularly thereafter, especially at election times and always in the form of oblique references and sly innuendos that were very difficult to combat. One recent writer, Francis Russell, considered the psychological effects of this rumor so central to an understanding of Harding's life that he called his biography *The Shadow of Blooming Grove.* But however this "shadow" may have affected Harding privately, he never publicly denied that he had Negro blood, and he made it plain to his associates, including Harry Daugherty, that he did not wish them to deny it either. He once remarked to an old friend, "How do I know, Jim? One of my ancestors may have jumped the fence." [32] It is probable that Harding never knew of Chancellor's book, or of Daugherty's swift suppression of it.

Samuel Hopkins Adams concluded his biography of Warren Gamaliel Harding with the following words:

> So turmoil, dissension, and recrimination followed that peace-loving, joy-seeking, and kindly soul, Warren G. Harding, to the last.
>
> Few deaths are unmingled tragedies. Harding's was not. He died in time. Not only was he relieved of a burden at all times beyond his strength, but he escaped an ordeal of accusation and heaped-up blame which must have crushed a soul never too sturdy. Had he remained, as he wistfully desired, a small-city editor, a local magnate, a greeter and conciliator and adjuster by virtue of his amiable nature and talent for friendliness, he would

---

[32] Quoted in Adams, *Incredible Era,* p. 280.

have died, warmly loved and sorely missed in his own environment. As President of the United States, he never wholly lost the public affection which he so craved, which was for him the reward most to be desired from life.

But it is the man, not the President, who is still loved and mourned.[33]

But few of the historians who followed Adams were so charitable. Consider, for example, the judgment of Eric Goldman:

Jesse Smith's friend in the White House did manage three positive achievements. The President, according to his mistress, left behind an illegitimate daughter, conceived in the Senate Office Building shortly before his nomination. He added "back to normalcy" to the American language because he misread the correct phrase that Professor Jacob Hollander of Johns Hopkins had written for him. And he took a firm stand on the tariff. "We should," the President of the United States told a reporter, "adopt a protective tariff of such a character as will help the struggling industries of Europe to get on their feet." The reporter rose and left the room, speechless.[34]

Warren G. Harding—An Alternative View

In 1965, a new biography of Harding appeared—Andrew Sinclair's *The Available Man: The Life Behind the Masks of Warren G. Harding*. Written with reference to correspondence and other documents previously unavailable to scholars, Sinclair's book was new not only because it had just been published but also because it presented a new interpretation of Harding both as a man and as a successful presidential candidate.

The Harding who emerges from Sinclair's book is largely the same man who emerges from Adams's book—he is no more intelligent, no less friendly, and certainly no

[33] Ibid., pp. 441–442.
[34] Eric Goldman, *Rendezvous with Destiny* (New York: Alfred A. Knopf, 1952), p. 221.

Warren Harding was thirty-five when this picture was taken in 1900. His newspaper was a success by then, and he had begun to play an active role in state politics.

BROWN BROTHERS

better qualified by education or experience for the presidency. But he differs from the traditional Harding in several important respects. He is, for one thing, politically ambitious. And he is, for another thing, politically shrewd, both able and anxious to set his own course toward high office. Harding's motto "boost, don't knock," his ever-present desire to "harmonize" conflicting factions and viewpoints, and his tendency to "trim" on an issue until he saw which way the wind was blowing—these were all natural enough to him, and they did indeed indicate a man more interested in the prestige of public office than in promoting a consistent political philosophy. But they were not necessarily the mark of a weak man. As used by Harding, they were invaluable political tactics which enabled him to remain on the winning side—whichever side that happened to be. They enabled him to *seem* weak, a definite advantage in a state and a party torn between rival political factions, without actually *being* weak. Harding, the friend of everybody, was the tool of nobody, except when he chose to be.

Even more interesting to Sinclair than *how* Harding became the Republican party's most "available man" for the presidency is *why*. Probably there were dozens of Republican politicians who could easily have matched him in adroitness. Why was Harding the nominee?

According to Sinclair, there existed in America certain "necessary myths"—some of them dating back as far as Andrew Jackson—which a presidential candidate had to embody, or appear to embody, if he wished to win the votes of the rural, Anglo-Saxon, Protestant middle classes whose influence dominated American politics until just after the 1920 election. And it happened that Harding, more than any other Republican contender, did genuinely possess many of the characteristics required by these myths.

Harding was, first of all, a Country Boy of relatively humble origins—the eldest of eight children of a none-too-successful country doctor. He was a Self-made Man, having through hard work, a flare for public relations, and the luck of being located in a town that had steadily attracted new industry, parlayed a small loan into a flourishing daily newspaper. Harding the prosperous small-town businessman, with his constant and perfectly sincere boosting of the values of Main Street, was particularly attractive in 1920 because he and his ideas represented a kind of compromise between the old, religiously based rural morality and the newer, more pragmatic morality of the spreading industrial society. "His life and vocabulary," as Sinclair expressed it, "nourished the Victorian and moral myths so dear to most American people that they could benefit from the machine without losing the values of the farm."[35] Harding was, furthermore, from the Presidential State, Ohio, which had supplied ten of the last thirteen Republican presidential nominees, seven of the twelve presidents since 1869. "Ohio was the Presidential state for fifty years because it produced Presidential nominees in the Republican Party who won elections and who looked after their own. Ohio believed itself to be the mother of Presidents and thus persuaded others that it was. In politics, nothing succeeds like boosting."[36] Like the majority of the American people, Harding believed in America First, and thought that the president should be guided by the Best Minds and generally subservient to the Guardian Senate. If he did not quite measure up to two more myths, those of the Political Innocent and the Reluctant Candidate, he could at least pretend to do so.

How well Harding and his advisors understood the importance of these "necessary myths" is revealed in the following press statement, released by Harry Daugherty in December, 1919, when Harding officially entered the presidential race:

> Senator Harding has practically been forced into every contest for high honors he has ever received. He has been generous in supporting others. He is a thorough-going Republican partisan who always supports his own party but never offends those who belong to other parties. In

Harding setting type at the *Star* office, shortly before his death.

[35] Sinclair, *The Available Man*, p. vii.
[36] Ibid., p. 30.

The Ohio political boss Marcus Hanna. A wealthy business-man with interests in mining and bank-ing, Hanna had his greatest impact on national politics in 1896–1901 when he was a close advisor of William McKin-ley, whose career he had guided to the presidency.

CULVER PICTURES, INC.

many respects that make men great and attractive, no man was ever as much like McKinley as is Harding. He is patient, he does not rush in with a positive opinion until he has taken all the time necessary to consider a subject and receive all the good advice he can find or is offered. He is a charming man to meet and people like him immediately upon meeting him. The liking lasts. As a clear, convincing, pleasing orator he has no superior in the United States. When he takes a stand he stands there until he advances. He was born a poor boy and knows all the hardships that accompany a man who makes his own way in the world. He is kindly, considerate, sympathetic and good-natured. He is a great American and for everything that is American. There is no man so humble that he would not stop and stoop to do a favor and help lift up in the world. He is well posted and sound on all the great questions of interest to the welfare of our country. He is sound in his ideas about finances. He is of the McKinley type in his ideas on the protective tariff. He is a good judge of human nature. He has lived a pure life. He has the very appearance of a president of the United States. Harding is the one man sure to carry Ohio if the great Republican Party were to nominate him.[37]

This eulogy, Sinclair observes, was "an admirable syn-thesis of the facts and fictions that made Harding both available and inadequate, the candidate who had not dared to be himself. Daugherty's statement was also something new in American politics. It was the first case of a manager selling his candidate as a winning image rather than as a great man."[38] It was largely because this image-making was so successful, Sinclair believes, that the "traditional Harding myths"—those of the Political Innocent, the Reluctant Candidate, the Dark Horse, the Smoke-filled Room, and the Solemn Referendum—were so widely accepted and have persisted in history books to this day.

[37] Quoted in ibid., pp. vii–viii.
[38] Ibid., p. vii.

Harding's credibility as a Political Innocent is under- mined by the simple fact of his success in Ohio state poli- tics. One of the reasons Ohio was the Presidential State was that it took a man of exceptional political skill to survive there, and during Harding's early years in politics the going was especially rough, with two powerful Repub- lican machines—those of Marcus Hanna, "the Red Boss of Cleveland," and Joseph B. Foraker, "the Black Boss of Cincinnati"—struggling for control of the state. By "har- monizing" and "trimming," by playing the innocent and leaving any necessary dirty work to Harry Daugherty, Harding managed to make himself useful to both bosses without permanently alienating either, and without iden- tifying himself in the public mind as a "machine poli- tician." According to Sinclair, Harding encouraged among his political associates the myth that he was only a plain, simple businessman whose career was guided every step of the way by Daugherty, just as he encouraged among his employees the myth that his wife made all the impor- tant decisions concerning the management of the Marion *Star*. That way, he was always the good guy, with any blame for meanness or failure to return a favor falling elsewhere. In reality, says Sinclair, "Harding, to the end of his life, kept all major financial decisions about the *Star,* and all major political decisions in his own hands."

Joseph B. Foraker, Hanna's rival for control of the Re- publican party in Ohio, was governor of the state from 1885 to 1889 and senator from 1897 to 1909.

> The myth that Harry Daugherty made Harding as a
> politician in Ohio and took him to the White House is as
> enduring as it is untrue. His relationship with Daugherty
> was, indeed, the most important relationship in Harding's
> life—not because it made him, but because it disgraced
> him. Without Daugherty, Harding would have been
> nationally known. Without Harding, Daugherty would
> have died an obscure lobbyist at Columbus.[39]

Harding had also made himself useful to the party's na- tional leaders, and in 1912 he was rewarded with the honor of nominating William Howard Taft for the presi- dency—Taft was considered certain to win both the nomi-

[39] Ibid., p. 37.

nation and the election, as in fact he did. In 1914, Harding proved his appeal to the voters of Ohio by being among the first group of United States senators to be elected directly by the people rather than by the state legislatures. In the Senate his "harmonizing" tactics continued to pay off. In 1916, he was given the prestigious job of keynote speaker and chairman of the Republican national convention.

Although mentioned as a possible contender during his early years as Ohio's junior senator, the probability of Harding's reaching the White House was not great until after the elections of 1916. At that time all of his serious state rivals were eliminated from the competition. Harding became the only Republican in high office from Ohio, the state's most available man for the presidency.

Assessing his chances, Harding decided to play the Reluctant Candidate in his pursuit of the nomination. He, not his future campaign manager, Harry Daugherty, developed the strategy. On numerous occasions, Daugherty unsuccessfully tried to convince Harding that a policy of intrigue was the best course to the nomination. But each time he was overruled by Harding's firm belief in the superiority of harmony and humility. Harding wanted no one to think him ambitious. His public speeches usually began with an avowal of his incapacity and unwillingness to accept the presidential nomination, but he concluded those same speeches with a conditional acceptance if his friends and the situation should wish it on him. He did not discourage early boosters but neither would he admit to having encouraged them. He liked supporters out working for him while he disclaimed ambition and pretended to be reluctant.

Harry Daugherty, photographed during the 1920 campaign.

UNITED PRESS INTERNATIONAL

Harding's campaign manager repeatedly underestimated the candidate he was guiding. Eighteen months before his nomination, Harding cautioned Daugherty:

> The trouble with you, my dear Daugherty, in your political relations with me, is that you appraise my political sense so far below par that you have no confidence in me or my judgment. Pray do not think because I can

and do listen in politeness to much that is said to me, that
I am always being "strung."[40]

Harding, confident that he could manage his own campaign, became disenchanted with Daugherty and on more than one occasion was ready to break off the relationship. Each time, however, Daugherty was able to mend the friendship and to continue as manager and advisor. On the basis of correspondence preserved in the Harding papers for the early months of 1920, Sinclair has stated conclusively that Harding planned his own campaign for the nomination. Although Daugherty later claimed that he managed the campaign without Harding's knowing much of what was going on, in reality it was Daugherty who did not know what Harding was doing. While Harding was carrying on a voluminous correspondence with associates in nearly every state of the union—and receiving reports from his territorial managers, Mannington and Forbes—Daugherty was left with the modest task of raising a campaign fund of $113,000.

Few contemporaries considered Harding a Dark Horse. Political commentators talked openly of a Harding or a Lowden candidacy. His service to the party, his small-town background, his presidential demeanor, and his position in strategic Ohio led many analysts to suggest that Harding was the logical choice for the nomination. Still, knowing that he would probably not be one of the front-runners, Harding thought that it might be useful to be regarded as a Dark Horse, someone on whom opposing factions could agree to compromise:

> The strategy of Ohio politicians at the Republican
> convention was often based on the theory of the deadlock.
> When neither of two leading contenders could gain the
> nomination, the convention always looked to the Buckeye
> State for its compromise candidate, for he, at least, could
> carry Ohio, the pivotal state of myth. Hayes and Garfield
> had both won the nomination by this tactic. . . . The
> potency of the Ohio myth always gave its favorite sons

[40] Quoted in ibid., p. 110.

a huge advantage in a deadlocked convention, even when the favorite son was not a frontrunner, such as Grant or McKinley or Taft.[41]

Throughout 1919, Ohio politicians made every attempt to force Harding's hand. Was he running for the Senate or the presidency? Daugherty advised him to declare for the presidency and forget the Senate. Harding ignored this advice and continued his strategy of evasion, refusing to announce his candidacy for either office. Many political deals were offered by other contenders, but Harding turned them down. Leonard Wood, for example, offered to support Harding's re-election to the Senate if Harding would deliver the Ohio delegation to Wood. Finally, the state delegation insisted on a decision, and the Reluctant Candidate announced in December, 1919, that he was available for the nomination—although he also filed for the Senate race. At this time he committed himself to Daugherty as his official manager. With Daugherty to make the deals, Harding could continue to play the role of the dignified, straightforward businessman-statesman.

To achieve the nomination, Harding believed that he had to do three things. First, he had to secure the support of the Senate's old guard—the conservatives—who, it was commonly thought, would have the power to dictate the nominee if the convention should deadlock. This had been true in the past, particularly in the cases of Garfield and Hayes. Next, he had to become the *second* choice of key delegations, particularly those supporting Governor Lowden. He spent a great deal of his time courting the Lowden delegates. Finally, he would have to prove his popular appeal by entering presidential primaries against Wood, Lowden, and Johnson. In the early months of 1920, Harding was confident of his nomination. Writing to a friend in February, he remarked:

I am bound to say that the whole situation looks
infinitely more promising than I have any reason to expect.
I am beginning to feel now as though I am afraid I will
be nominated.[42]

[41] Ibid., p. 41.

[42] Quoted in ibid., p. 131.

The famous prediction made by Daugherty that same month was merely an elaboration of Harding's own strategy for winning the nomination. By March, most of the delegates of Texas, Colorado, Missouri, and Ohio had declared in favor of Harding.

It was then that the campaign moved to Ohio. During the primary, Harding found that he had to fight for his life —he barely defeated Wood and got only thirty-nine of Ohio's forty-eight delegates. The Indiana primary which followed was even more disastrous, with Harding finishing last behind Wood, Johnson, and Lowden. The situation seemed hopeless, and the conservative political bosses began switching their support from Harding to Lowden. Harding's chances were salvaged, however, when Senator Borah's investigating committee charged Wood and Lowden with spending exorbitant campaign funds in an attempt to buy the nomination. By convention time, the reputations of both frontrunners had been badly damaged, and Harding was back in the picture.

Harding talking to reporters from his front porch in Marion.

That the old-guard conservatives did not completely control the convention was obvious from the outset— neither of the frontrunners, Wood or Lowden, was acceptable to them. (The other two contenders with substantial popular support, Johnson and Hoover, were even less acceptable but were not considered serious threats, being too progressive to win over a majority of the delegates.) When the convention looked as if it might deadlock, however, the old guard saw a chance to assert its power. Chairman Lodge, ignoring a vote against adjournment, simply walked away from the rostrum.

Sinclair then discusses the myth of the Smoke-filled Room. There were, he suggests, many smoke-filled rooms in the Blackstone Hotel that night. The suite of rooms important to the Harding myth was occupied by George Harvey, a party wheeler-and-dealer who later proved most inept as ambassador to Great Britain, and Senator Frank Brandegee of Connecticut:

> Throughout the night, in an ever-changing group, tired
> Senators came and went. Harvey, along with Senators
> Lodge, Brandegee, Curtis, and Smoot, was there most

of the time. Senators Wadsworth and Watson and
McCormick also called, as did less influential Senators.
There was no agreement between them, and there was no
formal meeting. They did not know what the convention
would do, what Wood and Lowden and Johnson would do,
or what compromise choice they would make. The
smoke-filled room was filled mainly with smoke.[43]

The following morning Senator Smoot announced to the
press, rather unenthusiastically, that Harding would probably be the nominee. But many other predictions were
made by many other senators that morning, any one of
which could have come true. The most interesting of
Sinclair's conclusions is that the old guard really did not
support Harding. They merely wanted to use him to stop
Lowden and Wood—and then submit the name of the
Republican national chairman, Will Hays.

In the balloting that followed, the old guard did not
help Harding. On the fifth through the ninth ballots,
Harding's strength grew because of the efforts he had
invested earlier in his campaign. Lowden, unable to reach
a compromise with Wood, allowed his delegates to move
to their second choice, Harding. Senator Penrose never
had controlled Pennsylvania's large delegation; if he had,
its favorite son would have been Senator Knox, not Governor Sproul. Chairman Lodge, supposedly one of Harding's most influential supporters, adjourned the convention after the ninth ballot in an effort to stop Harding. Not
until the tenth ballot did Lodge allow the Massachusetts
delegation to vote for Harding. Senator Brandegee tried
to convince his delegation to break for Hays on the tenth
ballot, but instead the entire delegation voted for Harding.
In the final analysis, it was the lack of power of the old
guard—plus their inability to communicate to the convention what they really wanted—that led to Harding's nomination. The selection of Calvin Coolidge as vice-president
only accentuated the ineffectiveness of their leadership:

> "The whole show at Chicago," Dwight Morrow wrote,
> "was a terrible jumble." In this terrible jumble, the myths
> of politics *believed by the delegates* were in command.

[43] Ibid., p. 142.

When Wood and Lowden deadlocked, two myths gave
Harding the nomination. The first: when in doubt, turn
to Ohio . . . ; the second myth was that the bosses of the
Senate *did* control the convention, when they did not.
Thus Harding became the most available man to break
the deadlock. The image of him as a small-town
businessman confirmed his appeal. And the personal
contacts, which he and Daugherty had assiduously
fostered before the convention, gave him the increasing
strength from *individual* delegates that started his
bandwagon rolling. . . .

Harding was certainly the popular second choice of a
majority of delegates at Chicago. He was not the popular
second choice of a majority of Senators. In fact, the
unbossed convention beat the Senators over both the
nominees. It was only after the fact that Harding's fellow
Senators claimed that they had seen to his nomination.
Daugherty knew that they had not, as did many others.
If, at any time, Wood and Lowden had agreed, or if
Johnson had joined either, Harding would have been
finished. He won by his subtle strategy of appealing to
all without pride and by treating false friends as though
they were true ones. Harding and the delegates believed
that he was the Senators' choice. Thus when the delegates
chose him, he became Senators' choice in legend and
retrospect. By playing the innocent, Harding outfoxed
the conspirators.[44]

Between the June convention and the November election, Harding added a new dimension to successful campaign strategy. His relations with journalists were excellent. As a former reporter himself, he was thoroughly
familiar with their deadlines, their problems, and the kinds
of copy they found most useful. According to Sinclair,
Harding "set a fashion in good press relations that was
not equaled until the time of Franklin D. Roosevelt and
John F. Kennedy." Sinclair further believes that the front-
porch campaign was Harding's own idea—it suited both
his temperament and his preconvention image as the Political Innocent and Reluctant Candidate.

[44] Ibid., pp. 150–151.

Sinclair suggests that President Wilson's announcement that the election would be a Solemn Referendum on the League of Nations has misled most analysts. It has been commonly assumed that Harding's victory was more than anything else a vote against Wilson. Sinclair argues that such an interpretation owes more to the progressive historians than it does to the facts. To many historians, the idea that a majority of the American people should have voted *for* Harding was distasteful, even incomprehensible:

> The legend of a referendum favoring isolation was created. And a second myth was also set up: that the vote was against Wilson and not for Harding. In fact, Harding's victory was more personal and positive. He confirmed the pattern of Party politics for the next decade and restored the Republican party to the position of ascendancy that it had had in 1908, before it was split by the Progressive movement. And he won through his own merits and shrewdness, by appealing to the nostalgia in people for normalcy—defined by a wit as the desire that everything should remain as it never was.[45]

With 60.2 percent of the vote, Harding's was one of the largest majorities ever recorded by a presidential candidate up to that time. It is perhaps worth noting that even H. L. Mencken cast his vote for Warren G. Harding.

Sinclair agrees with Adams that Harding tried to be a good president, but he also believes that Harding succeeded in this to a much greater extent than he is traditionally given credit for. Certainly he was more independent. At the end of his first year in office, Harding wrote a long and confidential letter to an old friend. In it he evaluated his position as president:

> I think perhaps it has been of some advantage to start into office so poorly appraised, because one does not need to accomplish very much to find himself somewhat marked up in value. I heartily agree with you that the party is not nearly so strong as it was last year. I may say to you, in the confidence which covers our correspondence, that the party is not much more than twenty-five percent

[45] Ibid., p. 156.

as strong in my own estimate, and there are a good many
people in Congress whom my experience has led me to
mark down to about ten percent of their normal appraised
value. In simple truth, I get discouraged sometimes about
the stability of popular government, when I come in
contact with the abject surrender of public men to what
appears to be about one-half of one percent of the voters
to whom they look for their commission to public service.
What this country needs more than anything else is a House
and Senate for ten years which gives at least as much
thought to the welfare of the Republic as is given to
individual candidacies for re-election. Nothing so
disheartens me as to have an extended conference with
men in responsible places, hear them admit of the
correctness of a policy or position and then frankly say
it is impossible to go through with the policy or maintain
the position and be assured of re-election. I have concluded
that I would vastly prefer a limited career with the
consciousness of having done the right thing, than to hold
on to the constitutional limit by playing to the favor of
those who do the fake work under our political system.
My own disappointment with the public estimate of me
lies in the fact that so many seem to think I can take a
whip and show Congress where to head in. It was possible
for my predecessor to follow such a course during the
war when men ofttimes put aside their petty interests to
perform what was believed to be a patriotic service.
Conditions are not quite the same now. Probably I am
lacking in the domineering traits which Mr. Wilson
possessed and found himself able to exercise for
considerable time. In the end he came to failure because
of the practices followed.[46]

Sinclair does not attempt to minimize Harding's responsibility for appointing such men as Harry Daugherty,
Albert Fall, and Charles Forbes to high office. He does
point out, however, that patronage was an old Ohio tradition and that the administration of at least one previous
Ohio president, Ulysses S. Grant, was far more corrupt.
To some extent, Harding, like Grant, was a victim of the

[46] Quoted in ibid., p. 238.

opportunism and relaxed moral standards of the times in which he lived. It is true that he was advised against appointing Daugherty, Fall, and Forbes, but it is also true that some of his best appointments—those of Hughes and Hoover, for example—were vigorously opposed by the Senate conservatives. Sinclair believes that the scandals which came to light after Harding's death, as well as the myths of the Guardian Senate and Best Minds which Harding promoted but did not entirely believe during his lifetime, have obscured Harding's real contributions to the accomplishments of his administration—such accomplishments as the Washington Conference, at which nine treaties relating to arms-limitation and naval disarmament were negotiated among the world's most powerful nations.

It might be pointed out, too, that Harding's tendency to put people above principle had its positive effect in a country that had just lived through a highly emotional war and a year of panic following the Communist revolution in Russia. In 1918, Eugene V. Debs, the leader of the American Socialist party, had been sentenced to ten years' imprisonment for opposing the nation's participation in World War I. Woodrow Wilson had refused to pardon him, saying "This man was a traitor to his country and he will never be pardoned during my administration." During his first year in office, Harding had Debs brought to see him at the White House and issued a pardon over the strong protests of Daugherty and many powerful groups such as the American Legion. Harding made sure that the pardon would be effective before Christmas, so that Debs could spend the holiday with his family. Debs' successor as head of the Socialist party, Norman Thomas, was a welcome guest at the White House, along with his wife. To Harding, the staunch Republican and champion of free enterprise, the facts that Debs was a good and sincere man and that Thomas had once been a newsboy on the Marion *Star* were more important than the fact that they were Socialists.

Sinclair's evaluation of Harding the man is quite different from that of Eric Goldman, quoted earlier in this chapter. After acknowledging that "Harding's name has

Eugene V. Debs.

UNITED PRESS INTERNATIONAL

become a byword as the worst American President, the prime example of incompetence and sloth and feeble good nature," Sinclair observes,

> The verdict of Harding's own time was different. And it cannot be the verdict of any historian who has looked at the evidence of the papers preserved at the Ohio Historical Society. Harding was a hardworking and shrewd Ohio politician. He was always his own master. He used compromise and humility as political tactics. He listened to the opinions of others in order to flatter their vanity and educate himself. He was a man of mediocre intellect, but of great presence, ambition, and political talent. He was exceedingly fortunate in rising so high, but he was helped by his own persistence and strategy of harmony. He was a good friend, and he was a formidable opponent in an election. He resembled in his abilities President Hayes, whom he thought had been misjudged because of partisanship and prejudice.[47]

Of Harding the president, Sinclair concludes,

> Warren Harding became the most notorious President in American history because the myths that had formed him were not adequate to meet with the power and responsibility of the Presidency after the First World War. As Will Hays commented when he was a member of Harding's Cabinet, "The government is like a corner grocery which a few years ago could be run by one man, and now we try to use the same system in running Marshall Fields." Harding could have run admirably a corner grocery, as he ran his small-town newspaper. . . . Unfortunately, the social and political myths washed him into the Presidency and left him stranded there. He could not cope with the international and industrial complexity of postwar America with the beliefs of small-town Ohio. It was too late to muddle through. . . .
>
> . . . Once in the White House, Harding was faced with the reality of power. The myths faded or turned on him. Main Street morality could not cope with Wall Street

UNDERWOOD & UNDERWOOD

Warren G. Harding, photographed in San Francisco just a few hours before he died.

[47] Ibid., pp. 297–298.

complexity. The "best minds" often disagreed. In an effort to prove yet another myth of democracy, that the office makes the man, Harding tried to free himself from the corruption and entanglements brought about by his small-town loyalties. He did too little too late, and he died too soon. After his death, this creature of myth became its victim, for the theories of conspiracy at the grass roots of democracy fed on new myths of the Poisoned President and the Ohio Gang. Harding, in his coming and going, was the apotheosis of the American rural dream.

In this way, the Harding story is like "an old Greek tragedy." The old gods struck down a folk hero. For in his time Harding did seem to be hero enough. He seemed to represent the truth of many legends: that Presidents did come from the backwoods, that opportunities were equal, that small towns were the homes of goodness and democracy. On his death, he was mourned more than any President since Lincoln. But his example proved that Washington had become a world city and could no longer be ruled by the man from Marion. Harding was a small man in a great place, which was daily becoming greater.[48]

Warren G. Harding—A Recent View

Historian Robert K. Murray has supplied the most recent interpretation of the Harding administration. In his *The Harding Era* (1969) and *The Politics of Normalcy* (1973), Murray asserts that Harding's achievements in office have gone largely unnoticed while myths and gossip abound. Among the accomplishments of Harding that Murray lists are the nation's economic recovery from a postwar recession, the creation of the Bureau of the Budget, the Washington Conference, peace treaties, and helpful agricultural legislation. The Harding administration, in Murray's view, provided a relatively smooth transition from the war years to peacetime and bequeathed a prosperous economy to Calvin Coolidge. Murray attacks the myth of "Harding the bumbling incompetent" by revealing that the president actually conducted a more successful administration than previously believed.

[48] Ibid., pp. vi, viii.

SUGGESTED READINGS

Adams, Samuel Hopkins. *Incredible Era: The Life and Times of Warren Gamaliel Harding*. G. P. Putnam's Sons, Capricorn Books.

Hicks, John D. *Republican Ascendancy: 1921–1933*. Harper & Row, Torchbooks.

Lewis, Sinclair. *Babbitt*. New American Library, Signet Books.

Lewis, Sinclair. *Main Street*. New American Library, Signet Books.

Link, Arthur S. *American Epoch: A History of the United States Since 1890*. 3 vols. Alfred A. Knopf.

Mencken, H. L. *The Vintage Mencken*. Edited by Alistair Cooke. Random House, Vintage Books.

Sinclair, Andrew. *The Available Man: The Life Behind the Masks of Warren G. Harding*. Quadrangle Books.

White, William Allen. *A Puritan in Babylon: The Story of Calvin Coolidge*. G. P. Putnam's Sons, Capricorn Books.

Three churches at Dixon, South Dakota, photographed by Dorothea Lange. The tension between country and city, between old values and new values, shaped the important issues of the 1920's.

CHAPTER THREE

THE LIMITS OF

INDIVIDUAL FREEDOM

During the first two decades of the twentieth century, the progressive movement sought to redress the balance between the individual and the power of big business. If World War I marked the beginning of progressivism's end as a strong political force, it also marked the beginning of a movement for reform that was to spread far wider and deeper. As a result of the nation's rapid transformation from a rural to an urban society, many people were replacing the ideas, manners, and morals of the country and small town with ways of thinking and behaving that were more suitable to life in the modern, industrial world —a world opened up to them by their war experiences, by the automobile, and by radio, motion pictures, and mass-circulation magazines. The goal of both movements was more freedom for the individual, but the emphasis had shifted from concern with political and economic freedom to concern with social and intellectual freedom.

The scene of protest shifted, too. It passed from the halls of government and the pages of muckraking books and newspapers to the living rooms of millions of homes across the country. Women, having gained the right to vote in 1920, cut their hair, shortened their dresses, went to work, and began to smoke, drink, and talk like men in sufficient numbers to convince their elders that the moral fiber of American womanhood had snapped. The popularity of jazz and the Charleston contributed to that impression. The work of Sigmund Freud added a new dimension to many people's attitudes toward themselves and others, making the old, religiously based standards of right and wrong seem narrow and unscientific. Writers and artists complained of the materialism, puritanism, and general lack of sophisticated taste in American society, and many sought their inspiration, often literally, in Europe. Silly and strange fads and fashions appeared and disappeared, sometimes obscuring by the attention they attracted the serious experimentation with new ideas, or the rebellion against old ideas, that they reflected. Some of the most basic assumptions of the American way of life were being challenged in the 1920's.

But to concentrate exclusively on either the new order, as expressed in the social revolution of the young, educated, urban, and comparatively affluent, or on the old order of God-and-business-as-usual conservatism that prevailed in Washington and throughout the nation, is to miss much of the tension that existed between the two. This tension was revealed again and again in the public's responses to the questions of individual freedom that arose during the decade: Should the freedom of some be abridged to assure the security of the many? Should the freedom of speech, press, or assembly be sacrificed to combat the dangers of internal subversion? How far should the government go in attempting to control an individual's social behavior "for his own good"? Should the law concern itself with what people ought to *think* or *believe*?

These questions were not new in the 1920's, nor were the answers given then their final solutions. But the *way* in which these questions were answered can tell us much about the period, and about the America which preceded and followed it.

The Great Red Hysteria

America had not entered World War I with the wholehearted approval of all Americans, yet, throughout the war, the government of Woodrow Wilson demanded absolute loyalty from all. Most people gave it unthinkingly, even blindly. Schools dropped the German language and German history from their curriculums; librarians removed German books from their shelves. The governor of Iowa issued a proclamation forbidding the speaking of German in public places. Symphony concerts no longer included selections from Wagner, and the director of the Chicago Symphony Orchestra lost his position simply because of his German ancestry. Group pressure against any behavior that smacked of disloyalty, or even nonconformity, was enough to keep most people in line.

Both the federal and state governments passed sedition and espionage laws to help enforce loyalty, and a number of these laws remained in effect after the war ended. The Sedition Act of 1918 made it a crime, punishable by a $10,000 fine and twenty years' imprisonment,

> for a person to utter, print, write, or publish any disloyal, profane, scurrilous, or abusive language about the form of government of the United States, or the Constitution of the United States . . . or any language intended to . . . encourage resistance to the United States, or to promote the cause of its enemies. . . .

A second act passed in 1918 made it legal to exclude from admission into the United States all aliens thought to be anarchists. This act further provided that

> any alien who, at any time after entering the United States, is found to have been at the time of entry, or to have become thereafter, a member of any one of the classes of aliens [above mentioned] . . . shall upon warrant of the Secretary of Labor, be taken into custody and deported. . . .

The armistice of 1918 did not end the fear of subversion, or of the harmful effects of foreign influence. The American public continued to suspect anyone who spoke with an accent or carried a foreign name. Cases resulting from the sedition and espionage acts began to come before the courts in 1919, serving to remind the nation that

Two posters issued by the United States government during World War I.

disloyalty—at least alleged disloyalty—had existed, and suggesting the possibility that it still did.

At the same time, the American people watched with increasing apprehension the events growing out of the 1917 Bolshevik Revolution in Russia. Many feared the possibility of a worldwide proletarian revolution. Such patriotic organizations as the National Security League, the American Defense Society, and the American Protective League, which had been so popular and successful during the war years, were fighting for survival in late 1918. Seeking to prolong their existence, they played up the threat of Bolshevism.

The success of the Bolshevik Revolution also injected new life into American left-wing movements, which at that moment were weaker than they had been for many years. Excited by the Bolshevik actions in Russia, some socialists and others boasted that a similar revolution would soon occur in the United States. In its alarm at such statements, the American public made little distinction among the various shades of political opinion of left-wing groups: they were all labeled "Communist" and/or "radical." Labor unrest, a flurry of general strikes, race riots in the nation's urban centers, and bomb explosions reinforced the fear that the country was seriously threatened internally by "Reds."

In his book *Red Scare: A Study in National Hysteria, 1919–1920*, Robert K. Murray summarized the events of 1919 in the following way:

> During 1919, there occurred a series of highly suspicious and spectacular events which so focused public attention on the issue of radicalism that all these contributing factors were ultimately welded together into a common mass from which emerged the public panic and paranoia known as the Red Scare.
>
> Each of these incidents was particularly important because of its peculiar contribution in exaggerating the radical menace and increasing doubts concerning the essential soundness of the nation. One must admit that at a different time, or in a different background, most

of these occurrences would not have elicited more than a passing response from the general public. But, occurring when they did, each of these events seemed to lay the foundations of fear for the next, and so on, until at last truly abnormal actions resulted.[1]

In January, 1919, 35,000 shipyard workers in Seattle, Washington, went on strike for higher wages. By then, the cost of living was more than seventy-five percent higher than it had been before the war, yet laborers had not received a substantial increase in wages since the war began. Workers all over the country muttered against low wages, but the Seattle shipyard workers were among the first to take positive action. The day after the strike began, the Seattle Central Labor Council, representing all organized labor in the region, voted to conduct a general strike to support the shipyard workers. Mayor Ole Hanson and the press immediately denounced the strike as a "Red conspiracy." One newspaper headline proclaimed: "REDS DIRECTING SEATTLE STRIKE TO TEST CHANCE FOR REVOLUTION."[2]

Ole Hanson. In 1920 he published a book called *Americanism vs. Bolshevism*, but after the Seattle strike he never again achieved national recognition.

When the number of workers on strike grew to 60,000, the city of Seattle was paralyzed. Mayor Hanson, who bore a deep and particular hatred for the International Workers of the World, declared that it was not a strike at all—rather, it was a Wobbly plot to fan the flames of revolution in America. He requested federal troops, got them, and used them to break the general strike. Overnight, Hanson became a hero to many people for his "single-handed" stand against the "Bolshevik-sired insurrection." He was called "the Savior of Seattle." He had succeeded in persuading the country that the strike was part of a Communist plot.

Robert K. Murray wrote of the Seattle strike,

[1] Robert K. Murray, *Red Scare: A Study in National Hysteria, 1919–1920* (New York: McGraw-Hill, 1964), p. 57. Copyright © 1955 by the University of Minnesota. Reprinted by permission of the University of Minnesota Press, Minneapolis.

[2] Quoted in ibid., p. 65.

UNITED PRESS INTERNATIONAL

Federal troops keep striking shipyard workers away from the docks during the Seattle strike of 1919.

For the first time, public attention was focused sharply and solely on the issue of domestic radicalism to the virtual expulsion of all other factors. At the same time a pattern of response and reaction was set in motion which would be standard for the rest of the Scare period. Labor was placed in the position of making some disastrous mistakes which constantly subjected it to public suspicion. Employers, in turn, were brought to the realization that the issue of radicalism could be helpful in their fight against unionism. To certain politicians it became obvious that radicalism would make an excellent political issue by which free publicity as well as votes could be obtained. The general press, meanwhile, found in the issue of radicalism an immediate substitute for waning wartime sensationalism and eagerly busied itself with reporting exaggerations instead of facts.[3]

A report in February, 1919, that Premier Georges Clemenceau of France had been wounded by a Bolshevik

[3] Ibid., p. 67.

agent helped to keep the Red Scare alive. Revolutionary uprisings in Hungary and Bavaria excited further alarm, as did the formation in March of the Communist Third International, or Comintern, a Moscow-directed movement dedicated to the promotion of an immediate, worldwide proletarian revolution.

Late in April, a package wrapped in brown paper arrived in Mayor Ole Hanson's Seattle office. The fact that it contained a homemade bomb was discovered in time to prevent injuries. On the following day, however, a maid in the Atlanta home of Senator Thomas W. Hardwick lost both her hands when the package she was opening exploded. Postal authorities soon discovered sixteen similar packages in the New York City Post Office and more elsewhere in the mails. Altogether, thirty-six bombs had been mailed, addressed to such men as

Frederic Howe, Commissioner of Immigration at Ellis Island;

Lee Overman, chairman of the Senate committee investigating Bolshevism;

Oliver Wendell Holmes, United States Supreme Court justice;

Albert Burlesen, Postmaster General of the United States;

William B. Wilson, Secretary of Labor;

A. Mitchell Palmer, Attorney General of the United States;

J. P. Morgan, Jr., financier;

J. D. Rockefeller, financier.[4]

Apparently the bombs were scheduled to arrive on May 1, the traditional marching and speech-making day for labor unions.

During the first week of June, bombs exploded in eight cities, killing two people. Attorney General Palmer's home in Washington, D.C., was partially destroyed. Although the pattern of the bombings did not suggest any sort of coherent strategy, rumor-ridden Americans saw them as part of an organized conspiracy to overthrow the govern-

[4] Ibid., p. 71.

ment. The sources of the bombs, both those that were mailed in April and those that exploded in June, were never discovered. Robert K. Murray concluded:

> The bombs were certainly not the result of a calculated plan to overthrow the government, but probably the work of isolated groups of terrorists who, inspired by the Russian experiment, insanely believed the unloosing of a few bombs would trigger such an upheaval here. Even the May Day riots, while displaying the enthusiasm of domestic radicals for the principles of international socialism, were in no way "dress rehearsals" for revolution but rather the product of precipitous action by police and angry citizens who foolishly made martyrs of them rather than permitting them to rave and parade.[5]

Rumor had it that a nationwide general strike would begin on Independence Day. Local governments put police forces on twenty-four-hour duty and swore in hundreds of private citizens as special deputies. The federal government sent troops into many cities, placing them on special alert. July 4 came and went without incident, but the antiradical emotion of the public did not diminish.

The summer of 1919 also brought race riots. In February, a million New Yorkers had lined Fifth Avenue to welcome home the troops, including the Negro 369th Regiment. Similar receptions were given returning veterans in St. Louis, Hoboken, and Buffalo, and in Chicago Negro soldiers of the 370th paraded through the downtown streets to the cheers of thousands. Five months later, twenty-three Negroes and fifteen whites, the victims of racial violence, lay dead on the streets of Chicago's black ghetto. During the last six months of the year, twenty-five race riots occurred in cities across the nation. The period of postwar brotherhood had been short-lived.

The Chicago riot was the worst. For thirteen days, mobs roamed the slum areas of the city, looting, burning, and killing, the National Guard unable to control them. In addition to the thirty-eight dead, more than four hundred

A wounded Negro, one of the victims of the Chicago race riot, being lifted into a patrol wagon.

UNITED PRESS INTERNATIONAL

[5] Ibid., p. 82.

UNITED PRESS INTERNATIONAL

Chicago policemen lead a Negro away from the riot zone.

people (almost two-thirds of them Negroes) were injured, and more than a thousand families were left homeless. Charles W. Holman described the riot with remarkable objectivity in an article for *The Outlook* magazine:

> Chicago has just finished her first week of rioting between Whites and Negroes. Already thirty-three people have lost their lives and more than three hundred have been injured. The death toll was slightly greater among the blacks, on Tuesday there being fifteen of them dead as against eleven whites. During this wild week mobs of whites pursued and beat and killed Negroes. Other mobs of Negroes pursued and beat and killed whites. From the upper windows of tenements, when darkness came, snipers picked off pedestrians or fired into squads of police sent to bring order to the Black Belt.
>
> On Monday rioting reached its height, and before noon twenty-four known dead had been taken to the morgue.
>
> The confusion of the city as a whole was heightened by a strike of surface and elevated street car employees

which paralyzed traffic, not a single car being in operation from midnight Sunday until the early hours of the following Saturday. During this time the people adopted any method of conveyance possible, and many of them got into trouble by being forced to walk through the districts where rioting was in progress.[6]

Marcus Garvey in a uniform he designed to go with the title he gave himself— "provisional president of Africa." Garvey raised millions of dollars from discontented black Americans who hoped to emigrate to Africa under his sponsorship, but their hopes came to nothing when he was convicted of using the mails illegally in 1923.

But few reports were so dispassionate. In this summer of bomb scares and strikes, it was not difficult for many people to believe the newspaper headline that read: "REDS TRY TO STIR NEGROES TO REVOLT."[7]

Actually, of course, the causes of the riots were far more complex. During the war, thousands of Negroes had moved from the South to seek jobs in northern cities. They were joined, after the war, by many of the 400,000 returning black veterans, who thought that because they had fought for democracy abroad they might now enjoy some of its benefits at home. Contrary to their expectations, these migrants from the South found little freedom and no equality in their new environment. Only ghetto housing was available. Only certain low-paying jobs were open to them, and what employment they did find was resented by white workers, many of whom were immigrants suffering from similar kinds of discrimination. Jim Crow laws prevented Negroes from taking advantage of the city's cultural and recreational facilities and often even its public transportation. Many blacks turned to organizations like the NAACP, which had become increasingly militant under the leadership of W. E. B. Du Bois. Others simply gave up hope, if never desire, for a better life in America. The thousands of people who were attracted to Marcus Garvey's "Back to Africa" movement, which turned out to be fraudulent, typified that despair. So much tension developed between blacks, who found their hopes frustrated, and whites, who saw the blacks as a threat to the security of their neighborhoods and jobs, that in many cities only a dim spark was needed to set off

UNITED PRESS INTERNATIONAL

[6] Charles W. Holman, "Race Riots in Chicago," *The Outlook*, 13 August 1919, p. 566.
[7] Quoted in Murray, *Red Scare*, p. 178.

UNITED PRESS INTERNATIONAL

A state militiaman directs traffic during the Boston police strike of 1919.

a riot. In Chicago, it had all started with an argument between a group of whites and a group of blacks on a Lake Michigan beach.

Conditions were no better in the South, where postwar Negro militancy—or simply the fear of it—provoked an even more violent and organized white response. Seventy blacks were lynched in 1919, some of them veterans still in uniform, and fourteen blacks were publicly burned. The Ku Klux Klan was revived, and during 1919 it grew from comparative insignificance into a powerful organization with a hundred thousand members and cells in twenty-seven states.

Along with racial violence, the autumn of 1919 brought three of the most spectacular labor disturbances in modern American history. The first of these was the Boston police strike.

After repeatedly requesting and not receiving any relief from long hours, poor working conditions, and low wages, the Boston police force voted to affiliate with the American Federation of Labor. Police forces throughout the

Governor Calvin Coolidge inspecting the military guard at the State House in Boston during the police strike.

UNITED PRESS INTERNATIONAL

country had been doing the same thing for several months without attracting the public's attention or arousing its hostility. On August 15, the AFL granted the Boston police a charter. Police Commissioner Edwin Curtis opposed the idea. He refused to tolerate any form of police unionism, and he was supported by the Boston press. On September 8, Curtis dismissed nineteen officers from the force, all of them union leaders. The following day, enraged policemen voted 1,134 to 2 to walk off their jobs. Immediately the strike became a Bolshevik plot and fear once again gripped the nation. Newspaper editorials declared that terror reigned in Boston, that Lenin and Trotsky were on their way to America, and that officials in Washington were convinced that a serious attempt to "sovietize" the government of the United States was underway.

On September 12, AFL president Samuel Gompers, who had just returned from Europe, urged the strikers to return to work and await negotiation. The policemen unanimously accepted his advice, and Gompers informed the mayor and Commissioner Curtis of their decision. But Curtis refused to reinstate the policemen. He was backed up by the hitherto little-known governor of Massachusetts, Calvin Coolidge, who telegraphed a message to Samuel Gompers on September 14: "There is no right to strike against the public safety, by anybody, anywhere, any time."[8] Coolidge became the nation's number-one hero, replacing Ole Hanson. Curtis recruited a new police force, mostly from war veterans, and the police strike died with the majority of Americans believing that it had been inspired by radicals and revolutionaries.

On September 22, 365,000 steelworkers went on strike to protest the firing of union leaders, twelve-hour work days, seven-day work weeks, and low wages—the average steelworker earned about twenty-eight dollars a week. Judge Elbert Gary, chairman of United States Steel Corporation, and other industry leaders refused to recognize

[8] Quoted in Donald R. McCoy, *Calvin Coolidge: The Quiet President* (New York: Macmillan Co., 1967), p. 94.

the union or to negotiate its demands. With some help from Attorney General Palmer, the steel companies successfully represented the strike to the public as another Red uprising. Federal and state troops were used to prevent picketing and to protect the tens of thousands of strikebreakers imported by the steel companies to keep the factories running. Eighteen strikers were killed. After two months of this, the strikers were forced to return to their jobs without a single gain.

The third major strike began when 394,000 soft-coal miners walked out of the mines in November. The mine owners, taking their cue from other industrial leaders, charged that the strike was the work of radicals and that it was being financed from Moscow. The miners did win something, however. Defying the courts, the attorney general of the United States, and their own union leader, John L. Lewis, they stayed away from their jobs until they received wage increases.

There were hundreds of strikes that year, most of them stimulated primarily by the worker's increasing inability to pay rising prices with low wages. Construction workers, longshoremen, subway men, telephone operators, and so many other groups adopted the walk-out tactic that by November, 1919, the number of men and women on strike was estimated at two million. And not all of them were striking for the traditional causes of higher wages and shorter hours. Some had aspirations, not always clearly defined, for a new industrial order, one controlled by the government—or by the workers themselves—rather than by capitalists. Such aspirations gave substance to the industrialists' charges of "Marxian influence" in the labor movement.

By November, many people had come to believe that the country was seriously threatened by a Communist-led revolution. Frederick Lewis Allen reported that in Indiana a jury deliberated only two minutes before acquitting a man who shot and killed an alien for yelling, "To hell with the United States!" William Leuchtenburg wrote that a minister called for the deportation of Bolshevists "in ships of stone with sails of lead, with the wrath of God

Billy Sunday, a former professional baseball player, was probably the best-known clergyman in America during the 1920's. His revival meetings attracted huge audiences, and his opinions on political matters carried considerable weight.

In 1924, J. Edgar Hoover became director of the FBI, a job he held until his death in 1972.

for a breeze and with hell for their first port." Evangelist Billy Sunday exclaimed, "If I had my way with these ornery wild-eyed Socialists, . . . I would stand them up before a firing squad and save space on our ships."

People were demanding action, and Attorney General A. Mitchell Palmer ("the Fighting Quaker") was ready to give it to them. After the June bombings, Palmer had asked for and received a $500,000 increase in his budget, and he had used it to create an antiradical division in the Department of Justice under the direction of J. Edgar Hoover. He had also won the cooperation of Secretary of Labor William B. Wilson, who had authority under the wartime sedition acts to deport alien anarchists. For months, planning the war against radicalism had been the chief occupation of the Department of Justice.

On November 7, the "Palmer raids" began. Federal agents seized 250 officers and members of the Union of Russian Workers in twelve cities. The move was bold and swift, and it met with the approval of the public, which was not in a mood to debate constitutional rights. Only 39 of those arrested were subsequently held for trial; the rest were released for lack of evidence.

Armistice Day, November 11, proved to be one of the most violent days of that violent year. In the lumbering town of Centralia, Washington, members of the International Workers of the World fought a bloody battle with members of the newly organized, fiercely patriotic American Legion. Four Legionnaires were killed. In the confusion, no one could tell for certain who had started the trouble. The Legionnaires claimed that they had been fired upon as they marched peacefully by the union's local headquarters, while the Wobblies claimed that they had been defending their headquarters against an unprovoked attack by the Legionnaires. Whatever the truth, the townspeople sided with the American Legion. Capturing one Wobbly who had escaped arrest, they beat him brutally, emasculated him, and hung him from a railroad bridge. They then riddled his body with bullets and left it hanging for two days. The coroner's verdict was suicide. More than a thousand IWW leaders were arrested in raids on union

UNITED PRESS INTE

Steelworkers waving strike notices on September 22, 1919. When the strike ended two months later, eighteen workers were dead, thousands were destitute, and not one of the workers' demands had been met.

offices throughout the state, and eleven IWW members arrested in the Centralia affair were convicted of murder and sentenced to long prison terms. The public, learning only of a "Centralia massacre" which cost the lives of four American veterans, found yet more evidence of radical revolution.

In late December, Attorney General Palmer secured from Secretary Wilson arrest warrants for three thousand aliens who allegedly were members of the Communist party. On the night of January 2, 1920, federal agents arrested more than four thousand alleged Communists in a dramatic series of raids in thirty-three cities across the country. The Department of Justice had been secretly planning the action for months. *The New York Times* described the department's strategy:

> The action though it came with stunning suddenness had
> been carefully mapped out, studied, and systematized.
> Every agency was ready and every operative at his post.
> For months Department of Justice men, dropping all other

work, had concentrated on the Reds. Agents quickly
infiltrated into radical ranks, slipped casually into centers
of agitation, and went to work, sometimes as cooks, in
remote mining colonies sometimes as miners, again as
steel workers, and where opportunity presented itself as
agitators of the wildest type. . . . The raiders were split
into parties; each had its leader and each its objective.
Locally, the raiders moved from their posts at the date
or time scheduled—moved in force directly on the halls
and meeting places, made rapid trips for individuals at
their homes, rushed down into the East side, and with
their warrants as their authority, climbed dark tenement
stairs and seized little groups. The agents acted in all five
boroughs and did it with amazing speed.[9]

Federal agents invaded private homes, union offices,
and meeting halls. They arrested people and held them
in jail for days without giving them the opportunity to
seek bail or legal counsel and without even informing
them of the charges against them. In many cases the
prisoners were denied food and treated with brutality.
Most of those arrested were later found to be simple
working-class immigrants with little or no involvement
in political movements. On very few if any occasions in
American history has such a violation of civil liberties
occurred. Yet the public condoned it. As Robert K. Murray
has pointed out, fear of communism had reached the proportions of a national hysteria:

Bolshevism actually had a stranglehold on the nation.
But, ironically enough, this was not the result of any
revolutionary activity on the part of Bolshevists or the
ideological appeal of their program. Instead it represented
the willful action of the American people themselves.
Through their unintelligent thinking and intolerant actions
they were rapidly accomplishing what no number of
domestic radicals could have achieved by themselves.[10]

---

[9] *The New York Times,* 4 January 1920. Copyright © 1920 by
The New York Times Company. Reprinted by permission.

[10] Murray, *Red Scare,* p. 166.

Nearly half of the aliens arrested during the January raids were released as a result of court decisions holding that people could not be deported on evidence that was illegally obtained—as most of Palmer's evidence had been. Secretary of Labor Wilson, alarmed at last by Palmer's high-handed tactics, refused to issue any more warrants for the arrest of aliens. But Palmer, who entertained ambitions of winning the 1920 presidential nomination, was not deterred. He continued to warn of dark and dangerous plots aimed at the overthrow of the United States government. None of these plots materialized, however, and eventually Palmer was accused of crying "wolf" much too often. Congress, instead of investigating the charges against alleged Communists, began to investigate Palmer. The "Fighting Quaker" was now referred to in less friendly terms, such as the "Quaking Fighter," "Faking Fighter," and "Quaking Quitter." Still, Palmer's zeal to catch Communists remained undiminished. Writing in *The Forum* in February, 1920, he declared:

A. Mitchell Palmer.

BROWN BROTHERS

> Like a prairie-fire, the blaze of revolution was sweeping over every American institution of law and order a year ago. It was eating its way into the homes of the American workman, its sharp tongues of revolutionary heat were licking the altars of the churches, leaping into the belfry of the school bell, crawling into the sacred corners of American homes, seeking to replace marriage vows with libertine laws, burning up the foundations of society.
>
> Robbery, not war, is the ideal of communism. This has been demonstrated in Russia, Germany and in America. As a foe, the anarchist is fearless of his own life, for his creed is a fanaticism that admits no respect of any other creed. Obviously it is the creed of any criminal mind, which reasons always from motives impossible to clean thought. Crime is the degenerate factor in society.
>
> Upon these two basic certainties, first that the "Reds" were criminal aliens, and secondly that the American Government must prevent crime, it was decided that there could be no nice distinctions drawn between the theoretical ideals of the radicals and their actual violations of our national laws.

CULVER PICTURES, INC.

Even Washington, D.C., was affected by the wave of frivolity that swept the nation in the early 1920's. Here, a congressman from Charleston, South Carolina, learns the fashionable new dance step that originated in his city.

My information showed that communism in this country was an organization of thousands of aliens, who were direct allies of Trotsky. Aliens of the same misshapen caste of mind and indecencies of character, and it showed that they were making the same glittering promises of lawlessness, of criminal autocracy to Americans, that they had made to the Russian peasants. How the Department of Justice discovered upwards of 60,000 of these organized agitators of the Trotsky doctrine in the United States, is the confidential information upon which the Government is now sweeping the nation clean of such alien filth. . . .[11]

Although Palmer did not tire of chasing Reds, the public finally did. Without the cooperation of the Department of Labor, Palmer could stage no more dramatic raids. Sports, automobiles, and radio and movie stars began to steal the headlines away from the Red Scare. In the lull that followed the first wave of hysteria, people

[11] A. Mitchell Palmer, "The Case Against the Reds," *The Forum*, February 1920, p. 63.

decided that perhaps the danger of communism "eating its way into the homes of the American workman" was not so great after all, and besides they were tired of thinking about politics, war, and the international situation. They began to turn their attention to the new fashions, fads, and gadgets that peacetime and increasing prosperity were bringing them. By the fall of 1920, the Red Scare was all over. A. Mitchell Palmer had not succeeded in winning the Democratic presidential nomination, and he passed into obscurity when the Republican administration of Warren G. Harding took office early in 1921.

Although the Red Scare did not last long, it left behind a bitter legacy. It left people suspicious of aliens, distrustful of organized labor, hostile toward reformers, and insistent upon political conformity. But perhaps its most disturbing effect was its impact on civil liberties, particularly on freedom of expression. The Red Scare spilled over into liberal universities, which were accused of being centers of Bolshevism. Many faculty members were charged with teaching Marxism and forced to resign their positions. State legislatures passed laws providing for the "purification" of history and civics textbooks, and book purges became commonplace. In many areas, public school teachers were required to sign oaths of allegiance. The scare had stimulated a trend toward ideological rigidity, and, it seemed, success in America during the twenties required at least apparent conformity. In 1922, in an article in *Harper's Magazine,* a writer, Katharine Gerould, lamented:

Flagpole sitting was one of the many frivolous amusements that attracted attention during the twenties.

America is no longer a free country, in the old sense;
and liberty is, increasingly, a mere rhetorical figure.
. . . No thinking citizen, I venture to say, can express
in freedom more than a part of his honest convictions.
I do not of course refer to convictions that are frankly
criminal. I do mean that everywhere, on every hand, free
speech is choked off in one direction or another. The only
way in which an American citizen who is really interested
in all the social and political problems of his country can
preserve any freedom of expression is to choose the mob

that is most sympathetic to him, and abide under the shadow of that mob.[12]

The interpretation of freedom of expression was narrowed by the courts as well as by public pressure. Several free speech cases reached the United States Supreme Court during the 1920's, the most famous being *Gitlow v. the State of New York.* In that case, Benjamin Gitlow, who was arrested for writing and publishing a tract entitled *The Left-Wing Manifesto,* challenged the New York anarchy law under which he was convicted. The law, he said, was unconstitutional because it abridged his personal liberty as guaranteed, by implication, in the Fourteenth Amendment. The Supreme Court disagreed with him. Justice Edward Sanford gave the majority opinion:

> It is a fundamental principle, long established, that the freedom of speech and of the press which is secured by the Constitution does not confer an absolute right to speak or publish, without responsibility, whatever one may choose, or an unrestricted or unbridled license that gives immunity for every possible use of language and prevents the punishment of those who abuse this freedom. . . .
> That a State in the exercise of its police power may punish those who abuse this freedom by utterances inimical to the public welfare, tending to corrupt public morals, incite to crime, or disturb the public peace, is not open to question. . . .
>
> Freedom of speech and of press . . . does not protect disturbances to the public peace or the attempt to subvert the government. It does not protect publications or teachings which tend to subvert or imperil the government or to impede or hinder it in the performance of its governmental duties. . . .[13]

[12] Quoted in Frederick Lewis Allen, *Only Yesterday* (New York: Harper & Row, Perennial Library, 1964), pp. 51–52. Copyright 1931 by Frederick Lewis Allen, 1959 by Agnes Rogers Allen. By permission of Harper & Row, Publishers.

[13] *Gitlow* v. *the State of New York,* 268 U.S. 652 (1925).

The Court's decision was not unanimous, however. Justice Oliver Wendell Holmes gave the dissenting opinion:

> It is said that this manifesto was more than a theory, that it was an incitement. Every idea is an incitement. It offers itself for belief and if believed it is acted on unless some other belief outweighs it or some failure of energy stifles the movement at its birth. The only difference between the expression of an opinion and an incitement in the narrower sense is the speaker's enthusiasm for the result. Eloquence may set fire to reason. But whatever may be thought of the redundant discourse before us it had no chance of starting a present conflagration. If in the long run the beliefs expressed in proletarian dictatorship are destined to be accepted by the dominant forces in the community, the only meaning of free speech is that they should be given their chance and have their way.[14]

Many questions emerged from the Red Scare experience, questions that would arise again during the McCarthy era of the 1950's. To what extent should a democracy restrict the civil liberties of its citizens, in peace or in war, to protect its national security? Who should determine the state of the nation's security and what restrictions that security does or does not require? Do our laws adequately protect persons accused of sedition or conspiracy? How narrowly can the limits of liberty be defined before liberty itself ceases to exist?

Prohibition

The Eighteenth Amendment to the United States Constitution reads:

> Section 1. After one year from the ratification of this article the manufacture, sale, or transportation of intoxicating liquors within, the importation thereof into, or the exportation thereof from the United States and all territory subject to the jurisdiction thereof for beverage purposes is hereby prohibited.

Justice Oliver Wendell Holmes, Jr., served on the Supreme Court from 1902 until his retirement in 1932 at the age of ninety-one. His regard for civil liberties, his independence of mind, and his plain common sense—expressed in tersely written, frequently dissenting opinions —helped to make the Court a creative instrument for social change.

[14] Ibid.

A 1919 liquor store advertisement urging customers to "buy now!"—"Uncle Sam will *enforce* prohibition."

Saloon-wrecker Carry Nation with a hatchet in one hand and a Bible in the other.

Section 2. The Congress and the several states shall have concurrent power to enforce this article by appropriate legislation.

Section 3. This article shall be inoperative unless it shall have been ratified as an amendment to the Constitution by the legislatures of the United States, as provided in the Constitution, within seven years from the date of the submission hereof to the States by the Congress.

The amendment was approved by Congress in 1917 and ratified by the legislatures of the required three-fourths of the states in 1919. From January, 1920, when the amendment went into effect, until December, 1933, when it was repealed, the United States was officially "dry."

The prohibitionist movement did not suddenly spring to life in the second decade of the twentieth century. It had been a part of the American scene for nearly a hundred years, and during that time it had developed an organized and effective political strategy as well as considerable popular support. Nor, "wet" cartoons to the contrary, was it wholly the creation of fundamentalist preachers, repressed maiden ladies, and frustrated matrons of the Carry Nation type. (Not content with verbal attacks on the saloons, Mrs. Nation used to attack them physically, with a hatchet.) Such people probably made up the hard-core of the movement, and they were the ones who refused to admit that the "noble experiment" had failed when everybody else could see plainly that it had. But from the beginning of the movement until well into the 1920's, prohibitionism drew support from many different groups of people for many different reasons, reasons that were both rational and irrational.

The prohibition movement first appeared in organized form in the 1830's in the rapidly industrializing, rapidly urbanizing Northeast, notably in Boston. There, excessive drinking among recent immigrants to the city, both from Europe and from rural America, was a serious social problem. Women and children went hungry, ill-clothed, and ill-housed because men spent their wages in the saloons. Many of the reformers recognized that drunkenness was more often the effect than the cause of poverty —whose true causes were to be found in the wretched working conditions, low wages, and tenement slums that immigrants were forced to accept. However, they believed that prohibition of the sale of alcohol would at least relieve some of the worst misery. At that time, the anti-liquor movement was only one of several social reform movements—for women's rights, for universal free education, for better conditions in prisons and insane asylums, for the abolition of slavery—and with them it spread from city to country. Prohibitionism was perhaps more successful in the country than the other movements because it threatened few established interests and accorded well with the puritanism of the Protestant evangelical churches which predominated in rural America. Before prohibitionism and the other social reform movements were overshadowed by the great abolitionist cause and the Civil War, thirteen states had experimented with "dry" laws prohibiting the sale of liquor within their borders.

A drawing from an early nineteenth-century book advocating prohibition.

After the war the movement grew up again, slowly at first, then more rapidly with the founding of the Prohibition party in 1869 and the Women's Christian Temperance Union in 1873. The impetus behind this second wave of prohibitionism came not from the urban Northeast but from the farms and small towns of the West, Midwest, and South. By 1893, when the Anti-Saloon League was organized, prohibitionism was no longer simply a movement for a social reform. It had become a moral crusade, overshadowing all other social issues as abolitionism had done forty years before. Nor was it simply a crusade against alcohol. As H. L. Mencken put it briefly and bitterly in 1928, "The battle for Prohibition was more than a struggle for a moral reform: it was a clear-cut combat between cities and the country, between the civilized centers and the areas of cornbread and revival."[15] The country was at war with the cities throughout the second half of the nineteenth century. On the political

[15] H.L. Mencken, *Prejudices: A Selection* (New York: Random House, Vintage Books, 1958), p. x.

and economic fronts, the battles were carried on by such organizations as the Grange, the Greenback party, the Farmers' Alliances, and the Populist party, over such issues as the regulation of trusts and monopolies and the free coinage of silver. They were, for the most part, losing battles. Andrew Sinclair wrote:

> There was a quality of desperation in the country's fear of the city after 1896. When Bryan was defeated by McKinley, the country seemed to have lost its chance to govern the nation. The Census of 1900 showed that nearly two in every five Americans lived in the great cities. In 1860, it had been one in five, and the cities were now growing faster than ever, as European immigrants poured into the urban slums. Within twenty years, more people would live in the cities than in the country, and the old rural America of the small farmer, on which the Republic had been founded, would become impotent. It is small wonder that denunciations of the city rose to the pitch of hysteria. . . .[16]

Prohibition was the country's battle against the city on the social front.

The Anti-Saloon League was the most effective of all the prohibitionist organizations, and its support shows clearly the rural and religious forces behind the dry movement. Calling itself "the Protestant church in action," the League drew most of its money and members from the Methodist, Baptist, Presbyterian, Congregational, Disciples of Christ, Christian Science, and Mormon churches, the Methodists being the most militant of the seven groups. Four out of five of the members of these churches lived either in small towns or in the country. The League and prohibition in general received little or no support from the Lutheran and Protestant Episcopal churches and were actively opposed by the Jewish and Roman Catholic churches, although clergymen of these faiths naturally

[16] Andrew Sinclair, *Prohibition: The Era of Excess* (Boston: Little, Brown, Atlantic Monthly Press, 1962), p. 19. Copyright © 1962 by Andrew Sinclair. Reprinted by permission of Atlantic-Little, Brown and Co., and Faber and Faber Ltd.

advocated temperance, or moderation in the use of alcohol. With the exception of the Lutherans, many of whom were German and Scandinavian immigrants who had settled in the Midwest, the members of these four churches lived predominantly in the cities, and by the second decade of the twentieth century they considerably outnumbered the combined members of the seven Protestant churches. And an increasing number of urban Americans—roughly three out of five by 1915—belonged to no church at all. To the rural Protestants who supported the League, atheism and "foreign" religions, city life, sin, and liquor were inextricably mixed and were threatening the moral integrity of the entire nation. The International Reform Bureau warned in 1911:

> In this age of cities it is to be expected that conversions will decrease if we allow needless temptations about our youth to increase, such as foul pictures, corrupt literature, leprous shows, gambling slot machines, saloons, and Sabbath-breaking. Instead of putting around our boys and girls a fence of favorable environment, we allow the devil to put about them a circle of fire; and then we wonder that they wither. *We are trying to raise saints in hell.*[17]

But, as the political observer Walter Lippmann wrote in 1927, after seven years of national prohibition:

> The evil which the old-fashioned preachers ascribe to the Pope, to Babylon, to atheists, and to the devil, is simply the new urban civilization, with its irresistible scientific and economic and mass power. The Pope, the devil, jazz, the bootleggers, are a mythology which expresses symbolically the impact of a vast and dreaded social change. The change is real enough. . . . The defense of the Eighteenth Amendment has, therefore, become much more than a mere question of regulating the liquor traffic. It involves a test of strength between social orders, and when that test is concluded, and if, as seems probable, the Amendment breaks down, the fall will bring down with

[17] Quoted in ibid.

it the dominion of the older civilization. The Eighteenth Amendment is the rock on which the evangelical church militant is founded, and with it are involved a whole way of life and an ancient tradition. The overcoming of the Eighteenth Amendment would mean the emergence of the cities as the dominant force in America, dominant politically and socially as they are already dominant economically.[18]

Samuel Gompers, the president of the American Federation of Labor, maintained at the time that the Eighteenth Amendment was class legislation, an attempt by the middle classes to impose their values and standards on the working classes. Gompers was not altogether wrong. If the main driving force behind prohibitionism was rural America's fear of the cities, the cause was certainly helped along, particularly in the cities, by social reformers and progressives who—like the early prohibitionists—believed that the members of the working classes had to be protected against their own worst instincts for their own good. To many middle-class reformers (and nearly all the reformers were middle-class), the enemy was not so much alcohol as it was the saloon. Probably a majority of middle-class men drank, but they did so moderately, on the whole, and in their own homes or with friends and social equals at parties and other private gatherings. The saloon was almost entirely a working-class institution. Excessive drinking may have been more common among workers, as the reformers believed, but it was also, because of the public nature of saloons, more conspicuous.

In 1910, there were over 150,000 saloons, licensed and unlicensed, in the United States, and some of them were fully as bad as the reformers claimed—natural breeding grounds of vice, violence, and crime. In the poorest parts of town, where competition among saloonkeepers was greatest, "barkers" or "shills" were sometimes employed to recruit customers—not always through force of

[18] Walter Lippmann, *Men of Destiny* (New York: Macmillan Co., 1927), pp. 28, 31. Copyright 1927 and renewed 1955 by Walter Lippmann.

words alone—from the street. Once inside, the customer
might find himself in the midst of a dirty, brawling crowd,
drinking cheap adulterated liquor that lacked even the
dubious protection of a brand name. And, once drunk,
he might find that his money had disappeared into the
hands of card sharps, pool hustlers, prostitutes, pick-
pockets, and other assorted criminal types.

Almost as alarming to the reformers as this moral
corruption was the political corruption fostered by the
saloons. In almost every city run by a political machine
or boss, selected saloons functioned as miniature city halls
for their wards or districts, and there jobs and other
favors were traded for votes. Around election times, saloonkeepers often set up "drunk coops" of alcoholics
and—with the connivance of dishonest election officials—
sent these men out to vote over and over again, reward-
ing them with drinks. Wandering around drunk, the writer
Edgar Allan Poe was picked up by an enterprising sa-
loonkeeper in Baltimore and thrown into such a "coop";
after five days he was finally recognized and rescued, but
by then his condition was so bad that he died in a
hospital.

But there were good saloons as well as bad, and at
their best the saloons filled a social need that other institutions available to immigrants and workingmen—including the churches—had been unwilling or unable to meet:

> In industrial cities, the saloon was often what the church
> was in a village. It was a center of faith and tradition,
> political rather than religious. It was a place of recreation
> and joy. Membership in the right saloon brought social
> prestige and good jobs, as did membership in the right
> church. . . .
>
> One reformer thought the church could learn many
> things from the saloon. There was human fellowship and
> equality in the saloon, little in the charity home. The saloon
> had no doorstep; the church hall had. The saloon had
> glitter; the chapel was drab. The saloon was easy to enter;
> the religious hall was locked. The saloon was active one
> hundred and forty hours a week, the church four. No one

A man enjoying a glass of beer and a free lunch in a Chicago saloon. The saloons were not wholly altruistic, however. The free food—pretzels, peanuts, salami, rye bread, beef jerky, hard-boiled eggs— was usually salty and dry, prompting patrons to drink more beer.

UNITED PRESS INTERNATIONAL

bothered about a man's business at the saloon. No one asked about his worries or his home troubles. Ragged clothes were not a mark of shame. Free lunches were given for a five-cent glass of beer; if the saloons of New York were closed, twenty-five thousand men would declare that the food had been taken out of their mouths. The saloon provided newspapers, billiards, card tables, bowling alleys, toilets, and washing facilities. And, above all, the saloon provided information and company. The bartender could direct and advise salesmen, pass the time of day with trucksters, enlighten strangers about the habits of the town. . . .

Exclusive of its psychological benefits, the saloon did great service, as well as great harm, to workingmen. It was, in particular, the friend of the immigrant, his only contact with the outer world. It is easy to forget how small and friendless the world of the immigrant was. . . .

The saloon provided immigrant votes to the city boss and corrupt politics to America; but it could only do so by providing jobs and help to the immigrants in return. The ward heelers and barkeepers were the first welfare workers of the slums. The saloons were the first labor exchanges and union halls. . . . The saloonkeepers had a near monopoly on small halls which could be used for labor meetings and lodges. They would charge no rent for these places in return for the privilege of selling liquor at the meetings. . . . In one sense, the attack on the saloons was the attack of capital on the haunts of labor.[19]

For the most part, only the reformers who worked directly with the poor—like General Evangeline Booth of the Salvation Army—understood the social value of the saloons. When national prohibition seemed imminent, General Booth announced plans to buy up a number of saloons across the country and to operate them, complete with spitoons and swinging doors, as soft-drink bars so that "the psychology of the brass rail" would not be lost. The great majority of middle-class prohibitionists,

[19] Sinclair, *Prohibition*, pp. 76, 73–75.

however, had no closer sources of contact with the lower classes than their daily newspaper, which told of labor unrest and crime in the streets; the dry literature, which attributed most if not all deprivation, depravity, and disease to alcohol; and perhaps an occasional unpleasant drive through a slum.

In addition to the moral crusaders and the social reformers, other groups supported prohibition for their own more specific reasons. Businessmen, for example, tended to support it because they hoped that it would eliminate "blue Monday" absenteeism and inefficiency among their workers; they also hoped that the workers, unable to spend their wages on liquor, would require less in the way of raises and would spend more on other consumer goods. Many white southerners supported prohibition because blacks got "uppity" when they drank. Many blacks, on the other hand, supported it because white southerners got vicious when they drank. Booker T. Washington observed, "Two-thirds of the mobs, lynchings, and burnings at the stake are the result of bad whiskey drunk by bad black men and bad white men."[20] Women in general were strongly behind the dry movement. Some, actively involved in the struggle for their own rights, endorsed it simply because the prohibitionists endorsed them. Others, forbidden involvement in the women's rights movement by their husbands or public opinion but bored at home, found in prohibitionism a morally unassailable cause that welcomed their brains and energy. Working-class women, of course, had more immediate reasons: the saloon not only took money that they and their children needed, but it also gave their husbands an escape from the dreary tenement home and a free and easy social life in which they, according to the standards of the time, could not share.

Progressive thinkers of both sexes, steeped in Social Darwinist philosophy, were impressed by the prohibitionists' scientific arguments against alcohol. Many of these arguments were perfectly valid—alcohol is a dan-

[20] Quoted in ibid., p. 30.

ONE DEATH
FROM ALCOHOL
EVERY EIGHT MINUTES

Drink is one Cause of Not Less Than
60,000 Deaths Every Year in the
United Kingdom.
**DO NOT LET US GO BACK TO
PRE-WAR CONDITIONS.**

A 1918 prohibi-
tionist poster.

gerous drug that can cause physical and mental deterioration and death. And it can, as the prohibitionists pointed
out repeatedly, cloud judgment and relax inhibitions,
which can lead to sexual license, which can lead to a
disease like syphilis, which can be passed on to the second generation. But the prohibitionists went further than
that in their journals and newsletters: they claimed to
have utterly reliable medical evidence demonstrating that
drinkers could pass on most of their acquired disabilities
and diseases to their children and that, in addition, even
moderate drinkers had a significantly greater number of
children with defects of all sorts—including epilepsy,
St. Vitus dance, idiocy, and physical deformity—than
the children of nondrinkers. If alcohol were not outlawed
soon, the prohibitionists warned, the once vigorous
American race would become so weak that it could no
longer compete in the fierce struggle for survival. In a
nation that was beginning to think of itself as a major
world power, having recently won overseas territories
from Spain, this argument had considerable appeal.

The political tactics of the prohibitionists were well
organized and effective on all three levels of government.
Community politics was particularly important because
a county or township could vote itself dry in a local
option election regardless of the policy adopted by the
state as a whole. On the local level, the prohibitionists
favored dramatic events, such as torchlight rallies and
the picketing of saloons by children. Children proved to
be an especially potent weapon for the drys. Joined together by their mothers in Cold Water Armies or Lincoln-
Lee Legions (the prohibitionists claimed, incorrectly, that
the two great leaders of the Civil War had supported their
cause), children marched and chanted temperance verses
on every possible occasion. In his novel *Look Homeward, Angel*, Thomas Wolfe described the way in which
children were used to shame known drinkers during an
election in the small town of Altamont, North Carolina:

As they approached the polls, glancing, like surrounded
knights, for an embattled brother, the church women of

the town, bent like huntresses above the straining leash, gave the word to the eager children of the Sunday schools. Dressed all in white, and clutching firmly in their small hands the tiny stems of American flags, the pygmies, monstrous as only children can be when they become the witless mouths of slogans and crusades, charged hungrily, uttering their shrill cries, upon their Gulliver.

"There he is, children. Go get him."

Swirling around the marked man in wild elves' dance, they sang with piping empty violence:

> "We are some fond mother's treasure,
>   Men and women of tomorrow,
> For a moment's empty pleasure
>   Would you give us lifelong sorrow?
>
> Think of sisters, wives, and mothers,
>   Of helpless babes in some low slum,
> Think not of yourself, but others,
>   Vote against the Demon Rum."[21]

In addition to the excitement of such direct action, the prohibitionists offered their supporters in the towns and villages a steady stream of visiting speakers—ranging from the glamorous William Jennings Bryan to reformed drunkards with fascinating tales of the wicked lives they had left behind—as well as a deluge of books, periodicals, and other literature. By 1915, the Anti-Saloon League alone was producing thirty-one individualized state editions of four journals (representing some 250 million pages a month), two national journals, and literally millions of pamphlets, newsletters, and leaflets. In the days before radio and the commercial mass-circulation magazines, the prohibitionists served as an important link between country dwellers and the larger world of affairs, a position they did not hesitate to exploit.

On the state and federal levels, the prohibitionists relied less on emotional appeals and more on practical

A "wet" cartoon showing William Jennings Bryan dragging the Democratic party into the desert of prohibition.

---

[21] Thomas Wolfe, *Look Homeward, Angel* (New York: Charles Scribner's Sons, 1929), p. 300.

pressure politics. The Anti-Saloon League, in fact, was one of the most efficient pressure groups the nation has ever known. League lobbyists in Washington and the state capitals, maintaining close contact with each other and with their fifty thousand field workers, could summon up, on a few days' notice, thousands of letters, petitions, telegrams, and telephone calls supporting or opposing some particular piece of legislation. The galleries of legislative chambers were always packed with drys whenever anything touching their interests was to be discussed, and League supporters were kept informed of the voting records of their representatives through hundreds of localized newsletters. Lobbyists buttonholed politicians who had not yet committed themselves firmly on the issue and demanded to know where they stood. Those who were not in favor of the *total* prohibition of alcohol, or who believed that the matter was not within the province of the federal government and should be left to the states or counties, were damned along with the out-and-out wets and could count on losing a measurable number of votes. Those who supported prohibition, on the other hand, could be fairly certain of gaining votes. The League's leaders were willing to endorse anyone, regardless of his special interests, personal character, or party affiliation, who endorsed them. League endorsement, at a time when the Democratic and Republican parties were about equal in strength in most parts of the country, frequently meant the difference between victory and defeat.

Although possibly a majority of Americans did not like the idea of prohibition, there was really no organized opposition to the antiliquor movement. Many influential people openly criticized the drys' methods and their insistence on banning all alcoholic beverages, but even the most committed wets could not entirely reject the drys' motives. No one, after all, *approved* of drunkenness, misery, or disease. The liquor manufacturers naturally attempted to counteract the dry propaganda with advertising campaigns, but their arguments were so defensive and their self-interest so apparent that nobody was sold. The wine growers asserted, for example, that their product was seldom drunk by the vulgar persons who patronized saloons; wine, they said, was a family drink, even a holy drink, sanctified by Christ himself at Cana and by the sacrament of communion. The brewers emphasized the low alcoholic content and "nutritious ingredients" of beer, which they advertised as "liquid bread." The distillers of hard liquor pointed out that the brewers owned seven out of every ten saloons across the country and thus were chiefly responsible for the shameful conditions that had made a prohibitionist movement necessary. Perhaps the only effect of such advertising was to create dissension within the liquor industry itself.

By 1917, twenty-seven states were wholly dry and local options were in effect in others, but the most populous states—including Massachusetts, Connecticut, New York, Pennsylvania, Ohio, Illinois, and California—remained stubbornly wet. The prohibitionists, realizing that they would never succeed in converting a majority of the people in these states, began to concentrate their efforts on forcing a constitutional amendment through Congress. The amendment they proposed was unique in American constitutional history, as one of its critics observed:

> It withdrew power from the states and from the people. It did not merely grant power but attempted to fix an implacable policy. It vastly increased the hitherto limited police power of Congress. It vastly curtailed the police power of the states. Unlike most other Constitutional prohibitions it was directed not to the national or the state governments but to individuals. It was a sumptuary fiat quite different from anything else found in the Constitution.[22]

At any other time, such an amendment probably would not have had a chance. As it was, however, the prohibitionists experienced a tremendous stroke of luck in the form of World War I.

The absolute moral certainty of the drys suggested to some people, like this cartoonist, that they were not asking for an Eighteenth Amendment so much as for an Eleventh Commandment.

[22] Howard McBain, *Prohibition, Legal and Illegal* (New York: Macmillan Co., 1928), p. 61.

The patriotic fervor and anti-German hysteria that accompanied America's entry into the war provided the prohibitionists with new and potent ammunition. The simple fact that most of the brewers had German names was enough to make them suspect, and many people found no difficulty in believing the rumor that the brewers were part of a conspiracy to divert grain supplies from the manufacture of bread, which was needed to feed Allied troops, to the manufacture of beer, which could be used to demoralize Americans both at home and abroad. H. L. Mencken did not exaggerate the irrationality of the public's reaction when he wrote:

> *Homo boobiens* was scientifically roweled and run amok
> with the news that all the German brewers of the country
> were against the [eighteenth] amendment; he observed
> himself that all German sympathizers, whether actual
> Germans or not, were bitter opponents of it. His nights
> made dreadful by dreams of German spies, he was
> willing to do anything to put them down, and one of the
> things he was willing to do was to swallow Prohibition.[23]

Even people who were not swept away by anti-German hysteria were persuaded by the argument that prohibition was necessary to conserve food supplies and to preserve the mental and physical purity of the American fighting man. One such convert was Theodore Roosevelt, who was widely regarded as an expert on all things military. As governor of New York and as president of the United States, Roosevelt had been a firm opponent of prohibition, and his endorsement of the amendment carried great weight. There was a spirit of self-sacrifice in the air. Americans were fighting and dying in Europe to defend the noblest of ideals, democracy. Should not those who remained safely at home also give up something in order to make human society more perfect?

Still, getting the amendment through Congress took all of the prohibitionists' political skill. The founder of the

---

[23] H. L. Mencken, *Prejudices: Fourth Series* (New York: Alfred A. Knopf, 1924), pp. 162–163.

Anti-Saloon League, Howard Hyde Russell, described one tactic that was especially effective. With the help of dimestore tycoon S. S. Kresge, Russell contacted 13,000 businessmen known to favor national prohibition:

> We blocked the telegraph wires in Washington for three
> days. One of our friends sent seventy-five telegrams, each
> signed differently with the name of one of his subordinates.
> The campaign was successful. Congress surrendered. The
> first to bear the white flag was Senator Warren Harding
> of Ohio. He told us frankly he was opposed to the
> amendment, but since it was apparent from the telegrams
> that the business world was demanding it he would
> submerge his own opinion and vote for submission.[24]

The wording of the amendment itself owed much to League diplomacy. The purchase and use of alcohol were not prohibited so that the average citizen—and legislator —would not feel that he had done, or might do, anything wrong. The amendment, the League insisted, was aimed at the liquor industry, not individuals. The word "intoxicating" was used instead of "alcoholic" to leave open the possibility that light wines and beer might be exempted when the enabling legislation was written. Section 2— which consisted of the simple statement "Congress and the several states shall have concurrent power to enforce this article by appropriate legislation"—was made as vague as possible to confuse states' rights arguments and to blunt the objections of farsighted men (and there were many) who feared the broad police powers that effective enforcement would require. Section 3, seemingly a purely perfunctory provision, was presented to senators and congressmen as an escape clause—it was not they who would make the final decision to impose nationwide prohibition but the people, acting through their state legislatures. This approach was reversed, of course, when the amendment came before the states. The legislators were told that Congress, in its superior wisdom, had already made the final decision; their function, indeed their sol-

[24] Quoted in Sinclair, *Prohibition*, p. 110.

An official prescription form for "medicinal liquor." Doctors prescribed such "medicine" freely, and soon druggists were dispensing a million gallons a year. This was one loophole that the federal authorities did not even try to close.

emn duty, was simply to ratify the amendment without wasting precious time in nit-picking debates. In any case, getting the amendment approved by the necessary thirty-six states was not difficult. The legislatures were heavily gerrymandered in favor of the rural areas, a fact that the drys had not overlooked when they insisted that the amendment be ratified by the legislatures rather than by statewide referendums. And by then, 1919, the Red Scare was in full swing.

The Volstead Act, Congress's "appropriate legislation" for enforcing the Eighteenth Amendment, was so complex that perhaps only its principal author, Anti-Saloon League attorney Wayne B. Wheeler, fully understood it. The act closed one of the amendment's loopholes by defining "intoxicating liquors" as those containing one-half of one percent of alcohol, which ruled out wine and beer, but other loopholes were left gaping. People could store and consume liquor in their own homes and could not be charged with conspiracy for buying it even though its sale was prohibited. People could even make light wines and hard cider at home as long as they did not attempt to sell, transport, or otherwise distribute these products. Ministers could serve wine to communicants at religious services and doctors could prescribe alcohol in various forms for their patients. Permits could be obtained for the manufacture of industrial alcohol, although the act required that this alcohol be denatured before sale to make it unfit for drinking. Beer could also be manufactured by permit as a first step in the production of near-beer, which was simply real beer with the alcohol removed. All of these loopholes and many more were fully explored and exploited before the prohibition era ended.

The formidable task of enforcing the Volstead Act went to the Prohibition Bureau, a new agency of some 1,500 men under the direction of the commissioner of internal revenue. The bureau was placed in the Treasury Department rather than the Justice Department as a way of emphasizing that the government was more interested in regulating the liquor trade than in chasing after individual citizens. But, since the Justice Department was still responsible for prosecuting offenders before the federal courts, the arrangement created problems. Penalties for bootleggers (those who dealt in illegal alcohol) were set at $1,000 and six months in jail for a first offense, $10,000 and five years in jail for a second offense. The enforcement powers and responsibilities of the state and local governments never were clearly defined. The states were supposed to contribute to the support of the Prohibition Bureau, and local police forces were supposed to assist the federal agents in tracking down and arresting local offenders. But from the beginning many cities and some whole states (including Connecticut, Rhode Island, and New Jersey) refused to cooperate.

"Santo Vino wine-grape bricks" could be purchased in several flavors—this one is sherry—in stores across the country. By adding a gallon of water and sugar according to taste, the purchaser could make his own wine.

The weakness of the Volstead Act and the even weaker provisions for its enforcement are often attributed to congressional hypocrisy, and to some extent that is true. Undoubtedly the members of Congress were glad just to get the drys off their backs and to be free at last to concentrate on the nation's really pressing business, such as demobilization, labor problems, and the League of Nations treaty. But the Volstead Act was also shaped by the lawmakers'—and the drys'—appreciation of what the American people would and would not tolerate. They knew that really rigid enforcement of the Eighteenth Amendment would mean giving the executive branch of the federal government unprecedented police powers —powers that would necessarily narrow the interpretation of cherished constitutional guarantees like the Fourth Amendment, which gave people the right to be secure in their persons, houses, papers, and effects against unreasonable searches and seizures. They knew that both the people and the states feared an increase in the power of the federal government, just as they themselves feared a further increase in the power of the executive branch, which had already been tremendously strengthened during the wartime administration of Woodrow Wilson.

The idea of moral perfection made the American people enshrine in their Constitution ideals which they could not fulfill, and made them outlaw habits in which they rather generally indulged. By their moral fervor as lawmakers, they made a large part of the people the allies and clients of lawbreakers. And, at the same time, they insisted that the federal government which executed the laws should remain weak. The very same voters and lawmakers who made laws which would defeat the powers of a despotism were jealous to the point of absurdity about giving their own executive and judiciary any power at all. Thus the United States had "the strongest laws and the weakest government of any civilized country."[25]

The drys themselves did not believe that rigid enforcement would be necessary. Forgetting for the moment their own political machinations and underestimating the temporary nature of their wartime support, they interpreted the triumphant passage of the Eighteenth Amendment to mean that most people welcomed the law and would obey it gladly, without coercion. They also assured Congress that the great majority of law-abiding people would assist the police and federal agents by reporting violations and by testifying against offenders in court. Had the drys been correct in their assessment of the public temper, and had that temper lasted, prohibition might well have worked.

The drys' optimism was borne out, superficially, by the relative quiet of prohibition's first year. The middle classes, if not enthusiastic enough to help enforce the law, at least seemed resigned to it. The rich were still drinking up the private stocks of liquor they had purchased before the amendment took effect. And the working classes, despite a general willingness to break the law, were limited in their opportunities to do so. Beneath the surface, however, tremendous changes were taking place.

First of all, the bootleggers were getting organized—arranging with foreign contacts for the smuggling of liquor on a massive scale, figuring out ways of diverting legal alcohol to illegal purposes, setting up their own breweries and distilleries, establishing systems of transportation and

[25] Ibid., p. 219.

Above, federal prohibition agents Izzy Einstein and Moe Smith inspect a still discovered in New York City. Below, agents on board a "rum runner," a 110-foot yacht that was captured before its $3,000,000 cargo could be smuggled ashore.

Above, prohibition agents James Coppinger and Edward Kelley in their own clothes. Below, the same two agents in disguise before a raid on a speakeasy.

distribution. The saloonkeepers, taking care to strengthen their friendships with police and other public officials through bribery, were busy opening up "speakeasies," as illegal bars were called. Soon it would be possible to buy almost any kind of alcoholic beverage, at any price, in any neighborhood.

Second and even more important, 1920 saw the beginning of the rapid technological development, explosive economic growth, and sweeping social change that would complete the nation's transition from a rural to an urban society before the end of the decade. Mass migration from the farms and small towns to the cities and suburbs, the automobile, the emancipation of women, radio, movies, glossy magazines, automation, the flood of new consumer products—all these things acted to blur the distinctions between social classes and between city and country lifestyles. As Andrew Sinclair wrote:

> It was the tragedy of the drys that the revolution in technology and communications made impossible the dry law in the very decade in which it was passed. National prohibition came as soon as it could, but its coming was already too late. As de Toqueville had noted in early America, it was not virtue which was great but temptation which was small. Temptation now flooded the land, and virtue was at the ebb.[26]

With each new convert to the prevailing urban morality, enforcement became more difficult until finally, when a majority of the middle classes had succumbed, it became impossible. But the Eighteenth Amendment was the law of the land, and the prohibition agents—ill-trained, overworked, and underpaid—attempted to see that it was obeyed. The definition of individual liberty in the United States was narrowed as a result of that attempt, as many people had feared it would be.

Despite the Fourth Amendment, some states allowed police to search private property without a warrant when bootlegging or illegal possession of alcohol was suspected

UNDERWOOD & UNDERWOOD

[26] Ibid., p. 414.

—and often the grounds for suspicion were no more tangible than an agent's sense of smell. Most cases based on evidence obtained in this way were thrown out of court, but only after the defendant had suffered arrest, jail, and attorneys' fees. The legal status of evidence obtained through wire-tapping was less certain, and the fundamental questions about invasion of privacy and self-incrimination raised by this practice—first used by the federal government to catch bootleggers in the 1920's—remain unresolved to this day. Undercover agents devised methods of entrapment which many people thought should be illegal, although they were not. To identify liquor distributors in New York, for example, the bureau operated its own speakeasy, catering, in the process, to the very vice it was supposed to be fighting.

Illegal search was not the only hazard to private property. Under the Volstead Act, property that had been used to transport liquor, such as boats, automobiles, and airplanes, could be seized and sold at public auction, the proceeds going to the government. To prevent a bootlegger from operating during lengthy court proceedings, the act also provided that a home, business establishment, or any other place where liquor was allegedly made or sold, could be closed down for one year by court injunction. "Padlocking" became a convenient way for the authorities to avoid the uncertain process of trial by jury. In 1925, agents reported padlocking 4,471 places, including a California redwood tree that contained a still.

An agent destroying beer barrels, 1924.

Owing to the vast number of offenders, the process of trial by jury proved far too lengthy—although the Sixth Amendment promised Americans that right. It was also, from the government's point of view, too uncertain. "Wet" juries often brought in verdicts of "not guilty" despite overwhelming evidence to the contrary. In 1930, *Periscope* magazine reported that a jury in San Francisco was itself put on trial for drinking up the evidence in a bootlegging case. Usually suspects were urged to plead guilty before a judge and were guaranteed nothing worse than a light fine in return. Some cases, of course, never reached the courts at all. If a suspect was rich enough, or powerful enough, someone in the police department or the district attorney's office could frequently be persuaded to drop the charges.

The drys had long argued that prohibition would be a deterrent to crime. It had the opposite effect. The cost of attempted prohibition was the cheapening of all the laws of the land and all the procedures of justice. Psychologically, if not legally, prohibition made every American who bought a glass of beer, or who failed to report his neighbor for doing so, a conspirator to a crime. It required thousands of public officials—including policemen, customs inspectors, judges, mayors, governors, and even some federal prohibition agents—to enforce a law in which they did not believe, thus weakening their resistance to corruption.

Prohibition also created bootlegging, a profession lucrative enough to make almost any bribe worthwhile. Country farmers, carrying on an ancient tradition, tended stills in lonely woods and abandoned barns, producing potent beverages that earned such names as Jamaica ginger (Jake), jackass brandy, soda-pop moonshine, panther whiskey, and yack-yack bourbon. In the cities, in countless tenement flats, whole families tended "alky-cookers." Usually they sold the liquor they produced to organized gangs, who in turn sold it to the speakeasies. Within a few years, battles for control of distribution rights in various sections of the cities left a few successful gangsters in command, each maintained in power by a private army of gunmen. Dutch Schultz and Frank Costello "owned" New York City. After a series of bloody battles which included the infamous St. Valentine's Day Massacre, Scarface Al Capone defeated the Dion O'Banion–Bugs Moran gang and became sole master of Chicago. Capone rode through the streets of the city like a dark lord, in an armor-plated limousine flanked by cars containing eighteen bodyguards with automatic pistols and submachine guns. From 1924 to 1929, in the greater Chicago area alone, there were between three hundred and four hundred murders and over a hundred bombings annually,

George "Bugs" Moran, who lost the battle for control of the Chicago underworld to Al Capone.

UNITED PRESS INTERNATIONAL

with rarely an arrest or a conviction.* Capone's domi-nance, like that of other big-city gang leaders, was made possible not only by terror and violence, but also by the active collaboration of public officials in city, county, state, and even federal government. "Prohibition," wrote Andrew Sinclair, "was the vehicle through which orga-nized crime planted itself in a position of incredible pow-er." By 1927, Capone was making about $60 million from illegal alcohol, mostly beer; $25 million from gambling houses and dog tracks; $10 million from houses of pros-titution and other roadhouses and resorts; and $10 mil-lion from "rackets," a general term for various methods of extorting money through threats of violence. In one common racket, gang members bullied their way into positions of authority in established labor unions and then threatened employers with strikes or sabotage un-less they paid large sums of cash to the union leaders. In another, owners of small businesses like dry-cleaning plants were threatened with bombings or even murder unless they paid for "protection" against such assaults. And already, in the 1920's, narcotic drugs like morphine were providing organized crime with a profitable sideline.

Alphonse Capone in 1928. Capone ruled Chicago until 1931, when he received an eleven-year prison sentence for income tax evasion. He was released in 1939, in poor health, and died in 1947.

Nor did prohibition reduce the more insignificant crime of drunkenness. Police records kept in Philadelphia be-fore and after prohibition reveal that crimes related to drunkenness increased in nearly every category:

	1919	1925
Intoxication	16,819	51,361
Intoxication and disorderly conduct	6,794	5,522
Intoxicated drivers	0	820
Habitual drunkards	127	814
	23,740	58,517[27]

* Not listed as murder victims, incidentally, were the innocent persons killed by overzealous prohibition agents; official statistics acknowledged about two hundred such deaths nationwide over a ten-year period, although some private groups estimated the num-ber at as many as a thousand.

[27] Joseph K. Willing, "The Profession of Bootlegging," *Annals of the American Academy of Political and Social Science,* May 1926.

The defects of prohibition—or at least of its enforcement—were apparent to nearly everybody within a very short time, and the subject was discussed constantly, in the press, on the radio, in homes and offices and speakeasies across the country. In 1924, New York City officials sponsored a public debate on the question, "Should the United States continue the policy of prohibition as defined in the Eighteenth Amendment?" Speaking in favor of prohibition was Dr. John Holmes, a leading clergyman:

> When the state declares, as it used to in the old Puritan days, that a man shouldn't kiss his wife between sunrise and sunset on a Sunday, when the state prescribes that a woman must wear her skirts not more than six inches from the ground, when the state undertakes to prescribe that a man's neck-tie shall be red and not black or black and not red—when the state does things of that kind it passes sumptuary legislation; it invades the sanctities of the individual life and deals with those habits and standards of the individual life which limit themselves absolutely to the conduct and ideas of the individual. . . . We all agree, do we not, that the liberty of the individual must bow in a complex society to the safety and happiness of all of us together? . . . The Eighteenth Amendment to the Constitution is not sumptuary legislation. It has nothing to do with sumptuary legislation. From beginning to end, it is social legislation.
>
> You say, "Why has the state any right to dictate to me what I shall drink?" The state hasn't any right to dictate to you what you shall drink, provided that what you drink affects yourself alone and does not affect society at large. . . . Legislation against whiskey was justified—justified by its social effects, justified by the fact that the safety and happiness of us all must be protected from the invasion of the one or the two. . . . Liquor is dangerous to public safety because it creates poverty, it cultivates crime, it establishes social conditions generally which are a burden to society. . . . Because liquor is a menace to public safety, and an exploitation of the weak, we have

got to get rid of it. And if you can show me a way of
doing that thing apart from doing what we did to the
slave trade, to the opium trade, I would like to know
what it is. I believe in liberty—absolute liberty of speech,
absolute liberty of assembly, absolute liberty of the press—
all of these essential liberties. But I have never believed
that democracy involved the liberty to guzzle when that
liberty to guzzle was a menace to me and to all other
men and to the integrity of that society which constitutes
the America we love together.[28]

Speaking against the continuation of prohibition was
Clarence Darrow, the nation's best-known liberal lawyer:

Now, suppose we admit, for the sake of the argument, that
sixty percent of the people do not believe in something
that the other forty percent believe in, should they send
the forty percent to jail for what they do? Now there is
your question. What proportion of a population should
believe that certain acts are criminal before passing a
criminal statute? If forty percent of the people of this
country believe that a thing is innocent, do you think
that the sixty percent that do not believe it would send the
forty percent to jail if they were tolerant people? I assume
that sixty percent of the people in this country believe in
either the Protestant or Catholic religion, or think they do,
and believe that it is very necessary to man's welfare on
earth and absolutely necessary to his welfare in the
hereafter. Are they justified in passing a criminal statute
and sending heretics to jail? . . . On how many questions
do two people think alike? They can only go a certain
way, when they branch off and leave each other. Men
ought to hesitate a long time before they vote that a
certain thing is a crime—and prohibition means crime. . . .
In this world of ours we cannot live with our neighbors
without a broad tolerance. We must tolerate their religion,
their social life, their customs, their appetites of eating
and drinking, and we should be very slow, indeed, when

[28] *Debate on Prohibition* (New York: The League for Public
Discussion, 1924), pp. 24–26.

we make criminal conduct of what is believed by vast numbers of men and women to be honest and fair and right.[29]

Despite all the discussion, nothing was done either to modify prohibition or to improve its enforcement, and toward the end of the decade the broad tolerance that Darrow recommended was even more noticeably lacking. The extreme drys, becoming desperate in face of growing sentiment for repeal, were driven to excesses that shocked their more moderate supporters. One woman, for example, suggested that the government should distribute poisoned liquor through the bootleggers. Although thousands of Americans would die, she thought this was exactly what they deserved and was necessary for effective enforcement of the law. To some extent the Prohibition Bureau agreed. Bureau chemists continued to require that wood alcohol and other poisons be added to industrial alcohol even though it was known that thousands of gallons of this alcohol, improperly detoxified, were reaching the public through the bootleggers and were causing blindness and death. Other dry proposals for toughening enforcement included whipping and branding offenders and executing drinkers along with their posterity to the fourth generation.

By 1928, the Democratic party felt confident enough of the antiprohibitionist sentiment around the country to nominate for president a man who might almost be called "the essential wet"—Al Smith, a Roman Catholic from the Lower East Side of New York City. Smith lost, but whether he was helped or hurt by his stand against prohibition remains problematical. The winner, Herbert Hoover, was a nondrinker himself, and he was the first president to make a sincere effort to strengthen enforcement. At the same time, however, he appointed a commission to study the entire situation and to recommend any modifications of the law that seemed to be necessary. But in 1931, when the commission's report finally appeared—

Alfred E. Smith, the "Happy Warrior," campaigning in Butte, Montana, 1928. The four-term governor of New York did not succeed in winning enough of the rural vote and lost by a wide margin—87 electoral votes to Hoover's 531.

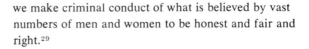

UNITED PRESS INTERNATIONAL

[29] Ibid., pp. 34, 43

with the rather inconclusive conclusion that prohibition, while not a wholly bad idea, was wholly unenforceable—the entire situation had changed. The nation was descending into the depths of the Great Depression, and a Democratic majority at last ruled Congress. In February, 1933, with a Democratic president, Franklin D. Roosevelt, on the way to the White House, Congress called for the outright repeal of the Eighteenth Amendment by submitting the Twenty-first Amendment to special state constitutional conventions. The necessary thirty-six states ratified the new amendment before the year was out.

The prohibition experience left deep wounds in American life, wounds that have not healed yet. By 1933, organized crime had become so powerful, and so diversified in its interests, that repeal was only a minor setback in its growth. Repeal could not restore the respect that municipal officials, law enforcement agencies, and the entire system of American criminal justice had lost during those thirteen corruption-filled years. Neither prohibition nor its repeal solved the problem of alcoholism. In 1978, alcohol was still considered the nation's most dangerous drug, with estimates of the total number of alcoholics in the United States ranging from six to ten million people.

THE FALL OF THE DESERT SHEIK

A cartoon celebrating the repeal of prohibition.

It is sometimes said that prohibition failed because it attempted to dictate morality, but all criminal laws—against murder, rape, assault, and so on—do that. Prohibition failed because, as Clarence Darrow pointed out, it attempted to define as immoral an activity which a substantial number of people did not feel to be immoral or socially harmful—however individually harmful that activity might be to the person who indulged in it to excess. Today, many lawyers and other students of the American legal system believe that the difficulties police are having in enforcing certain other laws—against gambling and smoking marijuana, for example, and against pornography, prostitution, and homosexuality—stem from a similar cause. A significant number of people no longer agree that these activities ("crimes without victims," as they are often called) pose a serious threat to society as a whole. When does an alleged individual error become a social evil requiring prohibitory legislation? It is a question that will have to be reconsidered in relation to many of our existing laws during the 1980's. And it seems certain, too, that the social consequences of our present total prohibition of hard drugs, particularly heroin, will continue to be debated throughout the next decade.

The Monkey Trial

The trial which took place on the lawn of a country courthouse in Dayton, Tennessee, in July, 1925, was officially known as the *State of Tennessee* v. *John Thomas Scopes.* Actually, it was the case of Clarence Darrow v. William Jennings Bryan, and it was better known to the millions of people who followed it in the daily papers or on the radio as the "monkey trial." Like prohibition and the Red Scare, the monkey trial dramatically illustrated the tension between old values and new which existed during the 1920's, and it, too, raised questions concerning civil and individual liberties which have yet to be resolved.

A fascinating book could be written on the many distortions to which Charles Darwin's theory of evolution has been subjected. In 1859, in his book *The Origin of Species,* Darwin postulated that higher forms of life had evolved from lower forms (as opposed to the prevailing belief that each species had been separately and divinely created) and that it was the ability to evolve or adapt in response to environmental changes which ensured a species' survival. In the writings of men like Herbert Spencer of England and William Graham Sumner of the United States, these scientific theories became social laws which held that only the fittest individuals within a species would survive and prosper, while the weaker and less fit would either die or struggle along on the lower plane of existence to which their own ineptitude had doomed them. Social Darwinism was naturally very popular among businessmen, who could justify low wages and wretched working and living conditions on the grounds that a really "fit" man would get ahead anyway. And it also appealed, in one form or another, to nearly everybody who was satisfied with things as they were and wished to see no

Charles Darwin.

fundamental changes in the social, economic, and political system. Thus, native-born white Anglo-Saxon Protestants could oppose unrestricted immigration on the "scientific" grounds that the influx of aliens from southern and eastern Europe (who were mostly Catholic or Jewish) was weakening the hardy American race that generations of struggle in the wilderness of a new continent had produced. So, too, prohibitionists could claim "scientifically" that the abolition of alcohol would strengthen the entire race by eliminating the frailties and diseases which drinkers acquired and (prohibitionists believed) passed on to their offspring. Curiously enough, however, many of the people who enthusiastically employed these distortions of Darwin's ideas to oppose labor or immigration, or to support prohibition, did not at all agree with Darwin's original theory. In the popular mind, Darwin's complex and carefully stated theory of evolution was reduced to the simple notion that "man was descended from a monkey" and was vigorously rejected as running counter to everything taught by the church and the Bible.

In 1924, a farmer named George Washington Butler was elected to the Tennessee state legislature. Butler, who was secretary of the Round Lick Association of Primitive Baptists, had based his campaign on a single issue: he had advocated a law that would prohibit the teaching of Darwin's theory of evolution in the public schools. Once elected, he immediately set about the task of preparing such a measure. The influential William Jennings Bryan went to Nashville to help draft the law and to support its passage, and on March 13, 1925, the Tennessee legislature approved the Butler Anti-Evolution Act by majorities of seventy-one to five in the House and twenty-four to six in the Senate. The act read in part:

"From Jungle to Civilization," a cartoon satirizing the Social Darwinist interpretation of the theory of evolution.

> Be it enacted by the General Assembly of the State of Tennessee, that it shall be unlawful for any teacher in any of the Universities, Normals [teacher-training colleges], and all other public schools of the State which are supported in whole or in part by the public school funds of the State, to teach any theory that denies the

story of the Divine Creation of man as taught in the Bible, and to teach instead that man has descended from a lower order of animals.[30]

Governor Austin Peay signed the measure into law with a statement which strongly implied that he did not expect it to be enforced. Although the state-adopted biology text, *A Civic Biology: Presented in Problems* by George Hunter, contained a description of Darwin's theory, the teachers of Tennessee anticipated little interference in their work.

According to the historian Frederick Lewis Allen, the Scopes trial occurred because a mining engineer, George Rappelyea, discovered that the American Civil Liberties Union would pay the costs of a test case of the law. Rappelyea persuaded his friend, John Scopes, to collaborate in bringing the statute to a test. Scopes, a young man of twenty-four, was a popular football coach and science teacher at Dayton High School. Partly in earnest and partly as a joke, it was agreed that Scopes would allow himself to be caught in the act of teaching the Darwinian theory from Hunter's book and that Rappelyea would then file a complaint. The two friends could not have foreseen the consequences of their scheme.

Upon hearing of Scopes's indictment, William Jennings Bryan quickly volunteered to assist the state in prosecuting the case. Bryan was a famous orator, a successful newspaper publisher, and a former secretary of state; he had been the Democratic party's candidate for president three times, in 1896, 1900, and 1908. Known as "the Great Commoner"—although he was a very wealthy man at this point in his career—he was enormously popular with rural Americans, whose attitudes and beliefs he genuinely shared and championed with thunderous eloquence. Bryan seemed the ideal man to present the state's case: as the author of a syndicated weekly column on the Bible, he had long been a leading spokesman for

John Scopes standing before the judge awaiting his sentence.

BROWN BROTHERS

---

[30] Quoted in Sheldon Grebstein, *Monkey Trial* (Boston: Houghton Mifflin, 1960), p. 3.

religious fundamentalism and a defender of the Scriptures as literal truth. He was also a strong supporter of prohibition.

The attorney for the defense, Clarence Darrow, hoped to demonstrate that the indictment against Scopes was so indefinite as to be incapable of proof and, furthermore, that the statute itself was unconstitutional. Darrow, the country's most famous criminal lawyer, was widely known as an agnostic, a bitter opponent of prohibition, and a defender of "radicals." He had defended Eugene V. Debs after the Pullman strike of 1894, had defended strikers on numerous occasions, and had even defended Wobblies accused of murder. He was also a most successful lawyer: during his long career he lost only one of the fifty murder cases in which he served for the defense.

The townspeople of Dayton did not greet Darrow's arrival with enthusiasm, as H. L. Mencken observed:

William Jennings Bryan cross-examining a witness.

> There is ample space about him when he navigates the streets. . . . All the local sorcerers predict that a bolt from heaven will fetch him in the end. The night he arrived there was a violent storm, the town water turned brown, and horned cattle in the lowlands were afloat for hours. A woman back in the mountains gave birth to a child with hair four inches long, curiously bobbed in scallops.[31]

The trial attracted over a hundred newsmen and many more Tennessee farm families and out-of-state curiosity seekers. Revivalists roamed the streets handing out leaflets and posting evangelistic slogans on lampposts and fences, while hot-dog and cold-drink vendors peddled their wares to the milling crowds. Owing to the heat, high humidity, and threatened collapse of the courtroom floor under the weight of spectators, the trial was moved out-of-doors, into the midst of the carnival atmosphere. Spectators

[31] Quoted in Charles Crowe, ed., *A Documentary History of American Thought* (Boston: Allyn & Bacon, 1965), p. 361. Copyright © 1965 by Allyn & Bacon, Inc. Reprinted by permission of the publisher.

cheered and booed the grandstand tactics of the participants. A small army of photographers captured every scene, and radio technicians captured every word—it was one of the first American trials to be nationally broadcast.

The highlight of the trial came when Clarence Darrow put William Jennings Bryan on the stand in an effort to reveal the inadequacy of a literal interpretation of the Scriptures.

Mr. Darrow: You have given considerable study to the Bible, haven't you, Mr. Bryan?

Mr. Bryan: Yes, sir, I have tried to.

Mr. Darrow: Well, we all know you have; we are not going to dispute that at all. But you have written and published articles almost weekly and sometimes have made interpretations of various things.

Mr. Bryan: I would not say interpretations, Mr. Darrow, but comments on the lesson.

Mr. Darrow: If you comment to any extent these comments have been interpretations?

Mr. Bryan: I presume that any discussion might be to some extent interpretations, but they have not been primarily intended as interpretations. . . .

Mr. Darrow: Then you have made a general study of it?

Mr. Bryan: Yes, I have; I have studied the Bible for about fifty years, or some time more than that, but, of course, I have studied it more as I have become older than when I was a boy.

Mr. Darrow: Do you claim that everything in the Bible should be literally interpreted?

Mr. Bryan: I believe everything in the Bible should be accepted as it is given there; some of the Bible is given illustratively. For instance: "Ye are the salt of the earth." I would not insist that man was actually salt, or that he had flesh of salt, but it is used in the sense of salt as saving God's people. . . .

Mr. Darrow: How long ago was the flood, Mr. Bryan?

Mr. Bryan: Let me see Ussher's calculation about it?

Mr. Darrow: Surely. . . .

Mr. Darrow: Let us make it definite, 2,348 years?

BROWN BROTHERS

Clarence Darrow and William Jennings Bryan pose for photographers, the tension of the trial showing in their faces.

Mr. Bryan: I didn't say that. That is the time given there [indicating the Bible] but I don't pretend to say that it is exact.

Mr. Darrow: You never figured it out, these generations, yourself?

Mr. Bryan: No, sir; not myself.

Mr. Darrow: But the Bible you have offered in evidence says 2,340 something, so that 4,200 years ago there was not a living thing on the earth, excepting the people on the ark and the animals on the ark and the fishes?

Mr. Bryan: There have been living things before that.

Mr. Darrow: I mean at that time.

Mr. Bryan: After that.

Mr. Darrow: Don't you know that there are any number of civilizations that are traced back more than 5,000 years?

Mr. Bryan: I know we have people who trace things back according to the number of ciphers they have. But I am not satisfied that they are accurate.

Mr. Darrow: You are not satisfied that there is any civilization that can be traced back 5,000 years?

Mr. Bryan: I would not want to say there is because I have no evidence of it that is satisfactory.

Mr. Darrow: I didn't ask you what you are satisfied with. I asked you if you believe it. . . .

Mr. Bryan: I am satisfied by no evidence that I have found that would justify me in accepting the opinions of those men against what I believe to be the inspired word of God. . . .

Mr. Darrow: Let me make this definite. You believe that every civilization on the earth and every living thing, except possibly the fishes [and except the people and animals] that came out of the ark, were wiped out by the flood?

Mr. Bryan: At that time.

Mr. Darrow: At that time. And then whatever human beings, including all the tribes, that inhabited the world, and have inhabited the world, and who run their pedigree straight back, and all the animals, have come onto the earth since the flood?

Mr. Bryan: Yes.

Mr. Darrow: Within 4,200 years. Do you know a scientific man on the face of the earth that believes any such thing?

Mr. Bryan: I cannot say, but I know some scientific men who dispute entirely the antiquity of man as testified to by other scientific men.

Mr. Darrow: Oh, that does not answer the question. Do you know of a single scientific man on the face of the earth that believes any such thing as you stated, about the antiquity of man?

Mr. Bryan: I don't think I have ever asked one the direct question. . . .

Mr. Darrow: Do you think the earth was made in six days?

Mr. Bryan: Not six days of twenty-four hours.

Mr. Darrow: Doesn't it say so?

Mr. Bryan: No, sir.

Here, Darrow caught Bryan in a fatal admission. Bryan, who had been holding firmly to a literal belief in the

Scriptures, now surprisingly offered an "interpretation" of the time element of creation. Darrow, sensing a breakthrough, drove the point home.

Mr. Darrow: Then when the Bible said, for instance, "And God called the firmament heaven. And the evening and the morning were the second day," that does not necessarily mean twenty-four hours?

Mr. Bryan: I do not think it necessarily does.

Mr. Darrow: What do you think about it?

Mr. Bryan: That is my opinion. I do not know that my opinion is better on that subject than those who think it does.

Mr. Darrow: You do not think that?

Mr. Bryan: No. But I think it would be just as easy for the kind of God we believe in to make the earth in six days as in six years or in six thousand years or in six million years. I do not think it is important whether we believe one or the other.

Mr. Darrow: Do you think those were literal days?

Mr. Bryan: My impression is they were periods, but I would not attempt to argue as against anybody who wanted to believe in literal days.

Mr. Darrow: Have you any idea of the length of the periods?

Mr. Bryan: No; I don't.

Mr. Darrow: Do you think the sun was made on the fourth day?

Mr. Bryan: Yes.

Mr. Darrow: And they had evening and morning without the sun?

Mr. Bryan: I am simply saying it is a period.

Mr. Darrow: They had evening and morning for four periods without the sun, do you think?

Mr. Bryan: I believe in creation as there told, and if I am not able to explain it I will accept it. Then you can explain it to suit yourself.

Mr. Darrow: Mr. Bryan, what I want to know is, do you believe the sun was made on the fourth day?

Mr. Bryan: I believe just as it says there.

Mr. Darrow: Do you believe the sun was made on the fourth day?

Mr. Bryan: Read it.

Mr. Darrow: [Reads aloud from Genesis 1:14–19.] Do you believe, whether it was a literal day or a period, the sun and the moon were not made until the fourth day?

Mr. Bryan: I believe they were made in the order in which they were given there. . . .

Mr. Darrow: Can you not answer my question?

Mr. Bryan: I have answered it. I believe that it was made on the fourth day, in the fourth day.

Mr. Darrow: And they had the evening and the morning before that time for three days or three periods. All right, that settles it. Now, if you call these periods, they may have been for a very long time. . . .

Mr. Bryan: Your Honor, I think I can shorten this testimony. The only purpose Mr. Darrow has is to slur at the Bible, and I will answer it all at once, and I have no objection in the world, I want the world to know that this man, who does not believe in a God, is trying to use a court in Tennessee . . .

Mr. Darrow: I object to that.

Mr. Bryan: [continuing] . . . to slur at it, and while it will require time, I will take it.

Mr. Darrow: I object to your statement. I am examining you on your fool ideas that no intelligent Christian on earth believes.[32]

Although the jury found Scopes guilty, he was fined only $100 and released; a higher court later overturned the verdict on a technicality without ruling on the law's constitutionality. William Jennings Bryan died, exhausted and demoralized, on July 26, 1925, five days after the conclusion of the trial. Clarence Darrow continued to fight for liberal causes until his death in 1938, turning his attention in several later cases—notably the Scottsboro case in 1932—to instances of racial injustice.

The confrontation between Bryan and Darrow has been described as a confrontation between literal and liberal

[32] Quoted in Grebstein, *Monkey Trial*, pp. 146–170.

interpretations of the Bible, between blind faith and free scientific inquiry, between country and city, between old and new. Bryan has been widely regarded as the loser, yet it is clear that the attitudes he represented did not die with him. The success of revivalists like Oral Roberts and Billy Graham proved that fundamentalism was still very much alive during the 1950's and 1960's and was in fact gaining strength in urban and suburban areas. The "Jesus people" movement of the early 1970's and the "reborn Christian" movement of the late 1970's gave further evidence of this trend. More than fifty years after the inconclusive conclusion of the Scopes trial, many young people, particularly in the South and Midwest, were entering college well armed against Darwinist teachings. In the 1970's, in so cosmopolitan a state as California, fundamentalist groups were strong enough to insist that state-adopted science textbooks must not present evolution as fact but only as theory, and that textbooks which discussed evolution must also discuss the alternative theory of Divine Creation. According to historian Paul Carter, the widespread assumption that fundamentalism is a dead or at least dying issue can be explained by the fact that the intellectuals who analyze these things have very little contact with fundamentalists.

The Scopes case also raised other, broader questions. Are church and state really separate in the United States of America? Should they be entirely separate? Prayers in the public schools, state aid to parochial schools, and other issues involving these questions were hotly debated during the 1960's and 1970's. Does a state have the right, even when supported by a majority of its citizens, to dictate what a teacher may and may not teach—and what a student may and may not learn—in the classroom? The controversy over the hiring of Angela Davis, a self-declared Communist, by the University of California at Los Angeles was only one of hundreds of cases involving academic freedom to arise during recent years.

There is an interesting sidelight to the Scopes case. The textbook used by John Scopes, George Hunter's *Civic*

Biology, discussed Darwin's theory of evolution on pages 194–195. Immediately following this discussion, on page 196, there was a paragraph entitled "The Races of Man":

> At the present time there exist upon the earth five races or varieties of man, each very different from the other in instincts, social customs, and, to an extent, in structure. These are the Ethiopian or Negro type, originating in Africa; the Malay or brown race, from the islands of the Pacific; the American Indian; the Mongolian or yellow race, including the natives of China, Japan, and the Eskimos; and finally, the highest type of all, the Caucasians, represented by the civilized white inhabitants of Europe and America.[33]

Exposure to Hunter's account of Darwinian theory might have broadened the intellectual horizons of the students of Tennessee, thus contributing in some measure to the general enlightenment of American society. That is what opponents of the "monkey statute" contended, and it is quite possibly true. But it seems equally certain that Hunter's reiteration of the myth of racial superiority— which gained added weight in the textbook through its implied association with modern biological theory—must have had a directly opposite effect, reinforcing a baseless superstition which had already had, and would continue to have, disastrous consequences for the students, for Negroes and other minority groups, and for American society at large. Yet nobody brought up that section of the text during the trial.

In each of the three episodes we have discussed in this chapter—the Red Scare, prohibition, and the Scopes trial —the power of the state and of established institutions was employed by people who opposed change in order to restrict the individual or civil liberties of people who welcomed or represented change. This play of force and counterforce, this tension between old and new, can be traced almost endlessly through the events and issues of the 1920's—it was at work in the case of Sacco and

---

[33] Quoted in ibid., p. 30.

CULVER PICTURES, INC.

With their fashionable short hair and short dresses, these girls, photographed in 1927, were part of a social revolution that enlarged the individual freedom of all Americans, and especially of women, during the 1920's.

Vanzetti, in the rise of the Ku Klux Klan, in the rebellion of youth, in the sex revolution, in the criticism of the era's literature and art, in the conduct of the nation's foreign affairs, and in controversies over tariffs, taxation, and other economic matters. For the twenties was, above all, a period of transition. Urbanization and industrialization, trends which had been underway in the United States since the 1830's, were rapidly accelerated in the 1920's, and as a result many people found it necessary to replace the values of the country and small town with new social practices, new economic habits, and new political ideas. Historian George Mowry has found the conflict between country and city clearly reflected in the nation's behavior during the Red Scare:

> The intolerance American society showed during the
> Twenties to minority groups, aliens of various types, and
> to all varieties of radicalism has often been explained as
> an inheritance of World War I, and as a product of the
> political conservatives who had been victorious in 1920
> in most of the states as well as in Washington. But perhaps
> a better and more inclusive explanation can be found in
> the rather frightened determination of the old and

essentially rural-minded majority to maintain its supremacy over rapidly increasing urban groups professing other social and religious faiths. The conflict was in some degree waged between an older North European American stock devoted to the Protestant ethic, with its emphasis upon individualism, hard work, sobriety, and frugality, and the newer immigrant folk crowding the cities, by origin from Southern and Eastern Europe, by religion Catholic and Jewish, and by temperament devoted to more personal indulgence and to paternalistic ways of thought inspired by either political or religious consideration. On another level the conflict was simply one between sophisticated urbanites of whatever racial origins and religious beliefs and rural folk—the first group devoted to the consumption and hedonistic ends of the new mass consumption economy, the second to the older, parochial economic and social dogma.[34]

And as Andrew Sinclair has observed of the prohibition movement:

The questions which occupied the American people in the first three decades of this century were not the questions which occupied their Presidents. While the White House was concerned with trusts and taxation and tariffs and foreign affairs, the people worried over prohibition and Romanism and fundamentalism and immigration and the growing power of the cities of the United States. These worries lay under the surface of all political conflicts. For the old America of the villages and farms distrusted the new America of the urban masses. Prohibition was the final victory of the defenders of the American past. On the rock of the Eighteenth Amendment, village America made its last stand. . . .

The Eighteenth Amendment was repealed by the Twenty-first. The old order of the country gave way to the new order of the cities. Rural morality was replaced by

[34] George E. Mowry, ed., *The Twenties: Fords, Flappers, and Fanatics* (Englewood Cliffs, N.J.: Prentice-Hall, 1963), p. 121. Copyright © 1963. Reprinted by permission of Prentice-Hall, Inc.

urban morality, rural voices by urban voices, rural votes
by urban votes. A novel culture of skyscrapers and suburbs
grew up to oust the civilization of the general store and
Main Street. A technological revolution broadcast a
common culture over the various folkways of the land.
It is only in context of this immense social change, the
metamorphosis of Abraham Lincoln's America into the
America of Franklin Roosevelt, that the phenomenon of
national prohibition can be seen and understood. It was
part of the whole process, the last hope of the declining
village. It was less of a farce than a tragedy, less of a
mistake than a proof of changing times.[35]

SUGGESTED READINGS

Allen, Frederick Lewis. *Only Yesterday*. Harper & Row,
Perennial Library.

Anderson, Sherwood. *Winesburg, Ohio*. Viking Press,
Compass Books.

Darrow, Clarence. *The Story of My Life*. Charles Scribner's Sons.

Hemingway, Ernest. *The Sun Also Rises*. Charles Scribner's Sons.

Leuchtenburg, William E. *The Perils of Prosperity*. University of Chicago Press.

Lewis, Sinclair. *Elmer Gantry*. New American Library,
Signet Books.

Murray, Robert K. *Red Scare: A Study in National Hysteria, 1919–1920*. McGraw-Hill.

Roth, Henry. *Call It Sleep*. Avon Books.

Sinclair, Andrew. *The Emancipation of the American
Woman*. Harper & Row, Colophon Books.

Sinclair, Andrew. *Era of Excess: A Social History of
Prohibition* (original title *Prohibition: The Era of
Excess*). Harper & Row, Colophon Books.

Wolfe, Thomas. *Look Homeward, Angel*. Charles Scribner's Sons.

[35] Sinclair, *Prohibition*, pp. 5–6.

"Rainy Night," painted by Charles E. Burchfield during the depression—a dark, dreary time in which, it seemed, almost all the lights were out.

CHAPTER FOUR

DEPRESSION

> By adherence to the principles of decentralized self-
> government, ordered liberty, equal opportunity and
> freedom to the individual, our American experiment in
> human welfare has yielded a degree of well-being
> unparalleled in all the world. It has come nearer to the
> abolition of poverty, to the abolition of fear of want, than
> humanity has ever reached before. Progress of the past
> seven years is the proof of it.[1]

Herbert Hoover spoke these words in a campaign speech
on October 22, 1928. One year later, the New York stock
market crashed. The nation's economic system faltered
and then began to shrivel up. By 1933, fear and poverty
had settled in on an enormous scale. Something had gone
badly wrong with "our American experiment in human
welfare," and the Great Depression seemed the proof
of it.

The Crash

The great bull market of 1928 and 1929 was, like the
Florida land boom of the mid-1920's, an inherently un-
stable thing. In many instances, the price of a stock no
longer reflected what a particular company was worth

---

[1] Quoted in Richard Hofstadter, ed., *Great Issues in American
History* (New York: Alfred A. Knopf, Vintage Books, 1958) 2: 342.

in terms of how much it owned, how much it was producing, how much it was selling, how well it was being run, or how valuable its product was. Instead, stock prices were based mainly on the expectation that stocks—no matter what their price—could be sold the next day or the next month for a still higher price. What did it matter if you bought stock worth $10 for $200, if tomorrow you could sell it for $250?

Much of this boom buying was done on margin; that is, a buyer put down a certain percentage of the purchase price and his broker or banker loaned him the rest. For example, if a man bought $1,000 worth of stock on a ninety-percent margin, he would put up $100 and his broker would put up the other $900. If the stock went up to $1500, for instance, the buyer would sell it; he'd pay back the broker his $900 and keep the other $600, of which $500 would be profit. If the stock went down, however, the broker could call upon the buyer for "more margin." If the stock fell to $800, for example, the broker would ask the buyer to put up at least $100 more, so that the broker could in a pinch sell the stock at $800 and still recover his $900 loan. If the stock continued to fall—say to $500—and the buyer could not give the broker more money, the broker could sell the stock out and keep the $500. But the buyer would still owe the broker $300. The buyer would therefore have lost his own $200, his stock, and be in debt besides. When the crash came in late October, this is exactly what happened to hundreds of thousands of buyers.

Sooner or later the speculative bubble had to break. Exactly what touched off the first selling wave is not clear, but it is not really important. Anything could have done it, even a spontaneous decision on the part of a group of shareholders that now was the time to get out of the market. On Monday, October 21, 1929, selling of all stocks was heavy. One issue that had closed at 335 on Friday was down 40 points; another, closing at 520, had declined 145 points in that one day. The market continued its general decline until "Black Thursday," October 24, when a huge selling wave occurred:

On Thursday, October 24, few speculators and brokers were in a mood to enjoy the "fine fall day." Before ten o'clock that morning brokerage offices everywhere were packed to the doors with anxious or frightened people. Almost every Stock Exchange member was on the trading floor, even the elderly ones who seldom appeared there. Every available employee and extra telephone operators were on hand. A curious public thronged the New York financial district and crowded the galleries of the two major exchanges. . . .

By eleven o'clock the rush to sell had become a mad stampede. Large and small stockholders alike, whose margins were disappearing or were about wiped out, gave up any last frayed hope they may have had and tried either to salvage something from the debacle or avoid being put in debt to their brokers for more than they could pay. Many probably were already thus in debt, and many more would become so during the day. "Sell at the market!" was about all that the beleaguered customers' men could hear, over the telephones and from those who crowded around them. To "get out" regardless of price was the desperate resolve of thousands of these trapped speculators. Many whose accounts a week before had been in a strong condition, but since then had been eroded by the decline, saw them completely wrecked by the precipitous drop. They had to abandon their shrunken holdings for whatever they could get.[2]

Traders at a ticker tape as stocks began to go up again in the afternoon of "Black Thursday," October 24, 1929.

At noon, five of the most influential bankers in New York met in offices across the street from the stock exchange. The crowd around the exchange noted their arrival. Rumors spread that the panic would be halted by the combined action of these powerful men, and some confidence was restored. An hour later, a broker for the Morgan Guarantee Trust Co., one of the largest banks in the nation, placed an order to buy 25,000 shares of United States Steel at 205 a share, although the stock had been selling at 193½. Brokers representing other bankers

[2] Robert T. Patterson, *The Great Boom and Panic* (Chicago: Henry Regnery Co., 1965), pp. 119–120.

Wall Street on October 29, 1929—the crash. One Wall Street broker wrote of the crash, "Like all life's rich emotional experiences, the full flavor of losing important money cannot be conveyed by literature."

began placing orders to buy and prices recovered by the end of the day. Although stock prices did come back, many people had already been wiped out, and did not profit from the afternoon recovery. Nearly thirteen million shares were traded on "Black Thursday," exceeding the previous record by more than four million.

On Monday, October 28, there was another heavy selling wave. Volume was more than nine million shares, and prices dropped very sharply, much more severely than on Black Thursday. Again the major bankers met, but decided that they could not stop the downward plunge. What they pledged themselves to do was maintain an "orderly market," one in which the offers to sell were matched by offers to buy.

On Tuesday, October 29, the crash came. Stock prices totally collapsed, huge blocks of shares were thrown into the market pell-mell, and many stocks had no buyers at all. More than sixteen million shares were traded. *The New York Times*'s estimate of losses suffered on that one day was between eight and nine billion dollars.

On Wednesday and again on Thursday, the market miraculously rose, more than recovering Tuesday's losses. On Friday and Saturday, the exchange was closed to enable the brokerage houses to catch up on the enormous volume of paperwork. The following Monday, much to the surprise and horror of the professional Wall Street community, the market took another deep drop. It now became clear that there was a lot of intrinsically worthless stock in the market which was in effect driving the price of sound securities down. On November 11, 12, and 13, the market took another deep plunge, and then levelled off. On November 13, 1929, the *New York Times* industrial average closed at 224; this average had been 452 in early September. By mid-November stock losses totalled thirty billion dollars, nearly equaling the cost of America's participation in World War I, and almost twice the amount of the national debt at that time.

For the next four months, until April of 1930, the market rose. People who had money were "shopping for bargains." By now, however, it was becoming clear that

The *Boston Daily Globe* headlines the "Black Thursday" crash. A major brokerage house took a front-page ad announcing: "We believe that present conditions are favorable for advantageous investment in standard American securities."

there was something drastically wrong with the economy as a whole. Backbone indicators like pig-iron, steel, coal, and automobile production were all shrinking steadily and fast. Consumer spending, especially for relatively expensive items like appliances and radio sets, had in some areas of the country fallen off by fifty percent. The Great Depression had begun.

In June of 1930 the market turned down again, and relentlessly went down for the next two years. In July of 1932 it reached a rock-bottom level that made the October-November "crash" look like a minor dip. *The New York Times* industrial average now stood at 58; in November, 1929, it had been 224. On October 29, 1929, U.S. Steel had closed at 174; on July 8, 1932, it was going for 22. Speculative stocks that had been selling for more than a hundred dollars a share had in many cases lost more than half their value on October 29, 1929; but in July of 1932 they were being offered for fifty cents.

The Crash and the Depression

There is considerable disagreement among economists about what caused the speculative boom that led to the stock market crash. Furthermore, economists do not agree about what caused the depression, a period of low industrial productivity and high unemployment that lasted until World War II brought about a full recovery. And they particularly do not agree on whether or not the crash caused the depression.

Many traditional economists blame "easy money" or liberal credit for the speculative boom, the crash, and the depression as well. Robert T. Patterson speaks for this view in his book *The Great Boom and Panic:*

> Many of the causes of the Panic and of the depression seemed remote and hardly related to the phenomena of American prosperity and of the stock market boom that led up to the panic. Even today economists differ in the emphases they give to the various influences that were at work. Most of those influences, however, were associated with the dominant one, namely, inflation; that is, an

unwarranted increase in currency and bank credit. Among
the immediate or precipitating causes were the unjustifiably
high prices of common stocks; the vulnerability of the
stockholders who had bought beyond their means and
carried their securities on thin margins. . . . If stock prices
had been less inflated, and if ideas as to future corporation
earnings had been more temperate, the panic would have
been less severe. . . .

More fundamental forces, however, were at work to
end the stock market boom and the era of widespread
prosperity. In the United States the inflationary extension
of credit, not only for stock speculation but for business,
real estate, and consumer purchases, had led to an
unwholesome . . . debt condition on an enormous scale.[3]

Economists who favor such a view place much of the
blame for inflation on the Federal Reserve System. The
Federal Reserve Board permitted the rediscount rate—
the interest rate at which the local banks borrowed money
from the Federal Reserve banks—to remain low. Thus,
it is charged, the government encouraged easy credit
throughout the economy during a period in which credit
should have been tightened.

John Kenneth Galbraith, author of *The Great Crash,
1929,* disputes this explanation, however, and proposes
that mass psychology had much to do with the boom in
the late twenties and the subsequent stock market debacle:

We do not know why a great speculative orgy occurred
in 1928 and 1929. The long accepted explanation that
credit was easy and so people were impelled to borrow
money to buy common stocks on margin is obviously
nonsense. On numerous occasions before and since credit
has been easy, and there has been no speculation
whatever. . . .

Far more important than rate of interest and the supply
of credit is the mood. Speculation on a large scale requires
a pervasive sense of confidence and optimism and
conviction that ordinary people were meant to be rich.

[3] Ibid., p. 174.

People must also have faith in the good intentions and even in the benevolence of others, for it is by the agency of others that they will get rich. . . . Such a feeling of trust is essential for a boom. When people are cautious, questioning, misanthropic, suspicious, or mean, they are immune to speculative enthusiasms.[4]

Many economists argue that the crash—for whatever reasons it occurred—did not of itself *cause* the depression that followed. Some, like Professor Patterson, suggest that factors like inflation and loose credit undermined the entire economy and that the crash was merely an alarming symptom of the more serious ailment. Other economists identify this deeper ailment as neither inflation nor easy credit, but rather as "underconsumption." According to the underconsumptionist theory, the American economic system is one primarily motivated by a demand for steadily rising profits. These profits ultimately come from an often ruthless competition for the consumer's dollar. But in order for profits to increase, the total number of consumer dollars also has to increase. However, in an effort to further increase profits, American business typically acts in such a way as to *decrease* the relative number of consumer dollars in circulation by (1) raising prices higher or faster than wages, (2) producing more goods than people need or can buy, (3) resisting wage increases, or (4) firing employees during slack periods. Thus, according to the underconsumptionist view, the system has a boom-and-bust cycle built into it: when times are good, producers glut the marketplace, raise prices too much, and otherwise reduce the number of consumer dollars in circulation. Consumers then find themselves with less to spend, and profits therefore decline even further, and so it goes until money is somehow pumped back into the system so that people can start buying things again. The Great Depression, these economists argue, was just the greatest of these "busts" and

---

[4] John Kenneth Galbraith, *The Great Crash, 1929* (Boston: Houghton Mifflin 1954), p. 174. Copyright © John Kenneth Galbraith 1954, 1955. Reprinted by permission of Houghton Mifflin and Hamish Hamilton Ltd.

otherwise was quite typical. In their view, the stock market crash was just an incident in the greater workings of the boom-and-bust cycle and had no cause-and-effect relationship to the depression.

Professor Galbraith, on the other hand, feels that the crash did seriously hurt the economy. He likens the crash to a hailstorm that destroys a greenhouse: although the hailstones may not have killed the plants inside directly, they have destroyed the special environment that sustains the plants' growth and life.

> The stock market crash in the autumn of 1929 has long been held to have been a somewhat secondary event. Beneath its froth more serious forces were at work. These, well prior to the market collapse and quite apart from anything that happened in Wall Street, were shaping things up for a serious depression. This explanation was attractive in downtown New York, for it at least partially absolved the stock market from the formidable responsibility of the depression. In my view, this puts the wrong face on matters. . . . Wall Street—as its prophets for other purposes concede—is of considerable importance in the American economy. The stock market crash and the speculation which made it inevitable had an important effect on the performance, or rather the malperformance, of the economy in the ensuing months and years.[5]

Galbraith agrees that there was a downturn of economic activity in the summer of 1929. But this mild and limited downturn, unlike many similar recessions in the past, snowballed and turned into a decade-long depression. Why? Galbraith concedes that the causes of the depression may probably never be adequately explained, but argues that the economy was peculiarly vulnerable to just the kind of shock represented by the stock market crash. There were, he notes, five basic weaknesses in the 1929 economy: (1) a lopsided distribution of income, (2) flimsy corporate organization, (3) a weak banking structure, (4) a not particularly healthy state of international trade, and (5) economic dogmas or formulas

[5] Ibid., p. 2.

incapable of dealing with a serious crisis. When the crash occurred, it snapped some of these weak links; these weaknesses then combined with each other to cause a downward-spiraling depression.

In 1929, five percent of the population received one-third of all the income earned in the United States. That meant that the economy was dependent for its growth upon high levels of spending by that five percent—investment in new business projects or spending on luxury items. As Galbraith notes, "This high-bracket spending and investment was especially susceptible . . . to the crushing news from the stock market in October of 1929." People in this bracket either lost their money or else decided to hang on to it. In either case the spending ceased, and the growing edge of the economy died.

In the late 1920's, much of American business was organized and interconnected by a series of holding companies and investment trusts that in turn owned or controlled actual working factories and productive industries. These holding companies and trusts issued their own stock and bonds, however. This stock became more or less worthless in the crash, and the holding companies had no money left to pay out to bondholders and other creditors, and therefore had to dig into the actual working factories for funds. This meant that there was no money left over to improve, repair, or replace factory equipment, and that the pressures to economize by cutting back production and reducing wages became intense. Thus precisely at the time when increased investment spending was necessary to stimulate the economy, the holding companies and investment trusts were sucking the working corporations dry to pay for their stock market losses.

Because most banks were totally independent of one another, bank failures had a tendency to become epidemic in nature. When news of one bank failure came the tendency was for depositors to run to *their* bank and get *their* money out. Since banks could not support each other effectively, a run on a small independent bank was likely to ruin it. A number of independent banks got caught in the crash, either because their officers had embezzled

A run on the Merchants Bank of Passaic, New Jersey, in late 1929.

depositors' funds to play the market, or because they had made loans for which the collateral was now worthless or greatly devalued stock. The Union Industrial Bank of Flint, Michigan, for example, had been looted by its officers of almost four million dollars, all of which was lost in the crash. Thus many millions of dollars of deposits were wiped out, and many more removed from circulation, at precisely the time when money in the form of loans was necessary to pave the way for an economic upswing.

Furthermore, major banks had made huge private loans to foreign governments. In order to pay back these loans, foreign nations had to do one of two things: either sell more of their products to the United States, or reduce the amount of imports they bought from it. President Hoover and Congress prevented governments from doing the first by raising the tariff, so that foreign goods became too expensive to sell in the United States. As a result, the debtor nations reduced their American imports. Since they had been buying largely agricultural products, the American farmer was especially hard hit at exactly the wrong time. Some foreign nations simply refused to pay back the loans they had received from American banks. Thus hundreds of millions of dollars which would otherwise have been available to the American economy just went down the drain.

As the cycle of declining production, increased unemployment, and reduced expenditure deepened, so did a general mood of pessimism and doubt. In 1930, payrolls in manufacturing industries declined by one-third. With six million workers unemployed and perhaps as many more reduced to part-time employment, people began to doubt that President Hoover knew what he was talking about when he said that "prosperity is just around the corner." But as Galbraith notes, "In the months and years following the stock market crash, the burden of reputable economic advice was invariably on the side of measures that would make things worse." People were solemnly told that the worst thing of all was not depression but an unbalanced budget and the danger of inflation.

Balancing the budget and avoiding inflation necessitated the following procedures: *reducing* government spending, or possibly *raising* taxes, and not "going off the gold standard" (putting dollars in circulation not backed by the gold in Fort Knox). These were procedures called for at exactly the time when more and more people needed jobs, relief, and money.

> The economic advisers of the day had both the unanimity and the authority to force the leaders of both parties to disavow all the available steps to check deflation and depression. In its own way this was a marked achievement— a triumph of dogma over thought. The consequences were profound. . . .
>
> When the misfortune . . . struck, the attitudes of the time kept anything from being done about it. Some people were hungry in 1930 and 1931 and 1932. Others were tortured by the fear that they might go hungry. Yet others suffered the agony of the descent from the honor and respectability that goes with income into poverty. And still others feared that they would be next. Meanwhile everyone suffered from a sense of utter hopelessness. Nothing, it seemed, could be done. And given the ideas which controlled policy, nothing could be done.[6]

Jobless People

The plight of the jobless factory workers is grimly recounted in the novel *The Disinherited,* by Jack Conroy:

> Factories did not open in the Spring, but the tides of the disinherited began to flow again. Hoboes captured freight trains and rode boldly through populous cities, defying both railroad bulls and city police. Flivver tramps clattered along the highways, breaking down, begging gas and spare parts. Usually the police would not allow them to light; often they were given gas and food in order to get them to move on. Like vagrant tumbleweeds they drifted along the highways from state to state. They had no place to stop.

[6] Ibid., p. 192.

UNIVERSITY OF WASHINGTON

A "Hooverville"
near the docks in
Seattle, Washington.

The highway that was to be built . . . drew job seekers
from hundreds of miles around, even before the
surveyors had finished driving the stakes. In hundreds of
. . . camps the word was spread that a new highway was
going through, and boomers gravitated to the site to squat
till the work began. Dozens of floaters piled off freight
trains and camped stolidly near the spot. The nights were
lighted with their jungle fires; you could hear them
muttering low and earnestly as they ate their mulligan
stew or drank java brewed in smoke-blackened tomato
cans. It was apparent that most of them were not
professional bums, but men who had held jobs as
machinists, carpenters, bricklayers, painters, railroaders,
and "white collar" workers.

When grading began, so many were assembled that it
was almost impossible to get near the boss. After the furor
of selection, the disappointed applicants dispersed.[7]

Unable to find work, many of the jobless gravitated to
make-shift shanty towns on the edges of the nation's cities.
These shanty communities, built of tarpaper and packing
crates, were cynically renamed "Hoovervilles."

[7] Jack Conroy, *The Disinherited* (New York: Hill & Wang,
1933), p. 282. Copyright 1933 Jack Conroy. Copyright © 1963 by
Hill and Wang, Inc. Reprinted by permission of Hill and Wang.

Among the wandering jobless were young single people who, in normal times, would be living at home as they began their first jobs or went to college. During the depression, many of these boys and girls left home in order to seek some form of employment, or at least not be an additional burden to their parents. These young transients were exposed to winter weather without adequate clothing; they didn't have enough to eat; they didn't get enough rest. The physiological effects of this kind of life were, in many cases, permanent. But the psychological effects were equally to be feared.

This 1933 "Hooverville" was located at 75th St. and the Hudson River, in Manhattan. It was called "Camp Thomas Paine."

When a boy is hungry and unable to obtain food by begging or working he must steal or starve.

To date, stealing has not developed many complicated techniques among the young tramps. In summer, the farmer's gardens and orchards are raided regularly. Chickens, turkeys, ducks, and even small pigs are picked up when they stray from the farmyards into a grove. They are run down, snared, or caught in any convenient fashion with as little noise and fuss as possible. Seldom, I suspect, do farmers miss the fowl. If they are missed, the farmer most likely blames a skunk or a fox.

Farmer John, it is true, is the most frequent and common victim of the young tramp's thievery, but there are others. Bakery trucks parked early in the morning before stores, vegetable trucks on the way to market before dawn, all furnish the youthful vagrant with some of his needed food. Sidewalk counters and tables inside stores are raided but not often. Produce trucks going to market early in the morning are the boy's best regular supply. Boys hiding in the culverts at grade crossings rush out, board the truck and are gone with an armful of supplies before the driver realizes he is being raided.[8]

People in America's industrial cities were particularly hard hit by the depression. Nearly everyone in Detroit, for example, depended to some degree on the auto in-

CULVER PICTURES, INC.

[8] David A. Shannon, ed., *The Great Depression* (Englewood Cliffs, N.J.: Prentice-Hall, 1960), pp. 63–64. Copyright © 1960. Reprinted by permission of Prentice-Hall, Inc.

dustry for his income. By 1931, with fewer Americans able to buy new cars, probably as many as two-thirds of the population of that city were out of work or only partially employed. Forty-five thousand families depended on the city welfare department for aid. Unemployed automobile workers waited in long lines gloomily outside factory gates. Skilled laborers who had made $1.10 to $1.40 an hour before the depression were eager to work for half their former pay.

Even before the depression, textile workers in New England's mills were among the poorest paid industrial workers. In 1929, the cost of living for a family of four or five persons was about $2,000; the average textile worker then had earned only a little over $1,000 per year. Edmund Wilson's book on the 1920's and 1930's, *The American Earthquake,* describes conditions in a New England mill town in October of 1931:

> The rent for a family tenement, unfurnished, with "nothing but the bare walls," seems to average about $7—which the workers . . . are particularly unfortunate in being obliged to pay weekly. The poverty of their homes is wretched. The women often make all the clothes and do all the housework and cooking, including baking the bread. They never get a chance to leave the house. The children who are old enough for school often cannot go for lack of shoes. If each child has a pair of his own—usually handed down from the next oldest one—the parents consider themselves lucky. Some of the families buy stale bread in bags. Some try to count on steak once a week and look forward to a chicken for New Year's; some are surprised if you ask them about meat, they get it so very seldom.[9]

In October of 1931, the textile mills announced a ten percent cut in wages. With winter coming on, nobody could afford to strike.

Predepression life had been equally poor in the coal mining regions of Appalachia. Coal mining was difficult

[9] Edmund Wilson, *The American Earthquake* (Garden City, N.Y.: Doubleday, 1958), p. 424.

Scenes like this one were common during the depression.

Jobless men in Grant Park, Chicago, in late fall, 1931.

and dangerous work. A miner worked from eight to twelve hours a day for $2.60 to $3.00. Many collieries paid their miners in "scrip," coins or pieces of paper, which could be traded for food at the company store or exchanged for money at a rate of perhaps 60¢ on the dollar. During the depression, conditions in the mining camps became even worse:

> The operators cut their rates and make up the difference to themselves and their stockholders by getting more work for less pay out of the miners. They put in mechanical cutters and loaders, and lay off as many men as they can. According to their practice, the first to go are the men over forty-five and the men who have been crippled in the mines. . . . And a medical examination weeds out other classes of workmen. If it is found, for example, that you are unable to read the bottom line of type on an oculist's chart—as comparatively few people can—you are likely to be eliminated. And the result is that the children . . . sometimes go without food for days and that they have so little to wear that they are sometimes more or less naked. . . . Even at the time when their fathers were working, they had no shoes to go to school, had hardly ever eaten

fresh meat or vegetables and had never known milk since they were weaned from their mothers. Their dish consists of sow belly, potatoes, and pinto beans. If they had been living in certain of the other camps, they would probably already have died from drinking water polluted by the outhouse and so escaped the pains of starvation.[10]

In northern cities, people who could not afford to buy coal to heat and cook with scoured the railroad yards for pieces of coal dropped from the trains. Shoeshiners and apple-sellers became familiar sights. Nineteen shoeshiners were counted in one block on West Forty-third Street in New York City. They charged a nickel a shine and sometimes earned a nickel tip. Employment agencies, soup kitchens, and city parks were crowded with men who had no jobs, no money, and no place to go. Many counted themselves fortunate when arrested for sleeping in the subway; it meant a night in jail with free meals.

The Farmers

For the farmer, the depression lasted longer because it had started sooner. But the early 1930's brought such low prices that southern cotton growers, midwestern corn farmers and dairymen, and western ranchers and citrus growers were all fortunate if they were able to break even —if they could sell their crops for enough to get back their seed and equipment costs. Corn brought 12¢ a bushel, and hogs 2½¢ a pound. A wagonload of oats at 10¢ a bushel would hardly pay for a pair of shoes. Farmers unable to sell their produce without actually losing money left it in the fields unharvested. Apples rotted on the trees in orchards in the fall of 1932, while millions of children did not eat a single apple all winter.

Ranchers had to pay more to ship an animal to market than the slaughterhouses paid them for the meat. Unable to feed his animals and unwilling to let them starve, many a rancher simply killed them. Yet at the same time, in New York, Chicago, and other cities, men were picking scraps of meat out of garbage cans.

[10] Ibid., p. 312.

An apple seller. Growers hired unemployed men to sell apples in many leading cities; it was not a bad job, considering the times. This young man, however, has taken over the stand for his pregnant, eighteen-year-old wife, who has disappeared. In the sign he gives her description and begs passersby to let him know if they have seen her.

A farmer could, of course, grow food for his own family, yet without an income he was unable to pay his debts and faced foreclosure. In Oklahoma, seventy percent of the farmers were unable to pay even the interest on their mortgages. One of the best collections of first-hand accounts of the depression years is David A. Shannon's *The Great Depression,* in which an article taken from *The New York Times* of September 25, 1932, describes how the depression affected Ole Swanson, a midwestern farmer:

> By 1912, Ole, then 35 years old and a renter, had accumulated some $2,000 in cash, two teams of horses, a reasonable supply of implements, a few good sows and some cattle. He decided to buy his deceased father's farm of 160 acres in Southern Minnesota for $20,000. He paid $2,000 in cash, gave an $8,000 second mortgage to the estate and a $10,000 first mortgage to an insurance company.
>
> Between 1912 and 1920, because of exceptional thrift and competence, Ole was able to pay off the entire second mortgage of $8,000, besides improving his barns, adding more cattle to his herd, increasing his equipment, building a porch to his home and making other improvements, as well as buying furniture, rugs and books, and giving his children an adequate education.
>
> But between 1920 and 1928 Ole found that his expenses, because of the industrial prosperity, were increasing. He had to pay more and more for labor and for goods. On the other hand, because of the drop in agricultural prices, his income was constantly falling. So, in those years, he was unable to amortize his remaining $10,000 mortgage, and, moreover, found that his standard of living was rapidly declining. By 1925 his net income for his labor had fallen to less than $400 annually. His 18-year-old daughter, who had become employed in town as a typist, with no experience whatever and without invested capital, was earning $15 a week, or nearly $800 a year, almost twice what Ole was earning for his labor during that period.
>
> In 1929 Ole was unable to meet a total interest of $600

and taxes of $300 and was compelled to give the insurance company, holding his mortgage, a chattel mortgage for the interest debt. In 1930 he was compelled to give an even larger chattel mortgage.

In 1931 his gross income was insufficient to meet either taxes or interest, and the insurance company, now having failed to get interest for three years, foreclosed the mortgage in the Spring of 1932. Ole, at the age of 55, was again a renter on his father's farm—the farm upon which he had been born and on which he had labored for a quarter of a century; having lost his entire equity of $10,000, he was left carrying a burdensome chattel mortgage.[11]

Not all farmers lost their farms in the depression, but all of them faced serious and even desperate financial situations. Many mortgage holders were reluctant to foreclose because they lost money as owners of these farms.

There was poverty amid plenty in the world's greatest industrial nation. The depression reduced industrial workers to poverty and their poverty increased that of the farmers. Neither had the money to buy the products of the other. The factories, though closed, were still capable of mass production. The rich farmlands could still yield abundant harvests. Yet people were going hungry, losing their jobs and their farms. People were beginning to lose confidence not only in themselves, but in traditional American values and systems. By 1932, increasing numbers of Americans were asking themselves "What is wrong?"

The Middle Classes

Community services, police and fire protection, highway maintenance, public building programs, schools, health services—all these are paid for by local taxes. In the early 1930's, many property owners and businessmen were unable to pay their taxes. Municipal tax revenues declined, and community services were curtailed. Public schools, for example, still received the largest portion of local

[11] Bernhard Ostvolenk, "The Farmer's Plight: A Far-reaching Crisis," *The New York Times,* 25 September 1932. Copyright © 1932 by The New York Times Company. Reprinted by permission.

revenues; nevertheless, the nation's educational system suffered along with other services. In the first years of the depression, school boards economized by lowering teachers' salaries; by 1933, those teachers who had not lost their jobs were receiving salaries that averaged from twelve to forty-three percent below those of 1930. New building programs were postponed; funds for building repairs and maintenance were slashed. By the 1932–1933 school term, schools had ceased to operate in some communities.

Until the autumn of 1931, most middle-class Americans remained comfortable and relatively well off. Although the salaries of professional people had been reduced and businessmen's profits had declined, many of these people did have savings on deposit in banks. They felt reasonably secure; their bankbooks would protect them if the depression should continue. Many depositors believed that things were so bad they could not get any worse. People were going to *have* to start buying again. A leading industrialist had asserted that the "dead center of the depression" had come and gone, and the secretary of commerce had said, "The banks of this country generally are in a strong position."

But the American banking system was slowly drawn in to the general economic crisis, which was by now international in scope. Some major American banks had made foreign loans which other countries could not or would not honor; other banks held foreign bonds whose prices had dropped drastically. Most banks had invested heavily in real estate mortgages and bonds, and real estate values had dropped so much—up to sixty percent in New York City—that banks could not regain the amounts of their loans through foreclosure. If, for example, a bank had loaned a man $50,000 to buy a $60,000 house, and the man could no longer keep up his payments, the bank would foreclose and take over the ownership of the house. But the house was now only worth $24,000; if the bank sold the house, it would lose $26,000 of its original loan. In order to avoid such losses, banks sold off their bonds instead—so many that bond prices fell twenty percent.

Worried depositors hurried to remove their money and bank deposits shrank by nearly $3 billion in the last months of 1931. Because banks reinvest most of their deposits in mortgages and bonds, many banks could not turn their investments back into cash quickly enough to cover the tremendous demand for withdrawals. They were therefore forced to close their doors, adding greatly to the snowballing panic. There were more bank failures in the last three months of 1931 than in the previous thirty years.

Though most banks were basically solvent, the secrecy then surrounding a bank's financial condition and the absence of effective outside controls on its business methods contributed little to restoring public faith. Confidence in banks and bankers was shaken by disclosures of embezzlement, insolvency, bad investments, and by the ever-increasing number of bank failures—nearly five thousand of them between 1930 and the end of 1932.

As more and more depositors withdrew their money, the situation grew worse and worse. Worried bankers could only continue to try to reassure their depositors, attempt to instill public confidence in their banks, and hope that unfounded rumors and gossip would not bring about fatal runs.

Perhaps more than any other one thing, bank failures brought the depression home to the comparatively well-to-do. Frederick Lewis Allen has described the effects of the depression on those whose incomes before had been over $5,000 a year:

> The great majority were living on a reduced scale, for
> salary cuts had been extensive, especially since 1931, and
> dividends were dwindling. These people were discharging
> servants, or cutting servants' wages to a minimum, or in
> some cases "letting" a servant stay on without other
> compensation than board and lodging. In many pretty
> houses, wives who had never before—in the revealing
> current phrase—"done their own work" were cooking and
> scrubbing. Husbands were wearing the old suit longer,
> resigning from the golf club, deciding, perhaps, that this

year the family couldn't afford to go to the beach for the summer, paying seventy-five cents for lunch instead of a dollar at the restaurant or thirty-five instead of fifty at the lunch counter. . . .

Alongside these men and women of the well-to-do classes whose fortunes had been merely reduced by the Depression were others whose fortunes had been shattered. The crowd of men waiting for the 8:14 train at the prosperous suburb included many who had lost their jobs, and were going to town as usual now merely to look stubbornly and almost hopelessly for other work but also to keep up a bold front of activity. . . . There were architects and engineers bound for offices to which no clients had come in weeks. There were doctors who thought themselves lucky when a patient paid a bill. Mrs. Jones, who went daily to her stenographic job, was now the economic mainstay of her family, for Mr. Jones was jobless and was doing the cooking and looking after the children (with singular distaste and inefficiency). Next door to the Joneses lived Mrs. Smith, the widow of a successful lawyer: she had always had a comfortable income . . . now she was completely dependent upon handouts from her relatives, and didn't even have carfare in her imported pocketbook.

The Browns had retreated to their "farmhouse" in the country and were trying to raise crops on its stony acres. . . . It was being whispered about the community that the Robinson family, though they lived in a $40,000 house and had always spent money freely, were in desperate straits: Mr. Robinson had lost his job, the house could not be sold, they had realized on every asset at their command, and now they were actually going hungry. . . .[12]

The deepening of the Great Depression from 1929 to 1933 can be shown statistically. Employment in manufacturing industries fell more than forty percent. Farmers lost more than seventy percent of their cash income.

[12] Frederick Lewis Allen, *Since Yesterday* (New York: Harper & Row, 1940), pp. 61–62. Reprinted by permission of Harper & Row, Publishers.

Prices dropped thirty percent. Total individual income fell more than fifty percent from $82 billion to $40 billion per year. Business and industrial failures rose from 20,000 per year in 1929 to 31,000 in 1932. The loss in value suffered by industrial and railroad stocks was nearly eighty percent. America's birthrate declined, and its suicide rate increased. But such statistics fail, of course, to convey the depression's fundamental effects upon a whole generation of men, women, and children. What were the physical and psychological effects upon breadwinners whose skills and talents were not wanted, upon fathers and mothers who could not keep their homes, who could not feed, clothe, and educate their children? What were once proud and independent people feeling as they stood in bread lines, or rooted in garbage cans, or begged on corners? And among those who had somehow managed to keep their jobs, there was often a feeling perhaps best described as "survivor guilt": an employed man could look around him and see perfectly decent human beings who, through no fault of their own, were reduced to desperation. *He* was certainly no better or wiser or more needful than they, and yet somehow he had been spared. It seemed impossible to help—or be helped—except in ways that seemed either inadequate or heartless or both.

Relief and Charity

To many people, the lack of adequate relief for many of those affected by the depression was perhaps the most severe indictment of our industrial and urban-centered society. Before the depression, needy persons had been helped by neighbors, local charities, or agencies of local government. But the depression created abnormal demands on these traditional sources of relief. Private charities simply lacked the money to cope with the huge volume of need. Local tax sources were inadequate to support relief programs on the scale that had become necessary, and the communities requiring the most relief were the ones least able to provide it.

The Great Depression was a national crisis. Yet the federal government failed to provide any type of relief until the summer of 1932, when Congress authorized the lending of $300 million to the states for relief purposes. By the end of 1932, however, only $30 million of this had actually been provided for relief. Critics of the government noted that in the same year, the federal government provided $90 million in loans to a Chicago bank.

The idea that "no one has starved"—often expressed by individuals not greatly affected by the depression—was contradicted again and again by newspaper accounts like this one, which appeared in *The New York Times* on Christmas Day, 1931:

> Attracted by smoke from the chimney of a supposedly empty summer cottage near Anwana Lake in Sullivan County, Constable Simon Glaser found a young couple starving. Three days without food, the wife, who was 23 years old, was hardly able to walk. The couple . . . had been unemployed since their formerly wealthy employer lost his money, and several days ago they invested all they had, except 25 cents for food, in bus fare to this region in search of work. Finding none, they went into the cottage, preferring to starve rather than beg. They said they had resigned themselves to dying together.
>
> An effort is being made to obtain employment for them, but if this fails they will be sent back to New York.[13]

Charitable organizations could not provide food, money, clothing, or lodging for all those in need. As the number of needy families continued to increase, private charities were forced to accept only the most pressing cases. One important and lasting social effect of the depression was to shift responsibility for aid from private to public agencies. But after 1931, even city and state governments were unable to meet demands. City and state governments could hardly provide ordinary services. By the winter of 1932, the additional burden of providing relief became impossible for most of them.

[13] *The New York Times*, 25 December 1931. Copyright © 1931 by The New York Times Company. Reprinted by permission.

This free kitchen, supported by private charity, was operated by the Brass Rail restaurant in New York City.

Social Discontent

After three years of assurances from the nation's economic and political leaders that the depression had run its course, public confidence in the national leadership sagged. The nation had abundant resources, a large and skilled supply of labor, and the most modern and productive factories in the world. Then why the depression? There was no famine—farmers actually were producing huge surpluses of food. Why were people hungry? What had happened to the nation's economic resources? Who was responsible for the depression? Even more disturbing questions were asked: Was our system of democratic capitalism and free enterprise capable of meeting the crisis? Could only authoritarian governments, like those in Italy and Russia, solve depression problems? One question frequently asked in 1932 was, "Will there be a revolution?"

Some Americans feared the possibility of a Communist takeover, since the depression offered Communists an opportunity to spread their revolutionary doctrines. Communist leader William Z. Foster outlined these doctrines to a congressional investigating committee:

> The bloody path that capitalism is traveling today over the lives of the workers is conclusive proof that when the workers, who are the majority, will become convinced

by their own experience of the necessity of changing the
capitalist order based upon private property and the
enrichment of the few, into a society based upon common
ownership of the means of production and the well-being
of the masses, then the capitalists will use their last gun
and their last dollar in defense of the only constitutional
principle they ever really held sacred—that is, the
unrestricted right to make profit out of the misery of the
masses. . . . The Communist Party is preparing the working
class for that day. . . . The Communist Party prepares the
working class to carry out in the proletarian revolution
that principle announced by the colonial revolutionists in
the Declaration of Independence: "it is the right, it is the
duty," of the working masses to throw off such government
and to provide new guards for their future security. The
only possible guard for the future security of the working
class is the dictatorship of the proletariat and the
establishment of a Soviet government.[14]

According to one contemporary journalist, ordinary
citizens were coolly critical of the Communist message:

He [the average citizen] examines carefully the text, "What
Is To Be Done," which a Communist acquaintance studies
so assiduously. This may have been of use in 1902, he
thinks, as an argument and plan of operation for a
newspaper run by exiles, but now! [In 1932.] Vainly the
citizen asks: Where are your engineers, statisticians,
managers, executives, teachers, and planners? If you
haven't them in full flower, where are you developing
them? And to all these questions there comes to the
citizen but one cry: Mass! Demonstrate! Protest! Words,
mass meetings, hunger marches, more masses, more
protests, more demonstrations. His ears roaring, the citizen
sits down on a curbstone and wonders what in God's name
he is going to do; and we may perhaps sit down on the
curbstone beside him and wonder too.[15]

[14] Quoted in Wilson, *The American Earthquake*, pp. 184–185.
[15] George R. Leighton, "And If the Revolution Comes . . . ?"
Harper's Monthly Magazine 164 (March 1932): 473.

It is more likely however that the average citizen knew nothing whatever about any Communist texts, or Bolshevik history, or a lack of statisticians; he probably didn't want to know, either. The only questions he wanted answered were, "Why did I lose my job? What am I going to do now? When will this thing end?" And for those questions, nobody seemed to have a convincing set of answers.

Accounts of "hunger riots" appeared in the nation's newspapers. Such incidents usually involved a crowd of jobless men breaking into a grocery store or gathering outside a city hall to organize a "hunger march." But much of the violent defiance of state and federal authority occurred not in the nation's industrial centers but in midwestern farm areas. Threatened with foreclosures and unable to obtain adequate prices for their products, farmers went on strike. They declared "holidays" during which they withheld food from markets. Farmers picketed and blockaded roads leading into cities. Sheriff's deputies attempted to escort delivery trucks into the cities, and in many instances were turned back by defiant farmers. Truckloads of milk were poured on the highways. Farmers reminded the nation that if such activities were illegal, so was the Boston Tea Party. They called U.S. Highway 20 in Iowa "Bunker Hill 20." And when farmers were arrested, they were hastily released as others marched on the jail. Masses of farmers attended foreclosure sales, as described in Conroy's *The Disinherited*:

Milk being poured down the drain— some 28,000 quarts.

"Gather up closely, ladies and what you brought with you," [the auctioneer] yelled. "So all can see and hear. This is where your money does double duty. You see what I hold in my hand? A bee-e-au-tiful cut-glass pitcher, and there's six glasses to match goes with it. . . . All right, ladies, gents, children, and bob-tailed hound dawgs, what am I bid? If you start off with less than a silver dollar, I'm going to be ashamed to own that I'm a resident of this fair county."

He paused expectantly and gulped a glass of water, slushing it about in his mouth and spitting it out. The farmers stood with folded arms. They had not laughed at his sallies as they usually did, and the auctioneer was bewildered. "I bid a dime," a farmer standing apart from the others called. Instantly a lanky fellow strode over to the bidder and muttered something to him, twirling his shilealah suggestively.

"Did I hear a bid?" asked the auctioneer, cupping his hand behind his ear and leaning forward.

"No," said the slim farmer. "He just made a mistake. Didn't you make a mistake, pardner?"

"Sure," answered the bidder, sullenly but submissively. "I reckon I just made a mistake."

"I like t' see a man own up to his mistakes. Gee Whiz! I wonder if that limb would hold up a two hundred pounder." The slim farmer raised his eyes to the branches of a hickory tree near the house. A rope knotted in a hangman's noose dangled from one of the high limbs. Several farmers held the loose end.

"Put up the whole shootin' match, auctioneer!" ordered the slim farmer. "No use of you wastin' yer time on one article at a time."

"I see we'll have to wait till the sheriff gets here," said the auctioneer, his urbane manner deserting him. "I know what you're up to, but you're not going to work any snide like that on me."

"We'll bid on the household goods now!" insisted the farmer firmly. "Come on!" He thumped on the ground with his cudgel and several of the others drew closer.

"How much am I bid on all these household goods?" muttered the auctioneer hurriedly.

"Well, without all the high-falutin' palaver you used tryin' t' sell the pitcher and glasses, it oughtn't t' be wuth much. I bid eight cents. Does anybody else wanta bid?" As he said this, he glared about him. Nobody spoke.

"Sold to this gentleman for eight cents," said the auctioneer mournfully.

"Now the implements and the hoss."[16]

Neighbors purchased the farm implements and horse for twelve cents and the farm itself for fifty cents. Then

[16] Conroy, *The Disinherited*, pp. 303–305.

they sold everything back to the owner for ninety-nine cents. The incident recounted above is fictional, but its real counterpart was repeated many times throughout rural America in the early thirties.

An incident that appeared especially ominous and revolutionary to government officials was the so-called Bonus March. This protest occurred in the spring of 1932, some fourteen years after World War I, and involved veterans of that war. The veterans, many of them jobless, favored a bill proposed by Representative Wright Patman that would pay them a bonus then and not in 1945 as originally scheduled. While the Patman Bill was being considered, a group of veterans from Oregon began a journey to Washington to demonstrate their support for the proposal.

As the Bonus March proceeded across the nation, thousands of sympathetic veterans joined it. When they arrived in the nation's capital, 8,000 of them organized a "Bonus Expeditionary Force" march down Pennsylvania Avenue. While awaiting action on the Patman Bill, 14,000 veterans, many of them with their families, camped on mud flats in Anacostia, an area outside Washington, and in abandoned buildings within the city itself. There was no violence or disorder; the veterans had adopted a military discipline and their behavior was orderly. Some people charged that the Bonus March was Communist-inspired, but actually the veterans were so anti-Communist that Communist organizers who tried to harangue the "B.E.F." were forced to appeal to the Washington police for protection.

When news of the defeat of the Patman Bill reached the veterans' camp, the men sang "America" and then a good number of them headed home. Congress had voted to pay their fares. But most remained in Anacostia. Some of the veterans had brought their families with them. President Hoover, who had for the most part ignored the marchers, finally ordered the army to clear the veterans out of Anacostia. Irving Bernstein in *The Lean Years* has provided an account of the operation:

Walter W. Walters, commander-in-chief of the "Bonus Army."

Bonus marchers gathered before the Capitol.

The armed forces that gathered in the vicinity of the White House consisted of four troops of cavalry, four companies of infantry, a mounted machine-gun squadron, and six whippet tanks. [General Douglas] MacArthur [Chief of the Army] himself was in command. At his side was his aide, Major Dwight D. Eisenhower, and one of his officers was the dashing George S. Patton, Jr. . . .

[MacArthur] led the troops in dramatic display down Pennsylvania Avenue before a huge crowd, arriving at the troubled area at 4:45 P.M. "We are going to break the back of the B.E.F.," MacArthur told [the Superintendent of Washington Police]. The soldiers, using tear gas, quickly cleared the old buildings and set them on fire. By 7:15, all the encampments within the city had been evacuated and burned.

MacArthur then sent his forces across the Anacostia bridge. Thousands of veterans, their wives, and children fled before the advancing soldiers. The troops attacked with tear gas and set fire to a number of huts. There was virtually no resistance. . . . By morning Anacostia was a smoldering ruin.[17]

[17] Irving Bernstein, *The Lean Years* (Boston: Houghton Mifflin, 1960), p. 378.

The Bonus March was ended, the marchers routed. Some state agencies provided trucks to remove the veterans, who were not allowed to stop at any of the towns along the way home. One resident of Washington, D.C., who was not a bonus marcher but who happened to get caught in the attack upon Anacostia, was trucked all the way to Indianapolis before he could escape. Railroads offered to carry the veterans home free of charge, but cities along their routes would not permit the trains to stop. A writer covering the story picked up two of the veterans along a Pennsylvania highway:

General Douglas MacArthur and his aide, Major Dwight D. Eisenhower, during the Bonus March.

> . . . One was a man gassed in the Argonne and tear-gassed at Anacostia; he breathed with an effort, as if each breath would be his last. The other was a man with family troubles; he had lost his wife and six children during the retreat from [one of the veterans' camps] and hoped to find them in Johnstown. He talked about his service in France, his three medals, which he refused to wear, his wounds, his five years in a government hospital. "If they gave me a job," he said, "I wouldn't care about the bonus." [18]

Many citizens who read about its activities in newspapers believed that the Bonus Army intended to start a revolution. But a great many others were repelled by the severity with which the federal troops had acted. Waiting in the wings, FDR noted that Hoover's decision was bad politics: you don't rough up war-heroes and their starving families and get *more* popular.

The question of why the Great Depression did not produce a revolution in America remains. Although attracting many of America's finest artists and intellectuals, Communist and Socialist movements failed to appeal to most American citizens. Why? In late 1933 an article appeared in *Harper's* that attempted to answer the question:

> Does the failure of the radicals to capitalize to any extent on the country's unquestioned unrest during a period of

[18] Malcolm Cowley, "The Flight of the Bonus Army," *The New Republic* 72 (17 August 1932):14. Reprinted by permission of the author.

such extreme provocation to radicalism prove, as so many
patriots love to believe, that there is something inimical
to radicalism in the American tradition and temperament,
or does it merely indicate that there is something
unrealistic—so far as the American scene is concerned—
in the methods of the revolutionaries?
    . . . We have, it is true, a radical, even a violently radical
tradition. But it is a tradition of individualistic, not
collectivistic radicalism. The individual buccaneer, not the
leader of unpopular causes, has been the American hero.
Anarchism is undoubtedly the philosophy most native to
our temperament, as it is the most futile in a complicated
industrial world. . . . From Bacon's Rebellion in 1676 down
to our latest disturbances in the Corn Belt, Americans
have flared out violently against specific injustices. Our most
frequent rebels have been, however, our hard-pressed
agrarians with a stake in the soil.[19]

Hunger riots by jobless in cities and the Bonus March
represented to many individuals immediate threats of
revolution, but it was generally conceded that the militancy of America's farmers posed a more immediate
danger. The farmers were not, however, calling for communism or any other form of revolutionary upheaval, as
Arthur M. Schlesinger, Jr. observed:

They were rather defending rights of property, especially,
the right of men to keep the homes they had carved out
of the prairie by years of labor and self-denial—a right
to be affirmed by force if necessary. . . . Theirs, as they
saw it, was the way not of revolution but of patriotism.
The foreclosure riots at Primghar, Iowa, thus came to an
end when a deputy sheriff sank to his knees before a crowd
of angry farmers and obediently kissed the American flag.[20]

[19] Lillian Symes, "Blunder on the Left," *Harper's Monthly Magazine* 168 (December 1933): 94.
[20] Arthur M. Schlesinger, Jr., *The Age of Roosevelt*, Vol. I: *The
Crisis of the Old Order* (Boston: Houghton Mifflin, 1957), p. 460.
Copyright 1957 by Arthur M. Schlesinger, Jr. Reprinted by permission of the author and William Heinemann, Ltd.

Norman Thomas of the Socialist party was an attractive, honest man, and what he said made a good deal of sense to thoughtful people: unemployment was the main problem, consumers not producers should be subsidized, the government should issue emergency grants of money each week, unused factories should be turned over to workers, there should be higher inheritance and income taxes, there should be a five-day work week, and so on. But the Socialist party was a shambles; it had little or no organization, no money to speak of, and no connection whatever with the real sources of political power in the nation. The Socialists got 885,458 votes in the 1932 election.

Norman Thomas in 1932, after having been chosen the Socialist party's presidential candidate.

The Communist party was even more splintered and impoverished. Even in the early 1930's, the party was composed of tiny, intensely ideological factions that seemed more interested in criticizing each other than in achieving a real voice in American politics. But communism as a *theory*—as a broad structure of thought having social, economic, political, and even religious elements—seemed to some intellectuals to provide a real answer to the great problems and failures of history. It promised to wipe the slate clean: there would be no more governments making wars, no more exploitation of the mass of humanity by a few greedy industrialists, no more poverty, injustice, ignorance, and soul-killing competition among men; man would at last be truly enlightened, truly free. Although nobody really knew what was going on in Russia at the time, it seemed as though communism actually might be working out there. In 1932 a pamphlet called *Crisis and Culture* was circulated, urging support of Communist candidates. It was signed by, among others, Edmund Wilson, Erskine Caldwell, Theodore Dreiser, Sherwood Anderson, John Dos Passos, Malcolm Cowley, Granville Hicks, Sidney Hook, Lincoln Steffens, Matthew Josephson, and Lewis Mumford. The Communist candidate got 103,000 votes.

People with real national power were not too worried about the radical left: the Communists and Socialists would orate to the wind, scare a lot of silly people, and get a handful of votes from some poets and philosophers. The real threat was from demagogues and from right-wing elements. In 1932, after Roosevelt had been nominated, and after the Bonus Marchers had been routed, he received a phone call from Huey Long, the enormously popular and powerful senator from Louisiana. R. G. Tugwell, one of Roosevelt's economic advisors, was present. When Roosevelt hung up, he told Tugwell, "You know, that's the second most dangerous man in this country." Roosevelt went on to explain Long's tremendous appeal:

> Huey's a whiz on the radio. He screams at people and they love it. He makes them think they belong to some kind of church. He knows there's a promised land and he'll lead 'em to it. Everyone'll be rich; there'll be no more work, and all they have to do is vote the way he says. He'll throw all the wicked Wall Streeters into a pit somewhere and cover it up. Then he and his folks can build their paradise. It's a time for that kind of thing. It's spreading.[21]

Senator Huey Long on nationwide radio.

UNITED PRESS INTERNATIONAL

Roosevelt rambled on about Long and the role Long had played at the Democratic convention. Tugwell then asked if he had heard Roosevelt correctly. Had he said Huey Long was the *second* most dangerous man?

> [Roosevelt] smiled. You heard all right. I meant it. Huey is only *second*. The *first* is Doug MacArthur. You saw how he strutted down Pennsylvania Avenue. You saw that picture of him in *The Times* after the troops chased all those vets with tear gas and burned their shelters. Did you ever see anyone more self-satisfied? There's a potential Mussolini for you. Right here at home. The head man in the army. That's a perfect position if things get disorderly enough and good citizens work up enough anxiety.
>
> He went on: I've known Doug for years. You've never heard him talk, but I have. He has the most portentous style of anyone I know. He talks in a voice that might

[21] Rexford Guy Tugwell, *The Brains Trust* (New York: Viking Press, 1968), p. 433. Copyright © 1968 by Rexford Guy Tugwell. Reprinted by permission of the Viking Press, Inc.

come from an oracle's cave. He never doubts and never argues or suggests; he makes pronouncements. What he thinks is final. Besides, he's intelligent, a brilliant soldier like his father before him. He got to be a brigadier in France. I thought he was the youngest until I read that Glassford was. There could be times that Doug would exactly fit. We've just had a preview.

No, if all this talk comes to anything—about government going to pieces and not being able to stop the spreading disorder—Doug MacArthur is the man. In his way, he's as much a demagogue as Huey. He has as much ego, too. He thinks he's infallible; if he's always right, all people need to do is to take orders. And if some don't like it, he'll take care of them in his own way. He has good officers. You saw that in Anacostia. There was a fine parade down Pennsylvania Avenue. There'll be order, all right.[22]

President Hoover and the Depression

Herbert Clark Hoover was born in West Branch, Iowa, in 1874. His blacksmith father died when Herbert was six. His mother, of Quaker background, supported the family for the next four years. When his mother died, Hoover went to live with relatives in Oregon. Hoover worked his way through Stanford University and became a highly successful mining engineer. During World War I he organized the Commission for Belgian Relief, the greatest relief program of the war. When the United States entered the war, Hoover was appointed food administrator and organized a program of food conservation. His interest in relief for the world's unfortunates continued during his service as a popular and efficient secretary of commerce under presidents Harding and Coolidge.

The depression was not Hoover's fault. He had been in office slightly more than half a year when the stock market crash occurred. As the depression worsened, how-

---

[22] Ibid., p. 434.

ever, the Hoover administration was increasingly criticized for its seeming inability to reverse the disaster, and was turned out of office by the voters in 1932.

Interpretations of Hoover's role in combating the depression fall into three main categories. First: that Hoover was a bumbler who did not understand the nature of the country's crisis and had nothing but hidebound platitudes to offer a desperate and frightened nation. Second: that Hoover was an astute student of the American economy, and proposed remedies that were potentially effective and were for the most part incorporated by the New Deal. But Hoover simply did not move fast enough and with enough style, vigor, and sympathetic concern to convince Americans that he knew what he was doing or that he really understood their plight. Third: that Hoover was a great man, controlled by a great and essentially correct vision of America, and that the American people failed him, not the other way around.

The first of these interpretations is well expressed by Robert E. Sherwood in his *Roosevelt and Hopkins*:

> Herbert Hoover, who had appeared to possess exceptional qualifications for the Presidency, had failed lamentably under the stress of major emergency. Although he had been honored as a "Great Humanitarian," his performance as President of a depressed nation was that of one who was pathetically inept in the exercise of common, human understanding. He first coldly assured the people that the depression was an illusion which it was their patriotic duty to ignore; then, when economic collapse occurred in Europe, he angrily denounced the depression as something un-American from which we should isolate and insulate ourselves; and, finally, he truculently scolded the people for blaming the depression on his own Republican party which had taken credit for the preceding boom.[23]

Sherwood, a playwright and biographer, was an intimate friend of FDR; his view of Hoover has been at least par-

---

[23] Robert E. Sherwood, *Roosevelt and Hopkins* (New York: Grosset & Dunlap, 1948), p. 38. Reprinted by permission of Harper & Row, Publishers.

tially supported by certain professional historians, however, most notably by Arthur M. Schlesinger, Jr.

What is perhaps the majority of historians incline toward the second interpretation, represented well by the following quotation from Broadus Mitchell's *Depression Decade*:

> President Hoover . . . did much, through domestic measures, to allay the effects and even to reverse the course of the depression; as indisputable need dictated, he more and more laid aside his inhibitions for direct, forthright government action. His policies, explicit and implied, came closer to the program of the New Deal than has been generally recognized. And he was more mindful of the need of international treatment of the depression than the New Deal was.[24]

Historians speaking for this second interpretation point out that Hoover realized that a business recession would follow the stock market crash. He immediately called the nation's business, industrial, financial, and labor leaders to the White House. He urged them to maintain production and spend $2 billion for business expansion. He asked businessmen to refrain from cutting wages and asked labor leaders not to demand wage increases. Later Hoover urged the nation's governors and mayors to expand their public construction projects. By mid-1931, however, the decrease in consumer spending forced the industrialists to reduce production; wage cuts and serious unemployment followed.

When, after two years of depression, hopes for a quick recovery faded, President Hoover proposed that the government assist businesses, industries, and financial institutions. In December of 1931, he proposed temporary government loans "to establish industries, railways, and financial institutions which cannot otherwise secure credit, and where such advances will protect the credit structure and stimulate employment." As a result, the Reconstruc-

---

[24] Broadus Mitchell, *Depression Decade* (New York: Holt, Rinehart & Winston, 1947), p. 57.

President Herbert Hoover throws out the first ball starting the 1931 baseball season in Washington, D.C.

tion Finance Corporation was established by Congress in January, 1932. The government advanced $500 million for loans to industry. Recalling that Hoover had refused to provide direct federal relief to the unemployed, critics labeled the RFC as a "breadline for big business."

Hoover had intended that RFC loans would primarily benefit the nation's smaller financial institutions. But the great banks and trust companies received the lion's share of RFC money. The largest single loan, some $90 million, went to a Chicago bank and trust company in which former vice-president Charles G. Dawes was an officer. This caused much criticism. The fact that the bank was a major national financial institution and needed the loan was outweighed, in the public mind, by the knowledge that Dawes had resigned from his position as president of the Reconstruction Finance Corporation to look after the bank's financial position.

The President's Emergency Relief Organization was created in late 1930 to coordinate, on a national scale, private giving to local relief organizations. But as one social worker explained, "Private philanthropy is virtually bankrupt in the face of great disaster." Equally ineffective was the "Give-a-Job" campaign of 1931 in which homeowners were urged to provide a few hours' employment to the jobless by giving them yard work or odd jobs around the house.

The president urged state and local governments to assume the responsibility for providing relief to their needy persons, yet local and even state resources were, in many instances, insufficient to provide the barest essentials of a relief program. The method by which local authorities distributed relief funds was sometimes grossly unfair. Even when federal funds became the major source of relief money, certain local authorities discriminated against minority groups: blacks and the foreign-born were often given smaller allowances on the theory that they had always been able to get along on less, or that relief payments might compete with the low wages being paid such persons. One large city reported, "Applications are not taken from unemployed Mexican or colored families."

Although he increasingly emphasized federal intervention after 1931, Hoover continued to place primary reliance for recovery on private business initiative. He urged state and local governments to undertake public works projects, especially those to be carried out by private industry and those that would produce income—toll bridges, for example—or those that would eventually pay for themselves, like municipal waterworks. But Hoover was opposed to such public works projects as municipal buildings, highways, and river and harbor improvements. These would produce no income and would burden the taxpayer. When the American Society of Civil Engineers appealed to him to consider an expanded public works program, President Hoover replied that in order to restore confidence and insure economic recovery, the federal budget must first be balanced and national credit be restored.

Professor Mitchell sums up the negative aspects of Hoover's depression policies in the following way:

> Hoover and his advisers were shortsighted in so long confining direct public financial relief to great business corporations, and in putting too much dependence on the percolation of public funds from these banks, insurance companies, and railroads [down] to the needy millions of the people. When it came to immediate relief of the unemployed, Hoover failed to recognize that the "situation demanded broad vision and comprehensive understanding of the problem, instant decision, bold and courageous action." The national economic calamity entailed wider acute suffering, and had deeper causes than he grasped. At such a time private relief was insufficient for great and little alike.[25]

A third view of Herbert Hoover has been presented by the historian William A. Williams in an article entitled "What This Country Needs . . . ," which appeared in *The New York Review of Books*, November 5, 1970.

According to Williams, Hoover was "an unusually intelligent and often perceptive conservative" who understood

[25] Ibid., pp. 80–81.

the principles upon which the total American system—
political, economic, and social—was based. What Hoover
saw to be the single overriding principle that could not be
abrogated without the eventual destruction of the system
was, in Williams' view, something that might be called
responsible brotherhood—a sense of responsibility for the
fate of one's fellow citizens and the capacity for joining
together in a cooperative endeavor that would act to fulfill
this responsibility. Hoover did not naively expect the system to operate smoothly at all times, nor did he believe
that the depression crisis would automatically fix itself.
But Hoover did believe that the main corrective action
against depression conditions would have to come from
the people themselves. Said Hoover,

> I want to live in a community that governs itself, that
> neither wishes its responsibilities onto a centralized bureau-
> cracy nor allows a centralized bureaucracy to dictate to
> that local government. . . . It is not the function of govern-
> ment to relieve individuals of their responsibilities to their
> neighbors, or to relieve private institutions of their responsi-
> bilities to the public. . . . You cannot extend the mastery of
> the government over the daily working life of a people
> without at the same time making it the master of the
> people's souls and thoughts.

Hoover's belief in the principle that the people must
ultimately be responsible for saving their system was so
strong that, according to Williams, it seemed the lesser evil
to him to let the system come apart at the seams rather
than save it *for* the people. Once the system was saved *for*
the people rather than *by* the people, it would no longer be
theirs; they would no longer rule but would instead *be
ruled*. Williams points out that Hoover was a Quaker, and
that honoring a commitment to principle is a crucial element in Quaker creed.

Williams argues that Hoover's actions as president were
consistent with a rigorous yet prophetic analysis of modern American society. In 1921, Hoover wrote that he
feared that the "great business units" could come to dominate American life and destroy "equality of opportunity."

President Hoover in 1932.

In 1909, Hoover had written that labor unions were "normal and proper antidotes for unlimited capitalistic organization"; he feared however that organized labor might also come to dominate American life. Big business and big labor were therefore the power blocs; Americans had to cooperate with each other in order not to be manipulated or dominated by either of them. The government's role had to be to umpire among business, labor, and the public, and, most importantly, to lead in the attempt to get these three groups to join in voluntary cooperation for the good of the whole society.

Williams states that Hoover's reluctance to move toward more sweeping governmental action stemmed from "his faith in the dream of a cooperative American community" and from his insight into what would happen if the people themselves did not "take charge of their immediate lives and then *join together* on cooperative action." Hoover believed that if the corporations took over and acted to save the system, the result would be fascism. If organized labor took over, the system would evolve into "a mutant, mundane, and elitist corruption of socialism." And if the government itself took over, Hoover foresaw what Williams calls "an elitist, bureaucratic, and community-destroying hell-on-earth."

Williams considers Hoover's analysis to have been a correct one. He implies furthermore that the New Deal solution involved a partial takeover by all three power blocs—corporate, trade unionist, and governmental—without any corresponding thrust from the people themselves; he asserts in this connection that our system today "is the worst possible combination of what [Hoover] saw as the three possibilities."

Williams concludes that the Bonus March was Hoover's great mistake. By 1932, the American people had not reacted in the cooperative, self-saving manner Hoover had expected of them, and had begun, in Williams' words, "to petition the government for salvation." The Bonus March therefore desperately confused Hoover. According to Williams, Hoover concluded that the Bonus marchers represented a military problem, if for no other reason than that "the people have done little serious marching except on the way to war." Hoover then turned the whole problem over to General Douglas MacArthur, whose solution was disastrous in terms of policy and in fact represented a usurpation of power, since MacArthur went beyond his orders. And Hoover failed to reprimand or otherwise discipline his general.

Professor Williams allows himself to wonder at the size and impressiveness of historical literature condemning Hoover. Why should it exist at all, if Hoover was such "a cold and feeble failure"? Why should the name Herbert Hoover have come to be a symbol for withdrawal, ineffectiveness, and obsolete silliness? Williams answers these questions in a rather figurative and roundabout manner. He points out that in the terrible days of late 1931, Hoover said, "What this country needs is a great poem. Something to lift people out of fear and selfishness." Williams then goes on to make a final, metaphorical assertion:

> If you kill a Quaker engineer who came to understand that—and to believe in and to commit himself to that—then you have murdered yourself.

The implication is clearly that the American people somehow failed a great test, and that Hoover himself did not. The result, Williams appears to be saying, is that Hoover is despised or criticized not because he was weak but rather because his career hints at an intolerable and irreversible American failure of will, principle, and brotherhood.

Whatever the merits of these varying interpretations of Hoover's depression policies, one thing is indisputable: Herbert Hoover was decisively rejected by the voters in 1932. Whatever it was that Hoover represented, a great majority of Americans wanted something else.

SUGGESTED READINGS

Bernstein, Irving. *The Lean Years: A History of the American Worker*. Penguin, Pelican Books.

Bird, Caroline. *The Invisible Scar*. David McKay.

Congdon, Don, ed. *The Thirties*. Simon & Schuster.

Conroy, Jack. *The Disinherited*. Hill & Wang, American Century Series.

Galbraith, John Kenneth. *The Great Crash, 1929*. Houghton Mifflin, Sentry Editions.

Guthrie, Woody. *Bound for Glory*. New American Library, Signet Books.

Shannon, David A., ed. *The Great Depression*. Prentice-Hall, Spectrum Books.

Sobel, Robert. *The Great Bull Market: Wall Street in the 1920s*. W. W. Norton.

Steinbeck, John. *The Grapes of Wrath*. Viking Press, Compass Books.

Terkel, Studs. *Hard Times: An Oral History of the Depression*. Avon Books.

This cartoon sums up FDR's changing relations with the Congress over an eight-year period. In the early years of the New Deal, FDR was able to have his way with Congress; later, congressional opposition to his programs became intense.

CHAPTER FIVE

THE NEW DEAL

I pledge you, I pledge myself, to a new deal for the American people. Let us all here assembled constitute ourselves prophets of a new order of competence and of courage. This is more than a political campaign; it is a call to arms. Give me your help, not to win votes alone, but to win in this crusade to restore America to its own people.[1]

With these words, spoken on July 2, 1932, Franklin D. Roosevelt became the Democratic party's candidate for the presidency of the United States. Roosevelt had been nominated on the fourth ballot, and he had flown to Chicago to accept the nomination in person, thus establishing two precedents. Presidential nominees had never appeared at nominating conventions before, and national figures did not travel by airplane in 1932. Trains were considered more dignified and safer. Roosevelt himself actually disliked air flight, and once nominated indulged his clear preference for surface transportation.

The 1932 Campaign

To most observers in 1932, it seemed clear that the Democratic nominee would be the next president. The Republicans had renominated Herbert Hoover, and it seemed

[1] *The Public Papers and Addresses of Franklin D. Roosevelt*, 13 vols. (New York: Russell and Russell, 1938–1950), 1: 623. Copyright 1938, 1966. Reprinted by permission of Random House, Inc.

likely that the voters were going to identify Hoover with the depression and get rid of him. Furthermore Hoover was strangely inactive, as though he did not consider Roosevelt a real threat. Nevertheless Roosevelt campaigned vigorously, traveling more than 25,000 miles and visiting almost every state. Roosevelt was a cripple, and although this fact was not made an overt campaign issue, it was also perfectly obvious. Clearly, FDR wanted voters to know that he was a strong active man who could get around and meet the people and run the country even if his legs were dead.

Rexford Guy Tugwell, one of the original and most clear-headed members of Roosevelt's "Brain Trust," suggests that there was a deeper reason for Roosevelt's strenuous campaign. It had become apparent that Roosevelt would win if he did not alienate any of the votes he had already had; people were going to vote *against* Hoover, and not *for* Roosevelt. His political advisors wanted Roosevelt to coast—to not say anything that would alienate any segment of the voting population. But Roosevelt had bigger game in mind, suggests Tugwell. Roosevelt wanted a huge vote *for* himself, because he wanted to break the stranglehold that the old-line, boss-ridden Democratic party organizations had on him. Roosevelt also wanted to reduce the tremendous influence of wealthy conservative Democrats like Bernard Baruch who, Roosevelt once declared confidently, "owned" some sixty congressmen. Roosevelt could do this by demonstrating that it wasn't the Democratic party that got him elected, but *the people*. If Roosevelt could get enough votes, *he* would be the Democratic party, and the people, not the old machines or Bernard Baruch, would be his real source of strength.

Some observers of the 1932 campaign found it hard to describe the position Roosevelt was actually taking on the issues. Reporter Elmer Davis wrote that he was sure Roosevelt was against prohibition, but for the rest, "You could not quarrel with a single one of his generalities; you seldom can. But what they mean (if anything) is known only to Franklin D. Roosevelt and his God." Professor

Arthur M. Schlesinger, Jr., on the other hand, has argued that although Roosevelt was perhaps evasive about specific programs, a powerful general policy direction emerged.

> It was perfectly clear from the campaign, for example, that he believed in positive government as a means of redressing the balance of the economic world; that he wanted federal relief as well as old-age assistance and unemployment insurance; that he planned a program of public works; that he would push the conservation of natural resources, including land utilization, reforestation and flood control; that he meant to tackle the crop surplus problem and to restore agricultural purchasing power; that he hoped to redistribute population between city and countryside; that he wished to regulate speculation and the security exchanges.[2]

Roosevelt campaigning in Hollywood, September, 1932.

Roosevelt frequently assailed Hoover for not recognizing the seriousness of the depression, for blaming the depression on international rather than domestic evils, and for delaying relief and forgetting reform. Very late in the campaign Hoover countercharged that Roosevelt's proposals were radical and collectivistic, that they meant a loss of traditional American freedoms and monstrous governmental interference in the private lives of individual Americans. Although Roosevelt sometimes hedged and swiveled in the face of these charges, he had, on September 24, 1932, made himself fairly clear in his famous "Commonwealth Club Speech." It was a speech that alarmed many conservatives because it outlined a broad "liberal" perspective on recent American history and hinted at "radical" departures from traditional governmental practices. Roosevelt did not write this speech, nor did he write most of his 1932 campaign speeches. On this occasion, however, his schedule was so tight that he did not have time to edit or even look at the "Commonwealth" speech. According to Tugwell, Roosevelt "never

[2] Arthur M. Schlesinger, Jr., *The Age of Roosevelt*, Vol. I: *The Crisis of the Old Order* (Boston: Houghton Mifflin, 1957), p. 13. Copyright 1957 by Arthur M. Schlesinger, Jr. Reprinted by permission of the author and William Heinemann, Ltd.

saw that speech until he opened it on the lecturn." The "Commonwealth" speech is therefore to be taken not so much as an indication of Roosevelt's thought but rather as a powerful formulation of the kind of ideas, beliefs, and perspectives that prevailed among some of Roosevelt's intimate advisors. In this speech, Roosevelt observed that

> The history of the last half century is . . . in large measure a history of a group of financial titans, whose methods were not scrutinized with too much care and who were honored in proportion as they produced the results, irrespective of the means they used.
>
> The financiers who pushed the railroads to the Pacific were always ruthless, often wasteful, and frequently corrupt but they did build railroads and we have them today. . . .
>
> As long as we had free land, as long as population was growing by leaps and bounds, as long as our industrial plants were insufficient to supply our own needs, society chose to give the ambitious man free play and unlimited reward, provided only that he produced the economic plant so much desired.
>
> During this period of expansion there was equal opportunity for all, and the business of government was not to interfere but to assist in the development of industry. . . .
>
> A glance at the situation today only too clearly indicates that equality of opportunity as we have known it no longer exists. Our industrial plant is built. The problem just now is whether, under existing conditions, it is not overbuilt. . . .
>
> Our last frontier has long since been reached, and there is practically no more free land. More than half of our people do not live on the farms or on lands and cannot derive a living by cultivating their own property. There is no safety valve in the form of a Western prairie to which those thrown out of work by the Eastern economic machines can go for a new start. . . . We are now providing a drab living for our own people. . . .

Recently a careful study . . . showed that our economic
life was dominated by some 600-odd corporations who
controlled two-thirds of American industry. . . .

More striking still, it appeared that if the process of
concentration goes on at the same rate . . . we shall have
all American industry controlled by a dozen corporations
and then by perhaps a hundred men.

Put plainly, we are steering a steady course toward
economic oligarchy, if we are not there already. . . .

It is the soberer, less dramatic business of administering
resources and plants already in hand, of seeking to
re-establish foreign markets for our surplus population,
of meeting the problem of underconsumption, of adjusting
production to consumption, of distributing wealth and
products more equitably, of adapting existing economic
organizations to the service of the people. . . .

If . . . we must restrict the operations of the speculator,
the manipulator, even the financier, I believe we must
accept the restriction as needful not to hamper
individualism but to protect it. . . .[3]

Although it may sometimes have been difficult for
voters to decide exactly what Roosevelt intended to do
if elected, one thing seemed clear: Roosevelt represented
some sort of a reasonable change.

People were insecure in their jobs, savings, and self-
respect; they wanted not only a change for the better,
but they also wanted change that promised to stabilize
the country, not throw it into even more confusion.
Roosevelt represented this kind of security: he was not
a vaguely "foreign-seeming" Socialist or a Communist;
he was thought of as an American aristocrat, a member
of a family of wealth, prestige, and a tradition of public
service. Roosevelt wasn't new to politics or to executive
decision-making; he had been a candidate for vice president in 1920, and had been governor of New York—then
the richest, most populous state in the union.

In 1932, Roosevelt carried forty-two of the forty-eight
states and received a heavily Democratic Congress as well.

[3] *Public Papers* 1: 747–755.

The 1932 Roosevelt campaign in action. FDR is driving in a political parade that stretched for two miles and contained 100,000 people.

Roosevelt was inaugurated on Saturday, March 4, 1933, a grey, drizzling day. There was a huge throng of on-lookers, and millions listened on the radio as Roosevelt delivered his first inaugural address.

In it, Roosevelt voiced his confidence in the American people—*they* had not failed, he said, and the depression was not their fault. They had voted him an overwhelming mandate for "direct, vigorous action," and they would, Roosevelt felt certain, unite to support his leadership in "arduous days" that lay ahead.

Roosevelt said harsh things about those who had brought about the depression, but cloaked the identity of these wrongdoers in vague, often biblical language. Although the country was rich, Roosevelt said, many people were poor or jobless, and this was "because the rulers of the exchange of mankind's goods have failed through their own stubbornness and their own incompe-tence." These people, Roosevelt asserted, had known "only the rules of a generation of self-seekers" but now "the money changers had fled from their high seats in the temple of our civilization"; the practices of "the unscrupulous money changers stand indicted in the court of public opinion, rejected by the hearts and minds of men."

Roosevelt promised to put "first things first." The first thing was "to put people to work." Close on the heels of this "greatest primary task" was to reduce urban overcrowding, to raise farm prices, to prevent the loss through mortgage foreclosure of "our small homes and our farms," to unify and equalize relief activities, to plan for and supervise on a national scale industries "which have a definitely public character," to strictly supervise all "banking and credits and investments," to put "an end to speculation with other people's money," and to provide for "an adequate but sound currency." Sandwiched among these priorities was an ambiguous sentence calling for drastic reduction of the costs of federal, state, and local governments.

Roosevelt promised to do these things and do them fast. Merely talking about them never helped: "We must act, and act quickly." Roosevelt promised to abide by the Constitution and hoped "the normal balance of executive and legislative authority" could be preserved. But if "Congress should fail," he would seek a vast though temporary enlargement of his executive power, and fight the emergency as though it were a "foreign foe."

The First Seven Days

During the 1932 election campaign, political commentator Walter Lippmann had written that Franklin Roosevelt was no crusader but was, instead, a pleasant man without any important qualifications for the office of president. One week after Roosevelt's inauguration, Lippmann wrote words of praise that summed up the reaction of many liberals and conservatives alike:

> At the beginning of March, the country was in such a state of confused desperation that it would have followed almost any leader anywhere he chose to go. . . . In one

BROWN BROTHERS

Frightened depositors gather outside their bank.

week, the nation, which had lost confidence in everything and everybody, has regained confidence in the government and in itself.[4]

What had the new administration done in such a short time to cause this surge of confidence?

Most of the president's activities during the first week were devoted to the banking crisis. Roosevelt instructed Secretary of the Treasury William Woodin to have ready an emergency banking bill to present to a special session of Congress, to be convened on March 9. The "bank holiday" Roosevelt proclaimed on Sunday, March 5— his first full day in office—closed all banks, including the Federal Reserve banks. Only those banks which had been examined and found solvent would be allowed to reopen.

On March 8, Roosevelt held his first press conference.

[4] Quoted in Arthur M. Schlesinger, Jr., *The Age of Roosevelt*, Vol. II: *The Coming of the New Deal* (Boston: Houghton Mifflin, 1958), p. 13. Copyright 1958 by Arthur M. Schlesinger, Jr. Reprinted by permission of the author and William Heinemann, Ltd.

FDR giving his first informal radio address, or "fireside chat," from his study in the White House, March 12, 1933.

From that date on Roosevelt met with the press about twice a week. In this first press conference, Roosevelt provided reporters with what he called "background" information (general facts not to be attributed specifically to Roosevelt) and "off-the-record" information (information not to be published or even repeated).

   Q. In your Inaugural Address, in which you only touched upon things, you said you are for sound and adequate. . . .

   The President: I put it the other way around. I said "adequate but sound."

   Q. Now that you have more time, can you define what that is?

   The President: No. *(Laughter.)* In other words—and I should call this "off the record" information—you cannot define the thing too closely one way or the other. On Friday afternoon last we undoubtedly did not have adequate currency. No question about that. There wasn't enough circulating money to go around.

   Q. I believe that. *(Laughter.)*

The President: We hope that when the banks reopen a great deal of the currency that was withdrawn for one purpose or another will find its way back. We have got to provide an adequate currency. . . . In other words, what you are coming to now really is a managed currency, the adequateness of which will depend on the conditions of the moment. It may expand one week and it may contract another week. That part is all off the record.

Q. Can we use that part—managed?

The President: No, I think not. . . .

Q. Now you came down to adequacy; but you haven't defined what you think is sound. Don't you want to define that now?

The President: I don't want to define "sound" now. In other words, in its essence—this is entirely off the record—in its essence we must not put the Government any further in debt because of failed banks. . . .

Q. Couldn't you take that out and give it to us? That's a very good thing at this time.

The President: I don't think so. There may be some talk about it tomorrow.

Q. When you speak of a managed currency, do you speak of a temporary proposition or a permanent system?

The President: It ought to be part of the permanent system—that is off the record—it ought to be part of the permanent system, so we don't run into this thing again. . . .

Q. Can you tell us anything about guaranteeing of bank deposits?

The President: I can tell you as to guaranteeing bank deposits my own views, and I think those of the old Administration. The general underlying thought behind the use of the word "guarantee" with respect to bank deposits is that you guarantee bad banks as well as good banks. The minute the Government starts to do that the Government runs into a probable loss. I will give you an example. Suppose there are three banks in town: one is 100 percent capable of working out, one 50 percent and another 10 percent. Now, if the Government assumes a

100 percent guarantee, it will lose 50 percent on one and
90 percent on the other. . . . Therefore, the one objective
is going to be to keep the loss in the individual banks down
to a minimum, endeavoring to get 100 percent on them.
We do not wish to make the United States Government
liable for the mistakes and errors of individual banks, and
put a premium on unsound banking in the future.

    Q. That is off the record?

    The President: Yes.

    Q. Couldn't you make it background? There is a demand
for the guarantee proposition.

    The President: As long as you don't write stories to give
the average depositor the thought that his own particular
bank isn't going to pay. That is what I want to avoid,
because, when you come down to it, the great majority of
banks are going to pay up. There will be many other banks
which won't pay out the whole thing immediately, but will
pay out 100 percent in time. There will be a very small
number of banks that will probably have to go to the
Examiner; but I don't want anybody to get the idea in
reading the stories that the average bank isn't going to
pay one hundred cents on the dollar, because the average
bank is going to pay it. . . .[5]

Meanwhile, Roosevelt had met with the nation's leading bankers, who could not agree upon what should be
done. It appeared that they had lost confidence in themselves and were willing to give up responsibility to the
federal government. There was talk of nationalizing the
banks. But the ultimate solution to the banking crisis
was conservative in nature and was highly acceptable to
the nation's bankers and businessmen. In his book *The
History of the New Deal*, Professor Basil Rauch writes:

The Emergency Banking Bill provided only such
government controls against export and hoarding of gold,
silver, and currency, and against the reopening of unsound
banks as would assist private bankers to regain control of

[5] *Public Papers* 2: 33–38.

the situation. Further panic was forestalled by providing for the issuance of Federal Reserve notes on the security of assets of sound banks, so that the latter could immediately reopen for business. Thus the money changers who had fled from their high seats in the temple were invited to return under government escort. Socialists could deplore the loss of an opportunity by the government to install itself in their seats.[6]

The Emergency Banking Bill was passed almost unanimously by Congress within four hours of its introduction on March 9. By nine o'clock that evening, the president had signed it into law. The only opposition came from seven progressive senators who voted against the bill on the grounds that it strengthened the New York bankers' control of the nation's economy. The speed with which the administration acted on this, and other legislation, inspired the humorist Will Rogers to comment:

> They know they got a man in there who is wise to Congress, wise to our so-called big men. The whole country is with him, just so he does something. If he burned down the Capitol we would cheer and say "Well, we at least got a fire started anyhow." We have had years of "Don't rock the boat," go and sink if you want to, we [might] just as well be swimming. . . .

Will Rogers.

At the end of the first week, on Sunday, March 12, Roosevelt went directly to the people in order to explain his banking measures. This was the first of many informal radio addresses which the press dubbed "fireside chats."

> I want to talk for a few minutes with the people of the United States about banking—with the comparatively few who understand the mechanics of banking but more particularly with the overwhelming majority who use banks for the making of deposits and the drawing of checks. I want to tell you what has been done in the last

[6] Basil Rauch, *The History of the New Deal* (New York: G. P. Putman's Sons, 1963), p. 62. Copyright 1963. Reprinted by permission of Farrar, Straus & Giroux, Inc.

[7] Quoted in Schlesinger, *Coming of the New Deal*, p. 13.

few days, why it was done, and what the next steps are
going to be. . . .

First of all, let me state the simple fact that when you
deposit money in a bank, the bank does not put the money
into a safe deposit vault. It invests your money in many
different forms of credit—bonds, commercial paper,
mortgages and many other kinds of loans. In other words,
the bank puts your money to work to keep the wheels of
industry and of agriculture turning around. A comparatively
small part of the money you put into the bank is kept in
currency—an amount which in normal times is wholly
sufficient to cover the cash needs of the average citizen.
In other words, the total amount of all the currency in
the country is only a small fraction of the total deposits
in all the banks.

What, then, happened during the last few days of
February and the first few days of March? Because of
undermined confidence on the part of the public, there
was a general rush by a large portion of our population
to turn bank deposits into currency or gold—a rush so
great that the soundest banks could not get enough
currency to meet the demand. The reason for this was
that on the spur of the moment it was, of course, impossible
to sell perfectly sound assets of a bank and convert them
into cash except at panic prices far below their real value.

By the afternoon of March 3rd scarcely a bank in the
country was open to do business. . . .

It was then that I issued the proclamation providing
for the nationwide bank holiday, and this was the first
step in the Government's reconstruction of our financial
and economic fabric.

FDR signing the
Emergency Banking
Bill on March 10,
1933.

The second step was the legislation promptly and
patriotically passed by the Congress confirming my
proclamation and broadening my powers so that it became
possible in view of the requirement of time to extend the
holiday and lift the ban of that holiday gradually. This law
also gave authority to develop a program of rehabilitation
of our banking facilities. . . .

The third stage has been the series of regulations
permitting the banks to continue their functions to take

care of the distribution of food and household necessities and the payment of payrolls.

This bank holiday, while resulting in many cases in great inconvenience, is affording us the opportunity to supply the currency necessary to meet the situation. No sound bank is a dollar worse off than it was when it closed its doors last Monday. Neither is any bank which may turn out not to be in a position for immediate opening. The new law allows the twelve Federal Reserve Banks to issue additional currency on good assets and thus the banks which reopen will be able to meet every legitimate call. The new currency is being sent out by the Bureau of Engraving and Printing in large volume to every part of the country. It is sound currency because it is backed by actual, good assets.

A question you will ask is this: why are all the banks not to be reopened at the same time? The answer is simple. Your Government does not intend that the history of the past few years shall be repeated. We do not want and will not have another epidemic of bank failures.

As a result, we start tomorrow, Monday, with the opening of banks in the twelve Federal Reserve Bank cities—those banks which on first examination by the Treasury have already been found to be all right. This will be followed on Tuesday by the resumption of all their functions by banks already found to be sound in cities where there are recognized clearing houses. That means about 250 cities of the United States.

On Wednesday and succeeding days banks in smaller places all through the country will resume business, subject, of course, to the Government's physical ability to complete its survey. It is necessary that the reopening of banks be extended over a period in order to permit the banks to make applications for necessary loans, to obtain currency needed to meet their requirements and to enable the Government to make common sense checkups.

Let me make it clear to you that if your bank does not open the first day, you are by no means justified in believing that it will not open. A bank that opens on one of the subsequent days is in exactly the same status as the bank that opens tomorrow. . . .

It is possible that when the banks resume a very few people who have not recovered from their fear may again begin withdrawals. Let me make it clear that the banks will take care of all needs—and it is my belief that hoarding during the past week has become an exceedingly unfashionable pastime. It needs no prophet to tell you that when people find that they can get their money— that they can get it when they want it for all legitimate purposes—the phantom of fear will soon be laid. People will again be glad to have their money where it will be safely taken care of and where they can use it conveniently at any time. I can assure you that it is safer to keep your money in a reopened bank than under the mattress. . . .

Remember that the essential accomplishment of the new legislation is that it makes it possible for banks more readily to convert their assets into cash than was the case before. More liberal provision has been made for banks to borrow on these assets at the Reserve Banks and more liberal provision has also been made for issuing currency on the security of these good assets. This currency is . . . issued only on adequate security, and every good bank has an abundance of such security. . . .

I hope you can see from this elemental recital of what your Government is doing that there is nothing complex, or radical, in the process. . . .

It has been wonderful to me to catch the note of confidence from all over the country. I can never be sufficiently grateful to the people for the loyal support they have given me in their acceptance of the judgment that has dictated our course, even though all our processes may not have seemed clear to them. . . . [8]

Will Rogers spoke for many people when he said that Roosevelt took a complicated subject like banking and made everybody understand it, even the bankers.

[8] *Public Papers* 2: 61–65.

The Hundred Days

The famous "Hundred Days" lasted from March 9 through June 16, 1933, when the weary Congress ended its special session. This period is unmatched in American history for the extent of legislative production. Congress passed, and Roosevelt signed, some fifteen acts of major legislation, many of them extending federal power into areas of national life hitherto considered off-limits to government. Some of this legislation provided immediate relief to the hungry and homeless, to those facing bankruptcy or foreclosure of their property. Other legislation was designed to produce recovery in the nation's economy or to correct economic abuses considered responsible in part for the present debacle.

In the following pages, some of the important Hundred Days legislation is discussed. The dates given are those on which Roosevelt signed the bills into law.

March 20: Act to Maintain the Credit of the United States Government. Roosevelt warned that the federal government faced a deficit that would exceed a billion dollars the next fiscal year unless immediate action was taken. He asked Congress for power to bring about governmental economies, especially in the Veterans' Bureau. Politically sensitive congressmen were particularly reluctant to enforce economies in this area; telegrams from veterans and veterans' organizations flooded the Capitol. But the measure was reluctantly passed. One congressional leader warned: "When the *Congressional Record* goes to President Roosevelt's desk in the morning, he will look over the roll call we are about to take, and I warn you new Democrats to be careful where your names are found."

It has been estimated that $300,000,000 was saved by the Veterans' Bureau through this measure, but it resulted in a second installment of the veterans' Bonus Expeditionary Force descending upon Washington. Arthur M. Schlesinger, Jr., contrasts this bonus march with the previous one:

The Roosevelt tactic, instant and instinctive, was to kill by kindness. Instead of the shacks at Anacostia and the hostility of the police and Army, Roosevelt offered the veterans an Army camp, three meals a day, endless supplies of coffee, and a large convention tent, where the leaders could orate to their hearts' content. The Navy Band played for the veterans; Army doctors ministered to their ills; dentists pulled their teeth; the President conferred with their leaders; and, as a climax, Mrs. Roosevelt and Louis Howe drove out one rainy spring day in a blue convertible. While Howe dozed in the car, Mrs. Roosevelt walked through ankle-deep mud and led the vets in singing "There's a long, long trail a-winding." "Hoover sent the Army," said one veteran; "Roosevelt sent his wife." [9]

Actually the economy act represented a bit of fiscal conservatism that can be regarded as largely a political gesture on Roosevelt's part. The plain fact was that vast amounts of money would be needed to provide relief and to finance emergency recovery measures; minor savings here and there were not going to do the trick, however pleasing they might be to old-fashioned economists. The government was going to have to go into debt.

March 31: Act Establishing the Civilian Conservation Corps (CCC). Conservation was one of FDR's most passionate and abiding concerns, and unemployment was perhaps the most critical danger then facing the nation. Between twelve and fifteen million people were jobless in the beginning of March, 1933, and things were actually getting worse, despite widespread public feelings of renewed hope and confidence. Roosevelt seized upon the CCC as a means of killing at least two birds with one stone: improving long-neglected natural resources, and providing a quick and beneficial reduction of unemployment.

Although there were objections to the idea from some quarters—especially from organized labor—the CCC got off the ground relatively quickly. The Labor Department

[9] Schlesinger, *Coming of the New Deal*, p. 15.

set up recruiting procedures; army reserve officers were called up to administer the camps. An agreement was reached with labor which called for the actual construction of the camps to be done by unionists at prevailing wages, and a labor leader was selected as director of the program. The Forest Service and the National Park Service were brought in to do large-scale planning of the projects to be undertaken.

The CCC was limited to unmarried men aged eighteen to twenty-five whose immediate families were on relief. By the end of July, 1933, some 300,000 men were enrolled; by 1942, when the CCC was finally discontinued, nearly 2.5 million people had worked in the camps.

Members of the U.S. Forest Service pose with CCC emblems. The Forest Service frequently selected projects for the CCC to do.

UNDERWOOD & UNDERWOOD

They discharged a thousand conservation tasks which had gone too long unperformed. They planted trees, made reservoirs and fish ponds, built check dams, dug diversion ditches, raised bridges and fire towers, fought blister rust and pine-twig blight and the Dutch elm disease, restored historic battlefields, cleared beaches and camping grounds, and in a multitude of ways protected and improved parks, forests, watersheds, and recreational areas.

They did more, of course, than reclaim and develop natural resources. They reclaimed and developed themselves. They came from large cities and from small towns, from slum street corners and from hobo jungles, from the roads and the rails and from nowhere. One out of every ten or eleven was a Negro. Some had never seen mountains before, had never waded in running brooks or slept in the open air. Boys from the East Side of New York found themselves in Glacier Park, boys from New Jersey at Mount Hood in Oregon, boys from Texas in Wyoming. Their muscles hardened, their bodies filled out, their self-respect returned. They learned trades; more important, they learned about America, and they learned about other Americans.[10]

Most of the CCC workers stayed in the Corps for six months to a year. Workers were paid less than the going

[10] Ibid., pp. 338–339.

rate and were required to send a portion of their wages back home to their families. Apart from its human and economic effects, the CCC reaped important political gains as well. As Rexford Guy Tugwell notes,

> The fact was that by the end of the summer [1933] there was hardly a family living in the same dread of the coming fall and winter as had been true a year before. This in itself was in such complete contrast to the last few oncomings of the cold season that good will for the author of this change spread like a benison over the land. And when there was added to this the prospect of real social security, [Roosevelt's] place in people's hearts became impregnable.[11]

May 12: The Agricultural Adjustment Act (AAA). The AAA bill as finally approved by Congress and signed by FDR contained three major parts. Title I contained provisions designed to raise farm prices by reducing huge surpluses in cotton, wheat, hogs, and tobacco. Title II provided for emergency loans for refinancing farm mortgages. Title III provided for measures that would increase the amount of money in circulation, so that more people would be able to buy farm products.

When the AAA bill appeared to stall in Congress— being frequently denounced there as communistic or un-American—farmers in Le Mars, Iowa, rioted in a manner showing just how desperate and close to civil war the farm situation was.

> On April 27 over five hundred farmers crowded the courtroom in Le Mars, Iowa, to demand that Judge Charles C. Bradley suspend foreclosure proceedings until the state courts had passed on recently enacted state legislation. When Bradley turned the farmers down and rebuked them for wearing hats and smoking in the presence of the court, a sullen murmur rose from the

[11] Rexford Guy Tugwell, *The Democratic Roosevelt* (Garden City, N.Y.: Doubleday, 1957), p. 279. Copyright © 1957 by Rexford Guy Tugwell. Reprinted by permission of Russell & Volkening, Inc. 551 Fifth Avenue, New York 10017.

crowd. A [farm] leader later described the reaction: "That's not his courtroom. We farmers paid for it with our tax money and it was as much ours at his. The crowd had a perfect right there." As the judge continued to scold the throng, men stepped forward, their faces masked in blue bandanas, and dragged him from the bench. In a fury they slapped him and mauled him, placed a blindfold around his eyes and threw him on a truck. Some shouted, "Get a rope! Let's hang him!" A mile from the city, they stopped, tossed a rope over a telegraph pole, fastened one end about his neck and tightened the knot till he nearly lost consciousness. Someone removed a hub cap from the truck and put it on his head, while others pushed him to his knees and told him to pray. Crowned with the cap, grease running down his face, thrust to the ground, he looked at the angry men around him and prayed: "Oh Lord, I pray thee, do justice to all men." And still he refused to pledge himself not to foreclose mortgages on their farms. They threw dirt on him, then tore off his trousers and smeared them with grease and dirt, till, weary and perhaps abashed, they went away.[12]

Title II (called the Emergency Farm Mortgage Act) was perhaps the most immediately successful of the AAA's parts. The Roosevelt administration had already combined a mishmash of agricultural bureaus into a single agency, the Farm Credit Administration. Title II served to confirm the FCA's powers, and it thereupon proceeded to disburse more than $100 million in seven months. The FCA also set up local committees for adjusting farm debts, persuaded creditors to settle for less, reduced interest rates on agricultural loans, and finally set up a series of regional banks to provide loans for all phases of agricultural production.

The boldest and most revolutionary provision of the AAA was the Title I subsidy mechanism. This was designed to simultaneously reduce surpluses and raise agricultural prices, thereby reducing the disparity between

[12] Schlesinger, *Coming of the New Deal*, pp. 42–43.

what farmers earned and what they could buy with their earnings. According to the subsidy principle, if a farmer would voluntarily reduce his acreage or production, the government would make direct cash payments to him, in effect renting the unused acreage from him. The funds for the subsidy came from a tax levied on the processors of certain farm commodities—on canners, millers, and textile manufacturers—which of course made this powerful group see red.

There were bitter disagreements among highly placed administrators within the AAA. The directors—first George Peek and then Chester Davis—were old-school agrarians. They wanted to solve the farm problem by traditional means—by creating inflation and by setting up international agreements allowing farmers to dump all their surpluses abroad. Peek and Davis argued that there could be no such thing as agricultural overproduction so long as there was one starving Chinaman in the world. They were less clear on exactly how that starving Chinaman was to pay for American farm produce, but they were willing to leave that up to governments to decide. The idea of cutting back production was hateful to them. They were not interested in viewing the farm problem in a total economic and political context; they wanted whatever would benefit the farmer immediately, and cared little about consumers or the international marketplace.

Another faction within the AAA, the legal division, was composed of brilliant young lawyers, many of them from prestigious Ivy League lawschools. Headed by Jerome Frank, the legal division included, among others, Thurmond Arnold, Abe Fortas, Adlai Stevenson, and Alger Hiss. This group had strong liberal commitments to social planning and most particularly to the relatively powerless groups like consumers and tenant farmers. Many of these lawyers knew nothing about agriculture, however; their ignorance alienated and infuriated the old-line agrarian administrators. A widely circulated story was told about one lawyer who, at a meeting about macaroni codes, angrily demanded to know what the codes would do for the macaroni growers! One evening, so another story goes, an AAA lawyer on a field trip cried out, "Good God! what's that!" It was allegedly the first time he had ever seen a firefly.

The legal division received much of its inspiration from Rexford Guy Tugwell, then assistant secretary of agriculture. Tugwell was strongly in favor of achieving a viable balance between agriculture and the rest of the economy. In many cases, this propensity to think in larger wholes brought the AAA lawyers into sharp conflict with the food-processing industry and with the old agricultural establishment, which served mostly the interests of the large farmers. It was clear to the lawyers that segments of the food-processing industry were gouging the public by using the processing tax as an excuse to pass unwarranted price hikes on to consumers. The legal division thus demanded full access to the financial records of the food processors, which caused a furious, intense reaction from this extremely powerful group. Eventually, the legal division was "purged" and its brightest members moved to other posts in the administration. Over the AAA's bitter internal disputes, Secretary of Agriculture Henry A. Wallace presided in a sometimes vacillating or indecisive way.

Despite the interagency struggles, however, the AAA enjoyed considerable success, at least on a short-term basis. Cotton was an especially critical problem. By early 1933, the U.S. cotton surplus was huge. And yet while the AAA was being debated in Congress, forty million acres of cotton had been planted; it seemed likely, furthermore, that the 1933 crop would be exceptionally large. If the 1933 cotton came onto the market, it was clear that cotton, already down to eight or nine cents a pound, would be worth almost nothing at all. The solution was to plow up much of the existing crop, an action that deeply disturbed many agrarians, including Henry A. Wallace. Wallace observed that "to destroy a standing crop goes against the soundest instincts of human nature." Nevertheless, thousands of farmers did plow up their fields and received in return some hundred million dollars in compensation from the AAA. In addition, governmental agencies loaned farmers money on their cotton at ten cents a pound, thus supporting the price of cotton and keeping part of the surplus out of the market as security for the loans.

Wheat was also critical: the surplus was so tremendous that the price of wheat had not been so low since the reign of Queen Elizabeth I of England. Although wholesale plowing under of the wheat crop was contemplated, it proved unnecessary. Drought and dust storms in the years 1933 to 1935 cut down the wheat crop by an average of nearly 300 million bushels a year. The existing surplus was absorbed, and wheat prices rose sharply; in 1935 and 1936, the United States had to import wheat to meet its needs.

Nature did not intervene so handily in the case of hogs and corn. It was clear that in 1934 there would have to be a substantial reduction in corn and hog production. But much corn had already been planted in 1933, and huge numbers of piglets were maturing which would, if slaughtered on schedule, completely glut the market in 1934. The solution was to pay farmers to plow up a portion of their corn acreage, and for the government to purchase and slaughter five or six million piglets in the fall of 1933. The proposed slaughter of baby pigs aroused considerable outrage in the public press, whose owners by the summer of 1934 had already become generally hostile to FDR and his policies. Henry A. Wallace, exasperated by the outcry against piglet-slaughter, complained that people seemed to think that "every little pig has the right to attain before slaughter the full pigginess of his pigness." Actually, Wallace deeply resented the measures that the AAA was forced to take. In 1934 he wrote that "the plowing under of ten million acres of cotton in August, 1933, and the slaughter of six million little pigs in September, 1933, were not acts of idealism in any sane society. They were emergency acts made necessary by the almost insane lack of world statesmanship during the period from 1920 to 1932."

Wallace agreed that the argument that there could be no agricultural surplus if people were starving at home

A sharecropper's cabin in Arkansas. This photograph was taken by Ben Shahn, who was one of many artists employed by the government during the New Deal.

UNITED PRESS INTERNATIONAL

Farm equipment buried by sand and dust blown from drought-ruined fields. This picture was taken in 1935, in Oklahoma.

and abroad was indeed a logical one. Yet most of the world functioned on some sort of an economic system that called for selling at a profit; if people could not buy food for prices that would enable farmers to recover their seed, equipment, and labor costs, farmers would just go under. They couldn't give their crops away. Farmers had no choice but go on producing, thus creating surpluses that drove prices lower, with the result that farmers got even poorer. Wallace further noted that no one objected when business curtailed its production by about $20 billion, but that for some reason the same right was denied to agriculture.

Actually, the farm subsidies allowed more people to eat than would otherwise have been possible. In October an agency called the Federal Surplus Relief Corporation bought more than 100 million pounds of pork and distributed it to people on relief.

The AAA did cause hardship to one segment of the farming population—the southern tenant farmer. As more and more cotton acreage was plowed under, more and more of these tenant farmers were "tractored" off the land on which they had lived and worked for generations. They had to shift for themselves or go on relief. Their situation has changed little from the early thirties to this day.

Despite this and other problems, the AAA was in large measure a success. From 1932 to 1936, farm income rose fifty percent. By 1936 the difference between the prices farmers received for their crops and the prices they paid for equipment and consumer goods had shrunk to ten percent. During the same interval, farm debts had fallen by a billion dollars.

May 12: Act Establishing the Federal Emergency Relief Administration (FERA). Under this act, Congress made available $500 million to be given as direct aid to state relief organizations. Harry Hopkins, a hard-bitten, sharp-tongued social worker, was appointed FERA administrator. Hopkins wasted no time—a *Washington Post* news story observed that Hopkins had spent more than $5 million during his first two hours in office.

Important as direct relief in the form of food and money was to starving families, Hopkins and many other officials were afraid that the country would not make it through the winter of 1933–1934 on direct relief alone. The demand for work as opposed to handouts was swelling to revolutionary proportions. Hopkins outlined a plan having for its objective the astonishing figure of four million men employed by December 15, 1933. Roosevelt quickly agreed, and thus the Civil Works Administration (CWA) was born. Hopkins quickly realigned his FERA staff, made extensive use of existing local relief agencies, and by the middle of January, 1934, the CWA had more than four million employed on its rolls. As one observer pointed out, Hopkins' remarkably flexible methods of administration had enabled him "to engage for employment in two months nearly as many persons as were enlisted and called to the colors during our year and a half of World War [I] mobilization, and to disburse to them weekly, a higher average rate of wage than Army or

Navy pay." CWA workers tackled over 40,000 projects, including road-building and school, airport, and park construction. Some 50,000 teachers were employed in county schools or in urban adult-education courses. Even artists and writers—some 3,000 of them—were put to work using their skills on state and local projects. Hopkins' comment was typical: "Hell. They've got to eat just like other people."

May 18: The Tennessee Valley Authority (TVA). The Tennessee River flows through seven southern states, forming an extended valley region some 40,000 square miles in extent. This valley, potentially one of the richest and most fertile regions of the nation, had been plundered time and again, first by loggers, then by oil and gas companies. By 1933, the Tennessee Valley was impoverished: the land was sterile; each year uncontrollable floods washed off yet more of the topsoil; the forests were overcut, and the resulting erosion was stripping away the higher ground. More than half the families in the valley were on relief; there were few schools, and only two out of every hundred farms had electricity. There was no industry to speak of; industry had come, raped the land, and left. The Tennessee Valley was a great rural slum.

During World War I the government had built a dam and a series of powerhouses on the Tennessee River near the town of Muscle Shoals, Alabama. Designed to produce nitrates for explosives, the Muscle Shoals installations fell into disuse when the war ended. For the next decade or so, Congress fought about what should be done with the now idle dam, powerhouses, and nitrate plants. Senator George Norris of Nebraska successfully prevented the Muscle Shoals site from being given away to private industry but was unable to get Presidents Coolidge or Hoover to accept his broader plan—government operation of the Muscle Shoals complex as a source of cheap electrical power that could thus serve as a "yardstick" for measuring the rates charged by private utilities.

Roosevelt's deep personal interest in the conservation of natural resources and in the development of public power combined in the case of TVA to produce one of the most successful and enduring of all the New Deal accomplishments. Roosevelt called upon the Congress to create "a corporation clothed with the power of Government but possessed of the flexibility and initiative of a private enterprise" which would make itself responsible for the total rehabilitation of the entire Tennessee Valley. This would mean producing and selling cheap electrical power, controlling floods, replanting forests, implementing a host of soil-conservation measures, and encouraging small private industries to come to the valley. And, despite heavy opposition from the private power companies, Congress delivered more or less what Roosevelt asked for.

TVA quickly became one of the New Deal's brightest showpieces. As Arthur M. Schlesinger, Jr., described it,

Norris Dam in Tennessee, one of the dams built and operated by TVA.

> New energy was pouring into the valley. In the first instance, it was the electricity produced at the dams, brought from the great generators along gleaming copper and aluminum wires to factories and farms in the farthest corners of the Tennessee basin. It was the clearing of the rivers, the rebuilding of the forests, the replenishment of the soil, the improvement of agricultural methods, the spread of schools, the development of recreation. But beyond this there was something less tangible yet even more penetrating: the release of moral and human energy as the people of the valley saw new vistas open up for themselves and for their children. The jagged river, flowing uselessly past worn-out fields, overcut forests, ramshackle huts, its muddy waters reflecting the dull poverty of the life around—all this was giving way to a shimmering network of green meadows, blue lakes, and white dams. The river, the destroyer, was becoming man's servant. The beaten and sour land was stirring with new hope. It was an eloquent symbol of the time—a symbol of man's capacity through the use of political and technical intelligence to change the conditions of life and transform defeat into possibility.[13]

[13] Ibid., pp. 338–339.

In small things as well as great, TVA administrators tried hard to work within local traditions and yet insisted upon certain minimal standards of fairness, as the following excerpt from a 1935 *Fortune* magazine article suggests:

> With white men by the hundreds out of jobs, TVA very quietly, but very firmly in line with its policy, began hiring Negroes by tens and twenties until their employment percentage tallied with the population percentage in those parts: about 20 per cent. Having hired them it proceeded to pay them the same wages and gave them housing precisely as good as that of the whites and training perhaps better. (Reason for good training: there are swarms of first-rate Negroes out of work; a Ph.D., for instance, heads the Negro training staff.) Meanwhile such TVA men as know the country at first hand were set for anything up to and including a lynching. Nothing happened, and they figured out why. TVA, and the Negroes too, had sense enough to stick absolutely to Jim-Crowism, which isn't necessarily edifying but which feels better, at any moment, than bright coal oil and buckshot. Moreover, TVA's workmen had no longer to fear that their jobs would be washed from under them by cheap Negro labor: TVA wasn't taking that advantage, so commonly taken, either of its Negroes or of them. TVA ran foul of some objection on the part of leading citizens of local towns when it began training them toward a higher possible standard of living— but it reminded them (a) that neither intermarriage nor insurrection was being preached and (b) that the Negro was undeniably a member of the community and might better be a decent than an indecent one, and went on about its business.[14]

May 27: Securities Act of 1933. This act had the purpose of preventing the issuance of worthless stock. It required that corporations issuing shares had to provide

[14] "TVA I: Work in the Valley," *Fortune*, May 1935, pp. 93–94, 145.

the public with all relevant financial information. The Federal Trade Commission was empowered to administer this law and to block the issuance of stock in cases in which information provided was either incomplete or misleading. In 1934 the Securities and Exchange Commission was created, and it took over this watchdog function. The Securities Act, although mild medicine indeed, aroused the financial community to apoplectic rage, a rage from which it seldom thereafter relented.

June 13: Act Establishing the Home Owners Loan Corporation. In 1932, more than 250,000 families had lost their homes to banks and insurance companies through mortgage foreclosure. In early 1933, families were losing their homes at the rate of more than a thousand a day. The Home Owners Loan Corporation bought up mortgages from banks and then refinanced these mortgages in such a way that people could meet the payments. Ultimately, one out of every five mortgaged homes was saved by the HOLC. Among the middle classes, the HOLC was perhaps the most popular of the New Deal measures.

June 16: The Glass-Steagall Banking Act. One of the provisions of this bill was designed to prevent banks from speculating in the stock market with depositors' funds. Another provision was the creation of the Federal Deposit Insurance Corporation, which guaranteed individual bank deposits in certified banks up to $2,500 (raised to $5,000 in 1934). Roosevelt himself was not happy with this latter provision but accepted it reluctantly. But the American Bankers Association denounced the idea of guaranteed deposits as "unsound, unscientific, unjust and dangerous," predicted catastrophe, and fought the measure down to the wire. In the words of Arthur M. Schlesinger, Jr., "The deposit insurance system turned out, of course, to be one of the most brilliant and successful of the accomplishments of the Hundred Days. Undeterred by the categorical predictions of disaster, the Federal Deposit Insurance Corporation entered into a markedly placid and effective existence."

June 16: The National Industrial Recovery Act (NIRA).
This act, the last major piece of Hundred Days legislation, was designed to be the industrial equivalent of the AAA. The purpose of NIRA was, in Roosevelt's words, "to put people back to work." Actually, the NIRA had larger goals: to put American industry and indeed the American economy as a whole on its feet again, and to put people back to work on decent jobs at decent rates of pay and under decent working conditions. As the depression deepened, those industries and workers still functioning were increasingly at the mercy of unscrupulous employers who slashed wages, increased hours, and made use of shoddy commercial practices. The bad was not only driving out the good but also spoiling the whole barrel.

The NIRA bill was divided into two parts: Title I and Title II. Originally designed to work as one unit under a single administrator, the two titles were separated and given to two administrators and their staffs. General Hugh Johnson was given Title I, which was responsible for fostering joint industry-labor cooperation; Johnson's bailiwick became known as the National Recovery Administration (NRA). Secretary of the Interior Harold Ickes was given Title II and made responsible for administering a massive program of public works as head of the Public Works Administration (PWA).

The NRA was supposed to prod each industry into formulating codes covering things like production, pricing, minimum-wage scales, acceptable working conditions, and ethical trade practices. Once written and agreed upon, these codes were to have the force of law and the NRA the responsibility of enforcing them. Although the NRA had certain licensing powers that could have been used to force industries to draw up and accept their codes, General Johnson decided that compulsion was too risky and probably unconstitutional. Hence he decided to seek industry's cooperation on a voluntary basis. The result was that industries drew up codes that, although containing provisions for minimum wages, maximum hours, and collective bargaining procedures, also contained agreements allowing price-fixing and monopolistic practices.

These latter agreements were not beneficial to the sort of long-range economic planning for the whole nation that NIRA had envisaged, since it meant that limited production and relatively high prices prevented goods from getting to consumers who needed them and hence prevented money and goods from circulating in sufficient quantities to get a large-scale recovery going.

Some major industries balked at the codes; other industries, especially smaller businesses, soon began to evade codes already accepted. General Johnson decided to embark on a massive publicity campaign designed to bring recalcitrants and chiselers into line. This was the ill-fated Blue Eagle campaign. The Blue Eagle (actually not an eagle at all, but a Navaho thunderbird emblem) was to be placed as a decal on all products produced by coded industries, and the public would therefore punish miscreants by not buying anything that didn't have a Blue Eagle on it. There was much ballyhoo—enormous rallies and parades—and many exalted promises: the Blue Eagle meant unity, prosperity, jobs for all, and in general an end to the depression. When the NRA's Blue Eagle didn't deliver any of these things, there was much general bitterness, and the Blue Eagle was shot down ignominiously. The complexity of the codes, and the difficulties in enforcing compliance, would have doomed the Blue Eagle anyway, even without all the fancy promises. For example, Henry Ford refused to join in the code for the automobile industry, and hence his Fords didn't rate a Blue Eagle sticker; yet Ford observed the wage-and-hour provisions called for by the codes for automotive workers. Some of Ford's competitors, however, did display the Blue Eagle, while at the same time violating the code provisions right and left.

One of the provisions of Title I was that labor had the right to organize and bargain collectively through representatives of their own choosing. This provision, called Section 7(a), infuriated employers and heartened organized labor. But employers quickly realized that 7(a) didn't say anything about their having to recognize unions, or indeed about their having to pay any attention to them

The Blue Eagle decal, indicating that a given product was produced by a coded industry.

Before and after shots of the city hall in Libby, Montana. The new city hall was built by PWA, which built everything from municipal swimming pools and woodsheds in national parks to the Lincoln Tunnel, Fort Knox, Boulder Dam, and the Triborough Bridge.

at all. Employers organized powerless company unions and frequently coerced their workers into joining them, thus meeting the vague letter of 7(a) without giving up any of their former prerogatives. The result was a rash of strikes—at a point more than two hundred a month— which the NRA was relatively powerless to deal with. Labor began calling the NRA the "National Run-Around."

When in 1935 the Supreme Court declared the code system of NRA unconstitutional, most people viewed the death of NRA without too much sorrow.

Although the NRA has generally been called a failure, at least as an economic recovery measure, it did make a few important contributions through its code system to worthwhile social ends. As Arthur M. Schlesinger, Jr., has written,

> The more enduring achievements of NRA lay not in the economic but in the social field. Here NRA accomplished a fantastic series of reforms, any one of which would have staggered the nation a few years earlier. It established the principle of maximum hours and minimum wages on a national basis. It abolished child labor. It dealt a fatal blow to sweatshops. It made collective bargaining a national policy and thereby transformed the position of organized labor. It gave new status to the consumer. It stamped out a noxious collection of unfair trade practices. It set new standards of economic decency in American life—standards which could not be rolled back, whatever happened to NRA. In doing these things, it accomplished in a few months what reformers had dreamed about for half a century.[15]

In contrast to NRA, the Public Works Administration created by Title II of NIRA got off to a relatively slow and unpublicized start. Presided over by the cranky, brooding Harold Ickes, FDR's secretary of the interior, the PWA was authorized to spend $3.3 million on roads, buildings, and other public projects. The money was designed to "prime the pump"—to stimulate the economy

---

[15] Schlesinger, *Coming of the New Deal*, pp. 174–175.

by injecting new wealth into it. Ickes did not spend freely or fast, however, and critics within and outside of PWA complained about what they considered Ickes' exasperating slowness.

Ickes was determined that all PWA projects be legal, economically valuable, and practical from an engineering standpoint. He was also determined that no hint of waste or corruption be associated with his PWA. To this end, Ickes personally scrutinized every single proposal and contract. Nevertheless, by 1934 engineers, contractors, and laborers were being helped by the PWA. Ultimately, some 34,000 projects were initiated—roads, highways, schools, bridges, power plants, flood-control projects, municipal water and sewage systems, dams, subways, hospitals and even a few aircraft carriers.

The Second New Deal

Historians have not wholly agreed upon what the "second" New Deal really was, how it was different from the "first" New Deal, exactly what its achievements were, or precisely when it ended. It is generally conceded, however, that many of the elements thought to be characteristic of the second New Deal came to the fore in 1935.

In many respects, 1935 was a key year in the American "depression decade." As business conditions improved, opposition to the Roosevelt administration hardened and indeed became fanatical within the American business community and among the American upper classes generally. At the same time, Dr. Francis Townsend, the Reverend Charles E. Coughlin, and Senator Huey P. Long each in his own way appealed to the millions of citizens for whom depression conditions had not substantially changed for the better, and each gained large and potentially troublesome followings. The U.S. Supreme Court began, seemingly for ideological reasons, to set its face against the New Deal, invalidating the NRA in terms that seemed to preclude almost all significant federal action. In 1935, Congress passed some of the most influential legislation of the decade, including the Social Security Act, the National Labor Relations Act (Wagner

Act), a tax package calling for steeply graduated income tax and increased taxes on large corporations, and the Emergency Relief Appropriation Act, which funded the Works Progress Administration, the Rural Electrification Administration, and the National Youth Administration. Partly as a result of this legislation, two groups—black Americans and organized labor—became important new members of the Roosevelt political coalition. The Democratic party became increasingly the party of "the little man" and of the urbanized northern areas, and Roosevelt himself moved slightly to the left of political center. Finally, also in 1935, Mussolini attacked Ethiopia, Adolph Hitler announced the re-establishment of the German air force, and the U.S. Congress passed the first of a series of Neutrality Acts designed to keep America out of any and all foreign wars.

Among the first organized antiadministration groups was the American Liberty League, a mixed group of conservative Democrats, including Al Smith, and wealthy Republican businessmen, including most of the Du Pont family. The League, founded in 1934, had two announced objectives: to teach respect for the rights of persons and property, and to remind the government of its duty to encourage private enterprise and protect the ownership of property. Many business leaders, believing that government should not interfere in the management of economic affairs, opposed the bothersome and expensive measures of the New Deal. They held the government responsible for the increasing strength of organized labor, at the same time ignoring any governmental responsibility for business profits, which had risen sharply. In addition, business leaders were alarmed at increased taxes and irritated by governmental forms, questionnaires, and restrictions. Many of these businessmen applauded the positions taken by the Liberty League.

But the League was obviously a spokesman for the rich and the superrich. Other extreme voices began to make themselves heard, among them those of Dr. Francis Townsend, Father Charles Coughlin, and Governor Huey Long. For the most part, these men addressed themselves to the poor. Since there were a great many poor people, by 1935 these men had attracted significant followings.

Dr. Francis Everett Townsend had come to Long Beach, California, from Belle Fourche, South Dakota, where his rural medical practice had included areas of South Dakota, Wyoming, and Montana. As with so many newcomers to southern California, Dr. Townsend had been attracted to the sunny climate for reasons of health. California had also attracted a great many midwestern farmers hoping to retire after a life of toil into a comfortable old age; instead, they had seen their modest savings wiped out by the depression. One morning Dr. Townsend looked out his window to see three women, stooped and haggard with age, rummaging through the garbage barrels in the alley below.

Within a short time, Dr. Townsend had founded an organization called "Old Age Revolving Pensions, Ltd." His plan ultimately evolved into a scheme designed to provide a pension of $200 per month to unemployed U.S. citizens over sixty years of age, a sum exceeding the income of most employed persons at that time; it was further proposed that the entire amount be spent within the month of receipt. Economists estimated that the scheme, which was to be financed by the government through a two percent sales tax, would require turning over half the national income to eight percent of the nation's population. In order to pay oldsters $50 per week, the average worker's salary of $16 a week would have to be reduced by a third.

Dr. Francis Townsend in 1936.

Townsend Clubs were organized all over the United States. The political balance of power wielded by the some ten million supporters of Townsend's plan could not be ignored. At their annual conventions, the old people sang:

> Onward, Townsend soldiers,
> Marching as to war,
> With the Townsend banner
> Going on before.
> Our devoted soldiers
> Bid depression go;
> Join them in the battle,
> Help them fight the foe!

And many politicians, attracted by the large block of voters, gave support to the Townsend plan.

Father Charles E. Coughlin, the "radio priest," had at first backed FDR with the slogan "Roosevelt or Ruin." But by 1934, Coughlin had begun to criticize the New Deal for not moving fast enough. Coughlin's popular denunciations of "international bankers" and Communists, both of whom he blamed for creating the depression, attracted millions of listeners to his regularly scheduled radio sermons. When his attacks became personally abusive, the radio network refused to renew his contract. But Coughlin had become so popular that listeners paid for his broadcast time and made it possible for him to create his own network. Radio receipts reached as much as $20,000 a week, and Coughlin was able to build a seven-story tower to house the offices of his Little Flower Radio League. Taking advantage of people's fear of poverty and hunger, Father Coughlin attracted listeners from all walks of life and from all faiths.

By 1935, at the peak of his popularity, Coughlin had extended his criticism from bankers, industrialists, and greedy politicians to include the nation's labor unions, whose activities he recommended be controlled by the government. Coughlin then organized the National Union for Social Justice. Designed as a "non-political" lobby, the NUSJ appeared to have been created primarily to further Coughlin's political ambitions. When William Cardinal O'Connell of Boston publicly criticized him, Father Coughlin announced that the cardinal had no jurisdiction outside his own archdiocese and went so far as to observe that the cardinal should do something about the welfare of his people rather than hobnob with the rich.

The most successful, and therefore the most dangerous, of the demagogues opposing Roosevelt was the shrewd and ruthless "Louisiana Kingfish," Huey P. Long. In 1928, Long had been elected governor of Louisiana. His campaign slogans had proclaimed "Every man a king, but no man wears a crown." From the time he became governor at the age of thirty five, Huey Long boasted that someday he would be president of the United States, and this boast was not entirely an empty one.

As governor, Long smashed all local political opposition and ruled the state almost as a dictator. Unlike most demagogues, he had made good many of his promises. He built new schools, more hospitals, good roads, and secured a generally higher standard of living for the people of Louisiana, most especially for the poorer and less educated citizens. But such accomplishments were not without their price: as governor and later as senator, Long controlled almost every aspect of Louisiana politics, as well as the state police, the militia, and the courts.

In 1932, the man who had bragged that *he* was the state constitution of Louisiana was elected to the United States Senate from that state. Within months, Huey Long ended his support of the New Deal. He ridiculed the president and the administration's leaders in a speech delivered from the floor of the Senate. When FDR cut off federal patronage in Louisiana, Long responded with his "Share Our Wealth" program.

Hodding Carter, whose Hammond, Louisiana, newspaper courageously opposed the "hillbilly dictator," wrote that "by the spring of 1935, Huey Long owned Louisiana." At about that time, Long declared his intention to run for president. Carter described the program by which Long hoped to win the presidency in the following terms:

The hazy concept of a national redistribution of wealth . . . took definable shape in a national "Share Our Wealth" organization. No dues were necessary. Huey produced the expense money as easily as the nation disgorged the followers, both by the hundreds of thousands. No matter that the Share Our Wealth program was demonstrably impracticable as presented. It *was* believable: a limitation of fortunes to $5,000,000; an annual income minimum of $2,000 to $2,500 and a maximum of $1,800,000; a homestead grant of $6,000 for every family; free education from kindergarten through college; bonuses for veterans; old-age pensions, radios, automobiles, an abundance of cheap food through governmental purchase and storage of surpluses. The Share Our Wealth members had their own catchy song, "Every Man a King," their

own newspaper, the mud-slinging *Louisiana Progress*,
expanded now to the *American Progress*.[16]

On the basis of a public-opinion poll, James Farley,
postmaster-general and Roosevelt's campaign manager,
predicted that Long might get three million votes in the
1936 presidential election. He took Long seriously, and
suggested that Long and his followers could conceivably
cost Roosevelt a second term. But in September of 1935,
Huey Long was assassinated in the Louisiana capitol building by a young man with a family grudge against Long.

Long's movement was carried on by one of his lieu-
tenants, and it was later combined with the Townsend and
Coughlin forces to make a united rabble-rousing front
against Roosevelt. Both the Townsend and Coughlin
movements were, however, touched by financial scandals.
By late 1936—after Roosevelt's tremendous electoral victory—all three demagogic movements had fizzled out.

From 1935 until its demise in 1943, the Works Progress
Administration—under the working control of Harry
Hopkins–was the principal agency of relief. Despite waste,
inefficiency, and occasional corruption, the WPA was
remarkably effective considering its scope; in the end it
provided some work for 8.5 million people, mostly unskilled or semiskilled workers, but also musicians, actors,
playwrights, painters, and writers. It was especially important that eighty-five percent of the money spent by
the WPA went directly for wages, and that the WPA
projects—the construction of roads, parks, buildings, and
airports—were designed in such a way as to employ a
maximum number of manual laborers rather than skilled
craftsmen. Only a few farsighted members of FDR's administration realized that a general business expansion
does not of itself significantly reduce unemployment
among the nonskilled; on the contrary, a growing *industrialized* economy merely places a premium upon those
who are already educated, skilled, or otherwise highly

[16] Hodding Carter, "Huey Long: American Dictator," *The
American Mercury*, April 1949. Reprinted by permission of *The
American Mercury*, Torrance, California.

trained or experienced. Their services become relatively more valuable and hence more highly paid. Since these are the people who do the great bulk of consumer spending, the effect is rising prices and inflation. Only a small percentage of the great numbers of unskilled and semi-skilled men and women participates in an expanding technological economy; the rest become relatively worse off.

Hopkins was theoretically supposed to work in connection with Harold Ickes and Ickes' PWA. In actuality, Hopkins often ran rings around Ickes, darting in to pounce upon or divert funds intended for PWA; projects involving more than $25,000 were supposed to go to the PWA, but Hopkins was a genius at splitting up his major projects or otherwise sneaking them through. Ickes was driven to monumental fits of rage or depression; he resigned a number of times, whereupon FDR coaxed, coddled, or shamed him back into the fold. Ickes insisted that Hopkins came up with the name WPA just so everybody would get it confused with Ickes' own PWA; such drollery would have been very like Hopkins, and the two agencies are still often confused in people's minds.

In 1934, two bills calling for unemployment insurance and old-age insurance had been introduced in Congress, and both seemed likely to pass. Key Roosevelt advisors were divided over what form social security should take, however, and managed to convince FDR that more study was needed. Some advisors favored an across-the-board federal system of old-age and unemployment and health insurance to be paid for out of the general tax revenues; others favored various contributory schemes to be administered cooperatively by the states and the federal government. The end result—the Social Security Act of 1935, sponsored by Senator Robert Wagner of New York and Representative David Lewis of Maryland—was a compromise affair. The unemployment insurance was a matter left essentially to the states to organize and operate, although the federal government would pick up ninety percent of the tab. Old-age insurance, now generally referred to as one's Social Security, became a wholly fed-

These WPA workers are farmers whose land had been ruined by drought and who had no way of earning a living.

FRANKLIN D. ROOSEVELT LIBRARY

Jobless men filing for unemployment insurance after passage of the Social Security Act.

eral program financed equally by employers and employees. Each employer and employee would contribute an amount equal to one percent—later three percent—of the employee's wages. The fund thereby created would then be used to pay out monthly pensions to retired workers or their beneficiaries after the age of sixty-five.

It was pointed out that since the poor and the well-to-do contributed the same percentage, the poor were actually paying a higher percentage of their total income to Social Security than the rich. The payroll deduction was in effect a sales tax, and like all sales taxes it penalized the poor. Roosevelt agreed that this was so but considered the political advantages of such a system irresistible. The payroll deductions or contributions were, he said, "politics all the way through. We put those payroll contributions there so as to give the contributors a legal, moral, and political right to collect their pensions. . . . With those taxes in there, no damn politician can ever scrap my social security program."

Manufacturers, representatives of the banking and insurance industries, and business leaders in general wailed that the unemployment and social security package would ruin the republic—people wouldn't work, wouldn't save, the moral fiber of the nation would be weakened, the Communists would creep in, and so on. In 1936, during the presidential campaign, some businessmen went further. Workers found slips of paper in their pay envelopes warning that they might not get their social-security deductions back from the government. Signs cropped up in factories telling employees that they had been "sentenced to a weekly pay reduction for all your working life." Newspapers suggested by word and picture that all people covered by Social Security would have to wear stainless steel tags around their necks.

This was the sort of claptrap that ultimately moved Roosevelt to an open attack on the business community. In a huge rally in Madison Square Garden, on October 31, 1936, Roosevelt lashed out with uncharacteristic severity. Never before, he said, had the spokesmen of "organized money" been so united against one candidate as they were now. "They are," Roosevelt went on, "unanimous in their hate for me—and I welcome their hatred. I should like to have it said of my first administration that in it the forces of selfishness and of lust for power met their match. I should like to have it said of my second administration that in it these forces met their master!" The crowd sent up a gargantuan bellow of approval.

About a week later, Roosevelt won every state in the nation but Maine and Vermont, and drubbed the Republican candidate Alfred E. Landon by a margin of about eleven million popular votes. Social Security had been made a campaign issue, and although millions of citizens were not covered—particularly migrant, seasonal, and domestic workers—many millions more *were* covered, and they voted in a landslide for the man who had made it possible.

In 1936, the worst of the depression seemed to be over. National income had nearly doubled since 1933, and unemployment had been almost halved, though it was still high. Although the fact that corporate profits were way up in 1936 seemed in some paradoxical way to increase the hatred of Roosevelt among businessmen, there is no doubt that improved economic conditions contributed to FDR's smashing electoral victory. In addition to Social Security and the success of the WPA, one other factor deserves mention in this connection—the 1935 Labor Relations Act, often referred to as the Wagner Act.

Prior to 1935, the Roosevelt administration—and Roosevelt himself—had not been especially sympathetic to labor. At best, FDR considered his role to be that of a mediator or peacemaker between industry and labor; more often than not, he considered the needs and demands of labor to be a threat to economic recovery. Almost single-handedly, Senator Robert Wagner of New York forced the Roosevelt administration into a prolabor stance. Wagner got help from the labor movement, of course; but the pigheadedness and hysteria of the business community helped too, increasingly alienating not only Roosevelt and his advisors but also the public and the Congress, therefore making the passage of "antibusiness" legislation easier.

Section 7(a) of the NRA law had been stuck in at the last moment to forestall a strong labor bill sponsored by Senator Hugo Black of Alabama. In 1934. FDR created the National Labor Relations Board, which was supposed to mediate disputes arising under 7(a). The NLRB had no enforcement powers to speak of, however; if a majority of workers elected to join a union, the NLRB could not compel a manufacturer to deal with that union as the sole representative of the workers, and the NLRB could not apply sanctions if its rulings were defied. In 1934. Wagner introduced a bill that would give the NLRB strong enforcement powers, but the administration managed to sidetrack the measure. In February of 1935, Wagner introduced a new version of the same bill which, despite administration coolness, was passed by a Senate vote of sixty-three to twelve in May. Later in May, the Supreme Court declared the 7(a) provision of NRA unconstitutional, and Roosevelt then demanded that the House act positively on its version of the Wagner bill. The House

UNITED PRESS INTERNATIONAL

Senator Robert E. Wagner of New York, appearing at a congressional hearing on behalf of the Social Security Bill.

passed it in June, and Roosevelt signed Wagner's National Labor Relations Act into law in July, 1935.

The Wagner Act reaffirmed the right of labor to organize and bargain collectively, and provided the NLRB with power to order elections, power to prevent unfair labor practices like setting up fake company unions or firing workers for union activity, and power to make its decisions stick. This was what organized labor had been looking for, and it brought trade unionists to Roosevelt and to the Democratic party in overwhelming numbers in 1936.

Industry hated the Wagner Act, of course; industry spokesmen cried that the new law out-Stalined Stalin and out-Sovieted the Red dictatorship, which is especially amusing in light of the fact that the American Communist party despised the Wagner law even more frenetically than American businessmen did. Industry, confident that the Supreme Court would strike down the Wagner Act as it had 7(a), instituted a whole rash of challenges to labor and to the new law. In 1937, however, the Supreme Court upheld the National Labor Relations Act and the authority of the NLRB.

As a legislative program, the second New Deal lasted until mid-1938, or perhaps even 1939, when a bill slightly extending social security coverage and benefits was passed. Most of the significant New Deal legislation in the years 1936 through 1938 was designed to replace agricultural or conservation programs dating from the Hundred Days that had been rendered unworkable by the Supreme Court, or to consolidate and improve upon gains made by the labor movement in 1935. In 1938, for example, a new AAA and a labor law establishing minimum wages and maximum hours—the Fair Labor Standards Act—were passed.

Decline of the New Deal

If 1933 and 1935 may be considered years of significant New Deal achievement, 1937 was also an important New Deal year, though important in a different way. 1937 may be looked at as a mixed bag of accomplishments and setbacks suggesting not only how far the nation had come in four years of FDR, but also the extent to which many things about American society had remained precarious or unsatisfactory.

On January 20, 1937, Roosevelt delivered his second inaugural address, a speech in which foreign affairs were not mentioned. In this speech, FDR said that he saw "one-third of a nation ill-housed, ill-clad, ill-nourished" (which was, if anything, an understatement of the facts) and called for increased social justice. Despite this reference to the many millions of disadvantaged Americans, general economic conditions had improved to the extent that soon afterwards Roosevelt recommended heavy cuts in government spending. As a result of the cuts, the economy went into a tailspin, and by August of 1937 an acute recession had set in, with unemployment approaching the ten million mark. On April of 1938, Roosevelt finally reversed himself: he expanded the WPA rolls and called for looser credit, an extra $3 billion for relief, and other measures involving increased government spending. By

June of 1938 recovery was underway, stimulated in part by war orders now beginning to trickle in from Europe. But the recession showed how fragile and tentative the economy's recovery had been. Full industrial production and full employment came four or five years later, as a result of World War II, not the New Deal.

The year 1937 also saw Roosevelt battling with the Congress over the Supreme Court, and losing decisively. Thereafter, Roosevelt's political relations with Congress and with key members of his party continued to decline. It was not until the early 1940's, when events in Europe and Asia became obviously threatening, that Congress began to rally once more behind Roosevelt—and not in support of his domestic program, but because the nation was almost certain to become involved in global war.

In 1937, the federal government also began to make some headway against the dust storms that had been raging in the southwestern Great Plains since 1934, ripping away almost a billion tons of precious topsoil and dumping it as far north as New York City and eastward hundreds of miles out into the Atlantic Ocean. Despite the limited success of government-sponsored conservation practices like contour plowing, windbreaks, and the planting of cover crops, refugees from the Dust Bowl continued to pour into California, Oregon, and Washington.

In 1936, a survey of seven agricultural counties in southeastern Colorado revealed that more than half of the farmhouses and homesites had been abandoned. Ironically, government money—AAA funds paid to farm owners to reduce farm acreage under cultivation—was used by the remaining farmers to purchase tractors, further reducing the need for farm labor. Thousands of tenant farmers were "tractored off" lands on which they had lived and worked for years, because owners found that by mechanizing their holdings they could greatly increase the yield of the acreage that remained in production.

What happened to those families who lost their farms to mortgage holders or who got tractored off their homesites? By 1939, the number of migrant refugees in California alone was greater than 200,000. In 1939, Nobel Prize

A farm in Cimarron County, Oklahoma, in 1936, its fields and pastures buried under tons of dust and sand.

Signs like this, the result of depression and drought, could be seen throughout the plains states in the 1930's.

A sharecropper from Oklahoma and his children stand beside their old car, which has stalled on the Mojave Desert near the California border.

A migrant farm worker in Oregon. This man once owned his own farm in Nebraska.

FRANKLIN D. ROOSEVELT LIBRARY

LIBRARY OF CONGRESS

winner John Steinbeck published his *Grapes of Wrath*, a novel about drought-stricken tenant farmers tractored off their Oklahoma farms who moved westward to California. What Steinbeck wrote of these people applies to all of the migrant refugees, wherever they came from:

The moving, questing people were migrants now. Those families which had lived on a little piece of land, who had lived and died on forty acres, had eaten or starved on the produce of forty acres, had now the whole West to rove in. And they scampered about, looking for work; and the highways were streams of people, and the ditch banks were lines of people. Behind them more were coming. The great highways streamed with moving people. There in the Middle- and Southwest had lived a simple agrarian folk who had not changed with industry, who had not farmed with machines or known the power and danger of machines in private hands. They had not grown up in the paradoxes of industry. Their senses were still sharp to the ridiculousness of the industrial life.

And then suddenly the machines pushed them out and they swarmed on the highways. The movement changed them; the highways, the camps along the road, the fear of hunger and the hunger itself, changed them. The children without dinner changed them, the endless moving changed them. They were migrants. And the hostility changed them, welded them, united them—hostility that made the little towns group and arm as though to repel an invader, squads with pick handles, clerks and storekeepers with shotguns, guarding the world against their own people.

In the West there was panic when the migrants multiplied on the highways. Men of property were terrified for their property. Men who had never been hungry saw the eyes of the hungry. Men who had never wanted anything very much saw the flare of want in the eyes of the migrants. And the men of the towns and of the soft suburban country gathered to defend themselves; and they reassured themselves that they were good and the invaders bad, as a man must do before he fights. They said, These goddamned Okies are dirty and ignorant. They're degenerate, sexual maniacs. These goddamned Okies are thieves. They'll steal anything. They've got no sense of property rights.

And the latter was true, for how can a man without property know the ache of ownership? And the defending people said, They bring disease, they're filthy. We can't have them in the schools. They're strangers. How'd you like to have your sister go out with one of 'em?

The local people whipped themselves into a mold of cruelty. Then they formed units, squads, and armed them—armed them with clubs, with gas, with guns. We own the country. We can't let these Okies get out of hand. And the men who were armed did not own the land, but they thought they did. And the clerks who drilled at night owned nothing, and the little storekeepers possessed only a drawerful of debts. But even a debt is something, even a job is something. The clerk thought, I get fifteen dollars a week. S'pose a goddamn Okie would work for twelve? And the little storekeeper thought, How could I compete with a debtless man?

And the migrants streamed in on the highways and their hunger was in their eyes, and their need was in their eyes. They had no argument, no system, nothing but their numbers and their needs. When there was work for a man, ten men fought for it—fought with a low wage. If that fella'll work for thirty cents, I'll work for twenty-five.

If he'll take twenty-five, I'll do it for twenty.

No, me, I'm hungry. I'll work for fifteen. I'll work for food. The kids. You ought to see them. Little boils, like, comin' out, an' they can't run aroun'. Give 'em some windfall fruit, an' they bloated up. Me. I'll work for a little piece of meat.

And this was good, for wages went down and prices stayed up. The great owners were glad and they sent out more handbills to bring more people in. And wages went down and prices stayed up. And pretty soon now we'll have serfs again.

And now the great owners and the companies invented a new method. A great owner bought a cannery. And when the peaches and the pears were ripe he cut the price of fruit below the cost of raising it. And as cannery owner he

The son of a destitute farmer in the foothills of the Ozark mountains in Arkansas. Most farm families who went west in the 1930's simply had no choice —they were forced from their homes by drought, bankruptcy, or, in the case of sharecroppers, by landowners who found machine labor more profitable than human labor.

paid himself a low price for the fruit and kept the price of canned goods up and took the profit. And the little farmers who owned no canneries lost their farms, and they were taken by the great owners, the banks, and the companies who also owned the canneries. As time went on, there were fewer farms. The little farmers moved into town for a while and exhausted their credit, exhausted their friends, their relatives. And then they too went on the highways. And the roads were crowded with men ravenous for work, murderous for work.

And the companies, the banks worked at their own doom and they did not know it. The fields were fruitful, and starving men moved on the roads. The granaries were full and the children of the poor grew up rachitic, and the pustules of pellagra swelled on their sides. The great companies did not know that the line between hunger and anger is a thin line. And money that might have gone to wages went for gas, for guns, for agents and spies, for blacklists, for drilling. On the highways the people moved like ants and searched for work, for food. And the anger began to ferment.[17]

The camp of a migrant family in California, 1935. The woman's husband is looking for work in the nearby pea fields.

FRANKLIN D. ROOSEVELT LIBRARY

Many of the farms of California's Imperial and San Joaquin valleys were not the family-size type of farm found in the Midwest, but were actually examples of industrialized agriculture. Highly mechanized, these farms were scientifically operated by managers just as any industry would be. Dispossessed farmers of the Dust Bowl were attracted in great numbers to California by widespread advertising conducted by labor contractors. The number of migrants far exceeded the available jobs and many, without work and without money, were stranded. Sick, starving, and angry, these refugees—called "Okies" or "Arkies"—drifted up and down the West Coast in search of food and work. Some resettlement camps were established in spite of great resistance from the major growers, but things did not really improve until business started to boom in the munitions and aircraft factories in 1940 and thereafter.

[17] John Steinbeck, *The Grapes of Wrath* (New York: Viking Press, Compass Books, 1958), pp. 385–388. Copyright 1939, © 1967 by John Steinbeck. Reprinted by permission of Viking Press and McIntosh and Otis, Inc.

The labor movement, despite major internal conflicts, made significant gains in 1936 and 1937, winning recognition from corporate giants like General Motors and U.S. Steel. But the labor movement also suffered a crushing setback in 1937, a violent and unsuccessful confrontation at Republic Steel that alienated public sympathy. Partly as a result of the hostile manner in which the nation's newspapers reported on the strikes of 1937, and partly as a result of FDR's increasingly noncommital stance on the issue, public opinion seemed to become more and more indifferent to the struggles of organized labor. It was not until the 1940's, when a labor shortage set in, that the unions were able to complete their organizing drive.

Black Americans had been harder hit by the depression than any other group. They had benefited somewhat from the CCC, the WPA, the TVA, and other New Deal programs, and, after 1935, had begun to receive some public recognition from the Roosevelt administration. Skilled Negro professionals were appointed to administrative positions in small but nonetheless unprecedented numbers. In 1937, the first Negro federal judge was appointed. Also in 1937, Joe Louis became the heavyweight boxing champion of the world, an event that caused a upswell of confidence and pride throughout the entire black community. Despite this progress, blacks remained at the bottom of the economic ladder; socially and politically, blacks continued to suffer discrimination of the most disgusting sort. FDR refused to jeopardize support for his domestic and foreign policies among southern Democrats by pressing for black political rights. In 1937, as in former years, an antilynching bill was filibustered to death in the U.S. Senate.

In October of 1937, Roosevelt delivered his "Quarantine-the-Aggressor" speech, a rather stern statement to the effect that the United States might find it good policy to discourage or even prevent armed aggression in the world at large. FDR had by this time become convinced that the United States would sooner or later have to take action against the military dictatorships gaining strength in Germany, Italy, and Japan. Japan was fighting an

Joe Louis, photographed the morning after he knocked out Jimmy Braddock to become world heavyweight champion. He held on to the title for twelve years and defended it twenty-five times; both are boxing records.

undeclared but vicious war in China; in Spain, the fascists under Franco were receiving substantial support from Germany and Italy; in Germany, Hitler was even then planning his conquest of Europe, and FDR seems to have read the Führer's appalling intentions correctly from the start. Nonetheless, American public opinion had never been so isolationist and so pacifist as it was during the thirties; Roosevelt's "Quarantine" speech laid a resounding egg. The negative public response to this speech convinced FDR that his paramount duty from that point on would be to prepare the nation—materially and psychologically—for war. From 1937 until late 1941, this effort consumed the greater part of FDR's energies and skills. Whenever he had to choose between his commitment to New Deal domestic goals and his commitment to a policy of collective security, he sacrificed the former. FDR could count on support for his foreign policy among conservative southern Democrats; increasingly, however, these same southern Democrats united with Republicans to kill or emasculate his domestic proposals. On the other hand, the midwestern and northern bloc of liberal or progressive congressmen who supported FDR's New Deal policies were on the whole flatly opposed to security measures likely to increase the chances of American involvement in European or Asian affairs. FDR's growing need to accommodate the conservative elements in his own party accounts in large measure for the death of the New Deal.

Two bitter struggles made the headlines in 1937—FDR's attempt to "reform" the U.S. Supreme Court, and organized labor's battle with the steel and automobile industries. Both these struggles, though fought on different battlegrounds, throw a good deal of light on the New Deal and on the strengths and weaknesses of the American system in the late thirties.

The Supreme Court Fight

Trouble between the New Deal administration and the Supreme Court had been brewing since 1935, when the Court had taken a case involving a small poultry business supplying kosher chickens to retail butchers and had used it to strike down the NRA. The Court held that Congress had unconstitutionally given over its law-making (code-making) authority to the executive branch, and that the Constitution did not authorize any legislation of the NRA type. Further Supreme Court decisions in 1935 and 1936 added up to an ominous and unacceptable pattern: namely, that neither the federal government nor state governments could regulate industry or agriculture for the benefit of workers or the economy as a whole. It seemed clear that vital and popular New Deal legislation like Social Security and the Wagner labor relations law would also be struck down.

Congress, the president, and the Supreme Court were clearly at loggerheads, but the basic problems involved were not new ones. The Constitution was an eighteenth-century document and had nothing whatever to say about labor unions, gigantic corporations, economic depression, unemployment, social security, or any of the other social and economic problems that the Congress and the executive were attempting to deal with. In cases like this, the Supreme Court had two choices. It could choose to uphold federal legislation dealing with new social problems largely on the basis of a single phrase in the Constitution —"Congress shall have the power to lay and collect Taxes, Duties, Imposts, and Excises, to pay the Debts and provide for the common Defense *and general Welfare of the United States. . . ."* Or it could choose to void such legislation and look for serviceable reasons within the Constitution.

When stymied by negative Supreme Court decisions, Congress had several options. It could rewrite or redesign a law so that the unconstitutional provisions were removed. Or it could draw up a constitutional amendment that would in effect reverse the unfavorable decision and then work to get this ratified in at least two-thirds of the state legislatures, a process usually taking several years. Or it could pass laws reorganizing the structure and procedure of the Court. The president could use the considerable powers of his office to persuade Congress to choose any of these options. He could also appoint to the Court—when and if vacancies occurred—men who were sympathetic to his general aims or philosophy of government. He could also rally or direct public opinion against the Court; hostile public opinion could have no immediate effect upon the Court, since its members were appointed for life, but, on the other hand, tradition and dignity forbade members of the Court from responding to public criticism. All that put-upon justices could do, as Rexford Guy Tugwell observed, was "wrap their robes about themselves and retreat into injured silence" and let other people do the arguing.

There is nothing in the Constitution specifically empowering the Supreme Court to declare state or federal laws null and void. In 1803, Chief Justice John Marshall asserted in the famous *Marbury* v. *Madison* decision that the Court did in fact have this power; his argument was in effect that somebody should have the final say, and it might as well be the Court. This argument, sensible in itself, also fitted in nicely with the power-wary consciousness of the age and was not seriously challenged. But the Court realized that it could retain this power only if it were not overused; fifty-three years passed before a Supreme Court again claimed and exercised its right to nullify a federal law. Thereafter, this right was exercised more frequently, but almost always conservatively—that is, in favor of those elements of society possessing the bulk of the nation's power. In the years between the Civil War and World War I, social power was heavily concentrated in the great industrial, commercial, and banking combines, and in protecting these interests the Supreme Court was not gravely violating either the cultural consensus or the power relationships of the time. People agreed for the most part that the way a man ran his business was not the government's affair. Furthermore, less than half the population lived in cities, and many of the city dwellers were immigrants or young people fresh from the farms who had almost no socioeconomic clout. By favoring industrial and banking interests, the Supreme Court was being, if not gallant, at least reasonable and prudent.

Although the Supreme Court is immune from "politics" of the small-time or grubby variety, it is nevertheless a political institution in the sense that it too must practice the art of government. Coequally with the Congress and the executive, the Court makes decisions that control or regulate the operations of men and institutions. Government is based upon the power to encourage certain kinds of behavior and discourage others; although government has many means of persuasion at its command, it is ultimately founded upon its ability to selectively apply controlled physical violence or force—to arrest, imprison, execute, or otherwise suppress those who violate its codes. The Court cannot implement its decisions without the cooperation of the Congress, the president, and the citizenry—the Court is an institution composed quite literally of nine legal scholars, usually aged ones. But the institutional violence available to government in the form of a police force or army cannot be applied to a majority or even a substantial minority: if it is, the result is civil war. As a political institution, the Court had in the past usually been careful not to stray too far from what was enforceable—because *acceptable*—in relation to the majority of citizens or at least the most powerful interest groups. During the depression, however, the Court had placed itself in an increasingly untenable position; by its decisions, it had alienated itself not only from the majority consensus but also from the enforcement arms of government. It had failed to recognize new power alignments; organized labor, for example, was already a force to be reckoned with. Furthermore, the great centers of industrial and commercial power, formerly in almost complete control, had been partially demoralized and discredited by events. The Congress and the president were clearly attempting to act for the benefit of the country as a whole, and the people knew it and approved. It was clear not only that something had to be done, but also that something *could* be done. But, in the end, nothing was.

The end result of the entire struggle was that neither the Constitution nor the Supreme Court nor the basic structure of government was altered. At the height of his power and popularity. FDR was successfully and eloquently defied by the Congress; thereafter, he found it extremely difficult to get what he wanted from it. This happened because FDR overreached himself; he made a series of political errors and was outmaneuvered by another politician—Chief Justice Charles Evans Hughes.

In 1937, the Hughes Court was old: five of its members had been born before or during the Civil War; only three were less than seventy years of age. Four justices—Willis Van Devanter, James McReynolds, George Sutherland, and Pierce Butler—were implacable conservatives and of dubious legal competence. Three justices—Louis Brandeis, Harlan Stone, and Benjamin Cardozo—constituted the liberal minority, and together represented a fund of legal and humanitarian acumen seldom equaled in the history of the Court. Brandeis was eighty-one years of age, and the oldest member. Chief Justice Hughes—seventy-five—and associate justice Owen Roberts provided the swing vote; until 1937, one or both had usually voted with the conservative four.

By mid-1936, many moderates in and out of government favored some sort of constitutional amendment that would clearly spell out the government's right to regulate in the public interest those economic or technological areas hitherto considered to lie within the realm of private wealth or property—wages, working conditions, hiring practices, production quotas, and so forth. This was *the* central issue, and many liberals within the administration wanted FDR to make it a subject of public discussion during the 1936 presidential campaign. Roosevelt decided not to, and, choosing the path of least resistance, ran on his record. He correctly anticipated a landslide victory and preferred to wait until he had this victory under his belt before taking action. But the huge vote of confidence he received may have caused him to overestimate his power. Whatever his reasons, Roosevelt chose a method that backfired disastrously: he tried to sneak a tricky little bill through Congress.

Although he rarely showed his true feelings about it in public, Roosevelt had been deeply angered by the Court's decisions; they had checkmated him in a way that was intolerable to his self-esteem, his presidential style, and

The Supreme Court in November, 1937, after FDR's attempts to change the Court had failed. From left, bottom row: George Sutherland, James McReynolds, Charles Evans Hughes, Louis Brandeis, Pierce Butler; top row: Benjamin Cardozo, Harlan Stone, Owen Roberts, Hugo Black. Black was appointed by FDR.

A cartoonist comments on Roosevelt's difficulties in "reforming" the Court.

his sense of historical importance. He wanted to injure the Court—to undermine its solemnity and dignity as an institution. He also wanted, it seems, a good deal more—to wrest from the Court its traditional prerogative to nullify federal or executive action. There had been a power vacuum in 1803, and Marshall had moved his Court into it. A similar vacuum had been created by the Court itself in 1935 and 1936, and Roosevelt thought he had the strength and support—both in Congress and among the people—to place his legislative program beyond the Court's reach. And he might indeed have been able to do this had he dealt with the issue widely and openly. But that was not, for the most part, Roosevelt's way.

On February 5, 1937, Roosevelt sent over to the Senate, with little or no warning to party leaders, a proposed bill for reorganizing the structure and procedures of the federal judiciary and an accompanying message urging the bill's passage. The provisions of the bill were complicated if not sly, but it was quickly understood by a few of the brighter senators that the bill would in effect allow the president to appoint six new justices to the Supreme Court and would probably give the executive the means to prevent unfavorable constitutional decisions in the future. Among other things, the bill provided that the president could, when any federal judge more than seventy years old had served on the same bench for more than ten and a half years, appoint a second or co-judge. The implication was that the aged jurist in question was no longer energetic enough to handle his case load or wise enough to recognize the fact and retire. Roosevelt's written message reinforced this implication explicitly, pointing out that old men couldn't understand the present or the future, and that their "lowered mental or physical vigor" resulted in judicial inefficiency and delay and hence considerable injustice. This argument was not only palpably unfair and false—Oliver Wendell Holmes had retired with great honor in 1932 at the age of ninety-one, and the octogenarian Brandeis was functioning very well indeed—but it also seemed egregiously beside the point.

There was a profound constitutional and governmental issue at stake, and the issue seemed to demand arguments of matching profundity and weight.

Most senators were lawyers, and many of them hoped to wind up with federal judgeships; they didn't like to hear that they could look forward to a time when they would be, as Roosevelt put it, old men of blurred vision looking through eyeglasses fitted for the needs and facts of a bygone day. Conservative southern Democrats, already disgruntled by FDR's liberal domestic program, were delighted to find an issue on which they could defy Roosevelt without being branded as reactionaries hopelessly out of touch with people's needs. Progressive and liberal senators were appalled at what they considered the low sneakiness of Roosevelt's message and furthermore had grave doubts about tipping the balance of governmental power so sharply in the executive's favor. After all, if the Court could be expanded or contracted at presidential will to sanction New Deal laws, it could also be used to okay laws of a very different sort. Senator Burton Wheeler, a man of long and valorous progressive credentials, led the fight against the bill.

Senator Joseph Robinson, the Senate majority leader, dutifully attempted to garner support for the bill and spent most of FDR's political credit—favors, patronage, and so on—to do it. But after several months of dealing, it was clear to Robinson that he didn't have the votes. Although a majority in the Senate was ready for some sort of compromise—two new permanent additions to the Court, or perhaps a requirement that the Court needed a 7–2 vote to nullify legislation—FDR would have none of it. He seemed unable to understand that his bill was in trouble. He "went to the people" in a fireside chat and other speeches and turned on the pressure. But his sources of organized power—the farm bloc, labor, and the big-city machines—responded unenthusiastically, giving him only token support. The debate in the Senate dragged on. Senator Robinson's stubborn, party-line labors on behalf of a bill he despised literally killed him; in July, he dropped dead of a heart attack, further disorganizing

Senator Joseph T. Robinson explaining his compromise Court bill to the press on July 12, 1937.

FDR's Senate following. Roosevelt wanted to win this one badly and seems to have assumed that his own deep commitment would, given his overwhelming electoral mandate, cause his bill to prevail. But despite heavy pressure from Roosevelt, fewer and fewer people saw any need for the bill at all, because meanwhile Chief Justice Hughes had been at work behind the scenes.

Hughes apparently persuaded Willis Van Devanter—perhaps the most fossilized of the conservative four—to announce his retirement in May thus giving FDR his first crack at appointing a Supreme Court justice. Hughes sent a letter to Senator Wheeler that very neatly punctured FDR's claim that Court members were overworked, behind schedule, or overtired; this letter was of course read to the Senate. More importantly, in March of 1937, the Court had begun to uphold New Deal legislation. It ruled in favor of a state minimum wage law, a farm mortgage act, the Wagner law, and Social Security. Hughes and Roberts were now voting with Brandeis, Cardozo, and Stone.

> Without admitting openly that it was being done. [Hughes and Roberts] solemnly, and with all the paraphernalia of legal exposition, reversed themselves. Going over to the liberal minority, they made it a majority. What had in 1935 been the reasoning of dissent now became the rule of law. . . . There is no sophistical argument capable of making this change anything but what it was—a political decision. The Chief Justice—and one of his associates—had decided not that the contentions of the President had a new force but that the Court as an institution must be removed from a looming danger.[18]

The reversals were dubbed "the switch in time that saved nine," and it is often suggested that FDR's court-packing scheme was responsible for the switch. This is almost certainly not the case. Roosevelt's bill would not have passed in anything like its original form. And the Court—or rather its chief justice, who had narrowly missed be-

[18] Tugwell, *Democratic Roosevelt,* p. 396.

coming president himself in 1916 and had been a highly popular governor of New York—could read election returns as well as anybody else. It is very likely that Hughes decided in November of 1936 that the Court had placed itself too far out in right field, and was determined even then to move it back within the consensus and social realities of the times.

In late July, the Senate voted to send FDR's bill back to the Judiciary Committee, which had already flogged it to death in the following terms:

SUMMARY

We recommend the rejection of this bill as a needless, futile and utterly dangerous abandonment of constitutional principle.

It was presented to the Congress in a most intricate form and for reasons that obscured its real purpose. . . .

It would subjugate the courts to the will of Congress and the President and thereby destroy the independence of the judiciary, the only certain shield of individual rights.

It contains the germ of a system of centralized administration of law that would enable an executive so minded to send his judges into every judicial district in the land to sit in judgment on controversies between the Government and the citizen.

It points the way to the evasion of the Constitution and establishes the method whereby the people may be deprived of their right to pass upon all amendments of the fundamental law.

It stands now before the country, acknowledged by its proponents as a plan to force judicial interpretation of the Constitution, a proposal that violates every sacred tradition of the American democracy. . . .

Its ultimate operation would be to make this Government one of men rather than one of law, and its practical operation would be to make the Constitution what the executive or legislative branches of the Government choose to say it is—an interpretation to be changed with each change of administration.

It is a measure which should be so emphatically rejected that its parallel will never again be presented to the free representatives of the free people of America.[19]

Roosevelt was able in the following years to fill seven vacancies on the Court and to give it his own liberal imprint. The New Deal was unquestionably safe. But it was almost over.

In the 1938 congressional elections, Roosevelt attempted to "purge" members of his own party who had sided against him in the Court fight and other controversies by campaigning against them in their home states; for the most part, he was unsuccessful and merely increased congressional enmity. Rexford Guy Tugwell has this final, somewhat tantalizing comment:

> When [Roosevelt] came to write ... his *Public Papers*, he could claim that the 1937 defeat had been only temporary and that ultimately all the changes he had advocated had been accepted. But he certainly knew that the vital one had been refused; and I have often wondered whether, if he had lived on into the post-war period, he would have tried again.[20]

Labor Upheaval

1937 was a critical year for the labor movement. A conflict among union leaders about how to organize the mass of workers—according to their skills or according to the industry in which they worked—burst into the open and was then settled by events: *both* forms of organization would prevail. The sit-down strike, a novel and generally successful technique in which workers shut down their machines and then barricaded themselves inside a plant or other work-site, flashed briefly across the 1937 scene. For the first time, labor contracts were signed with key industrial giants like U.S. Steel and General Motors; thereafter, it was clear that organized labor had become

[19] Quoted in Richard Hofstadter, ed., *Great Issues in American History* (New York: Alfred A. Knopf, Vintage Books, 1958), 2: 380–381.

[20] Tugwell, *Democratic Roosevelt,* p. 407.

Strikers occupying the Ford plant in Flint, Michigan, in January, 1937. They were demanding union recognition but had to give up when they ran out of food. Company guards forcibly prevented sympathizers from getting supplies to them.

a permanent and powerful interest-group within the national fabric. Also in 1937, old-style industrial managers made their last and temporarily victorious stand, employing the standard nineteenth-century repertory of heavy-handed foremen, goon squads, and private security thugs to intimidate individuals, and court-ordered injunctions and local police forces to do the large-scale dirty work.

During the 1920's, the trade union movement had not prospered; a decade of Red Scares, company unions, unfavorable court decisions, Pinkerton spies and thugs, economic prosperity, blacklisting, and hostile public opinion had left organized labor in a deathly coma.

In the early thirties, the horrible depression-bred labor surpluses now threatened to destroy the remaining pockets of union strength. The AFL, by far the largest union, had lost more than half its membership by mid-1933.

In the nick of time, labor took heart from Section 7(a) of the NRA package and, energized by leaders like John

Sidney Hillman, president of the Amalgamated Clothing Workers of America.

L. Lewis, Sidney Hillman, and David Dubinsky, bounced back with spectacular membership gains. As Cabell Phillips writes:

> The long-dormant labor movement came suddenly to life. From national headquarters of the big unions and on down through the musty, cobwebby warrens of state and city centrals and the hundreds of grimy local union halls, many of which had been boarded up and in disuse for years—an intense activity burst forth. Recruiters and organizers fanned out in every direction, posted themselves at mine tipples and factory gates, called shop meetings and public rallies, and passed out bales of leaflets and membership blanks. Coal miners coming off their shifts in West Virginia and Kentucky had fliers thrust into their hands proclaiming, "The President says you must join the union." Dropouts, holdouts, and those with no present job responded eagerly. Defunct locals came back to life. Shop stewards and walking bosses asserted their authority, and union buttons were openly worn on the job without fear of reprisal.[21]

The alert sympathy of Frances Perkins, FDR's secretary of labor, the passage in 1935 of the Wagner Act, and the administration's sharpening antibusiness tone convinced labor that the federal government was now, if not fervently prolabor, at least no longer firmly allied with the corporate interests. But this brightened prospect also brought to the surface a long-smouldering power-feud between the old craft-oriented unionists and those who correctly saw great potential in organizing the mass of semiskilled workers on an industry-wide basis. In 1935, a small group of dissidents within the AFL leadership formed the Committee for Industrial Organization (CIO), which proceeded to coordinate and to fund the organizing drives of a handful of existing unions in the mining, steel, automobile, and garment industries. The CIO-sponsored

---

[21] Cabell Phillips, *From the Crash to the Blitz, 1929–1939* (London: Macmillan & Co., 1969), p. 514. Copyright © 1969 by The New York Times Company.

unions immediately ran afoul of the older and for the most part impotent craft unions which also represented some workers in these industries. In 1936, the CIO—which later renamed itself the Congress of Industrial Organizations—was kicked out of the AFL.

The CIO unions forged ahead, however, and scored a number of exhilarating successes. John L. Lewis privately persuaded Myron C. Tyler of U.S. Steel to sign a contract with the CIO Steel Workers Organizing Committee. The contract granted union recognition, a ten percent wage increase, a forty-hour week, and time and a half for overtime. It was one of the most significant contracts in labor history and represented a huge boost for the fledgling CIO.

While the CIO was planning its campaign against steel, another CIO affiliate, the United Auto Workers, moved spontaneously against General Motors. In December of 1936, workers "sat down" in the Fisher Body Plant in Cleveland; the strike quickly spread to other GM plants. In Flint, Michigan, the UAW local under the leadership of the Reuther brothers—Roy, Victor, and Walter—outmaneuvered the GM security force and occupied the key Chevrolet engine plant, Plant Number Four, thus virtually crippling GM production.

Michigan Governor Frank Murphy, a Democrat and labor sympathizer, refused to call in the National Guard to evict the strikers. A local judge ordered the Flint sheriff to arrest the workers, but he refused. GM officials, inhibited by the fear that violence would result in the destruction of their machines, yielded to Murphy's plea for mediation. During the ensuing six-week negotiations, FDR applied great pressure upon GM management for a settlement, and one finally came about. The United Auto Workers union won recognition as the bargaining agent for all GM workers, and collective bargaining procedures were set up. The GM settlement did not produce any immediate wage-and-hour gains for the workers, but as one participant in the strike put it, "When Mr. Knudsen [GM president] puts his name to a piece of paper and

John L. Lewis, president of the United Mine Workers' Union, served also as president of the CIO from 1935 to 1940.

says that General Motors recognizes the UAW-CIO—until that moment, we were non-people, we didn't even exist. That was the big one."[22] The journalist Murray Kempton has described the Flint UAW victory in similar terms:

Joe Sayen, a Chevrolet Four worker thereafter unheard upon any great stage again, climbed the spiked fence outside Chevrolet and told the pickets that the bastions had fallen:

"We want the whole world to know what we are fighting for. We are fighting for freedom and life and liberty. This is our great opportunity. What if we should be defeated? What if we should be killed? We have only one life. That is all we can lose and we might as well die like heroes than like slaves."

For his little while, the auto worker was speaking a language beyond the dreams of the Reuther boys, his words like those Shakespeare put into the mouth of the tailor called to the wars: "By my troth I care not; a man can die but once; we owe God a death; . . . and let it go which way it will, he that dies this year is quit for the next."

The seizure of Chevrolet Four meant the end of the GM strike; the company recognized that it had lost the ascendancy; John Lewis came in to invest the men in its plants with his own heroic effrontery, to strut and fret and wangle a settlement. The union had won very little on paper. Outsiders wondered if it had won anything at all. But the men in the plants knew that this was a victory; it was summed up for them in the words of a striker who announced that he would slug the first foreman who looked cockeyed at him.

On February 11, 1937, they marched out in the twilight, down Chevrolet Avenue, the beards still on so many of their faces, the cigars in their mouths, the confetti sifting down from the gates of Chevrolet Four, on into the center

[22] Quoted in Studs Terkel, *Hard Times: An Oral History of the Depression* (New York: Avon Books, 1970), p. 161. Copyright 1970 by Studs Terkel. Reprinted by permission of Pantheon Books, a division of Random House, Inc., and Penguin Books, Ltd.

of Flint, and no one who watched them could doubt who the winners were.[23]

The UAW went on to strike Chrysler and won there too. But Henry Ford held out. His "service department"— a group of heavies and ex-convicts hired by Ford to spy upon and coerce his workers—managed through a combination of efficiency and terrorism to forestall UAW organization of Ford workers until 1940.

In 1937, a number of the greatest corporations read the handwriting on the wall with something like the statesmanship that might be expected of such enormously powerful institutions, and realized that unionization of their labor forces would neither ruin them financially nor seriously undermine the essential prerogatives of management. It was assumed that small and medium-sized companies would quickly follow the example of industry leaders, but that was not the case. The following account, by a man who in 1937 was a thirty-two-year-old vice-president and general counsel of one of those companies, suggests that plain ignorance was one of the main problems:

There was a wave of sit-down strikes. Newspapers and respectable people said it was bad enough to have strikes, but it was clearly immoral as well as unlawful to seize property. In those days, strikes were broken by the importation of strikebreakers. Sitting down in a factory kept strikebreakers from getting in. It was a new technique. When suddenly the rules of the game, which the unions had always lost, were altered by the sit-down, there was an outcry. . . .

There was a sit-down strike at one of our plants. We had a plant manager who dealt with these labor troubles. In his way, he was a nice guy, but his appearance was that of a cartoon factory boss: cigar in the corner of his mouth, a big square face and a big square frame. He had ways

[23] Murray Kempton, *Part of Our Time: Some Ruins and Monuments of the Thirties* (New York: Simon & Schuster, 1955), pp. 286–287. Copyright 1955 by Murray Kempton.

of beating the strikers that were not generally published, but known to manufacturers.

There was a police detail in Chicago known as the [Red Squad], in charge of a lieutenant, Make Mills. When a strike occurred, Mills would arrange to arrest the leaders. They'd beat them up, put them in jail, make it pretty clear to them to get the hell out of town. Mills got tips, $1,000, or if it was a serious thing, $5,000. He made a hell of a lot of dough to get the agitators, as they were called.

These were organizers, some of whom didn't work in the factory. With his plainclothesmen, Mills would get them in a saloon. They'd have free drinks, then a fight would break out.

His uniformed men would come in and arrest the organizer, beat hell out of him, put him in jail. They got a lot of people out of town. There was an awful lot of rough stuff going on.

The factory was shut down. I was drawn into it. The union had filed a complaint with the National Labor Relations Board. The issue was union recognition. The complaint: blacklisting.

The company sent letters out in very fancy language: we will pay the best wages, we will always discuss grievances with employees, but will allow no outside intervention. Newspaper editorials were urging employees to return to work. Each day of the strike was costing them money they'd never recover.

I was handed a stack of cards to take downtown to our attorneys. Some of those I examined had notations: "Union agitator, do not rehire." Others were marked with little round dots. The employment manager told me they indicated a union sympathizer. Many of them had been or were to be fired. If any prospective employer were to ask about them, he'd be told: "Don't hire him—troublemaker, agitator." The word "Communist" wasn't used much at the time. "Red," though, was a common term.

I took the cards to [the legal firm of] Twynan, Hill and Blair. The operating head of the thing, Blair, came out of the Northwest as a successful railroad attorney. He represented many big companies and was a member of our board. A tremendous bore, a funny little guy, about five feet four, small mustache. All his clients were saints, under attack. He was about seventy at the time. . . .

Blair told me the cards were harmless. It dawned on me that he didn't know of the existence of the Wagner Act. When I told him, he said, "There cannot be any such law. And if there were, I would not hesitate to advise you it would be unconstitutional because it would be an impingement upon the freedom of contract." I said, "There is such a law. It's sometimes called the Wagner Act." He said, "I never heard of it." And I said, "It was adjudicated in the Supreme Court and its validity was upheld." He howled, "That is impossible!" He swiveled around and grabbed for his mineral water.

He called in an associate. "This young man tells me there is a law by the name of the Watson Act." "The Wagner Act." The other nodded. "There is? This young man goes further and claims the United States Supreme Court declared it constitutional." The other nodded. "That, sir, is impossible!" His associate said it was so. "It's a fine thing!" With that, Blair slapped the stack of cards on his desk, bang. "Well that's one more of these left-wing New Deal activities. Respectable citizens who built up this country can come in and testify, and their testimony won't be believed." The other said, "That's the way it would go." Blair said, "We sent the president of the company to deny these charges, and he wouldn't be believed?" I said, "Mr. Blair, one of the reasons he wouldn't be believed is because it would be a lie."

"What do you mean a lie?"

"Look at these cards. It identifies union men."

"Is something wrong with that?"

"Yes, it's prohibited."

"That has to be adjudicated."

"It was adjudicated. And all these people who were fired. It says on the face of it: Don't rehire."

"But they are *former* employees."

Well, this is the way it went. He called in a detective, who was on the company payroll and said, "Take these cards. I don't ever want to see them again. I don't want to know what happened to them, and I don't want you to ever know anything about them."

The National Labor Relations Board did find the company engaged in unfair labor practices. The union was recognized. A large sum of money was awarded in back wages to employees who were fired. There were tremendous legal fees, of course.

There was a curious aftermath. The people went back to work. But there persisted an attitude of bitterness and resentment. A continuing hostility. Each side wished the worst of the other. . . .

Most people don't become vice presidents until their late fifties. I was one of the few college-educated men in the company. There was a lot of suspicion of me: I had to be watched. . . .

This was a time when people who went to Yale or Harvard went into brokerage, not into manufacturing. In contrast to now, the industrialists were basically men who came up from the bench. The hard way, they called it.

That had a lot to do with their tone and attitude. If anybody has the impression that a man who had come up the hard way had an easy way of looking at the working man, he's completely mistaken. His view was: I got ahead. Why can't you?[24]

Although U.S. Steel had recognized the CIO steel-workers' union, Bethlehem Steel, Republic Steel, and the Youngstown Sheet and Tube company—collectively known as Little Steel—did not. Tom Girdler, head of Republic Steel, threw down the gauntlet in these terms: "I won't have a contract, verbal or written, with an irresponsible, racketeering, violent, communist body like the CIO."

The strike against Little Steel was violent and costly. The worst episode was the so-called Memorial Day massacre at Republic Steel, on May 30, 1937. *The New York Times* gave the following account of the Memorial Day events:

[24] Quoted in Terkel, *Hard Times,* pp. 151–154.

4 KILLED, 84 HURT
AS STRIKERS FIGHT
POLICE IN CHICAGO

—

STEEL MOB HALTED

—

1,000 MARCHERS FAIL
IN EFFORT TO CLOSE
REPUBLIC PLANT

Chicago, May 30—Four men were killed and eighty-four persons went to hospitals with gunshot wounds, cracked heads, broken limbs, or other injuries received in a battle late this afternoon between police and steel strikers at the gates of the Republic Steel Corporation plant in South Chicago. . . .

The union demonstrators were armed with clubs, slingshots, cranks and gear shift levers from cars, bricks, steel bolts and other missiles. Police charged that some of the men also carried firearms.

After their repulse in the march, which began at 4 P.M., the strikers tried to reassemble for another attack on the plant, but gave it up with the arrival of police reinforcements.

The police said they stood their ground but made no effort to harm the invaders until showered with bricks and bolts. The police then used tear gas; when the rioters resorted to firearms, the police said, they were forced to draw their revolvers to protect themselves. Even then, the police declared, they first fired into the air as a final warning.

At a late hour three of the dead were unidentified. Police interpreted this as a confirmation of reports that outside agitators had played a leading part in the raid on the plant. . . .

Informed of the riot, Mayor Kelly, at his summer home at Eagle River, Wis., attributed it to "outside mobs who came into Chicago to make trouble."

He expressed confidence that "the well-disciplined police" would fulfill its duty to "protect life and property"

Above, things are still orderly as police and demonstrators confront each other outside the gates of Republic Steel on May 30, 1937. Below, the scene a few minutes later.

and added that "we can settle our troubles if we are left alone."

Several women and several boys were among the injured. Some of these were mere observers. . . .

Carrying banners and chanting "C.I.O., C.I.O.," the strikers drew within a block and a half of the gate to find the police lined up awaiting them. Captain Kilroy stepped forward and asked the crowd to disperse.

"You can't get through here," he declared. "We must do our duty."

Jeers greeted his words. Then the demonstrators began hurling bricks, stones and bolts.

The police replied with tear gas. The crowd fell back for a moment, choking, and then, the police say, began firing at the officers. The officers fired warning shots and, when, according to the police, the strikers continued firing, they returned it.   .   . . . .

Men began dropping on both sides. The strikers fell back before the police bullets and swinging police clubs.

Police wagons then raced onto the field and began picking up the injured. . . .

Officer Cleary saw a brother officer beaten to the ground by one of the crowd wielding a metal rod. The striker was disarming the prostrate officer when Cleary went to the rescue. . . .

Inside the plant, J. L. Hyland, vice president of the Republic Corporation, addressed the loyal workers today. He said:

"I imagine you men are interested in how long this plant will operate. I am here to tell you that it will continue to produce steel just as long as you men want to work."[25]

Dr. Lewis Andreas, a Chicago physician who observed the march on Republic, and later treated the wounded, tells it this way:

A few days before Memorial Day, 1937, some steel workers picketed Republic Steel on the Far South Side. I

---

[25] *The New York Times,* 31 May 1937. Copyright © 1937 by The New York Times Company. Reprinted by permission.

received a call: "We've got a very nasty situation here. There're probably going to be some injuries. There's not a hospital for miles around, not even a drugstore. Would you come and get a few first aid stations started?"

There was a tavern called Sam's Place. I took a few supplies and got a first aid station started. The men who picketed that day got clobbered. There were a few split skulls and a few fractures. Everybody got mad and then decided to try it again on Memorial Day.

It was a holiday, so we had them from Indian Harbor and Gary and all kinds of places. Some were looking for trouble, but for many it was simply a family picnic sort of thing: little kids, people dressed up in their Sunday shirts. Many came just for the fun of it; they weren't expecting anything.

The police were standing in line in front of Republic Steel, quite a distance from the others. It was a hell of a hot day, about ninety. They had their winter uniforms on. The sun was strong, and all I could see were their stars glittering.

The people began wandering out. A long line. This was a mixed bunch. Some of them may have been planning to use the sticks they were holding the signs on for other purposes, for clobbering somebody. Nobody was armed. But the police got the idea these people were armed. At least, they were told so by Captain Mooney and Lieutenant Kilroy, who were managing this thing. Mayor Kelly was out of town.

I stayed behind. All of a sudden, I heard some popping going on and a blue haze began rising. I said: My God, tear gas. What do you do for that? I couldn't remember what the medical books said. I ran back to Sam's Place. About three minutes later, they started bringing the wounded, shot. There were about fifty shot. Ten of them died. One little boy was shot in the heel. I took care of him. One woman was shot in the arm. They were lying there, bleeding bullet wounds in the belly, in the leg and all over. All sorts of fractures, lacerations. . . . I had absolutely no preparation at all for this. . . . I jumped on a chair and said: Get all the gun shots out of here right

away to the nearest hospital. I can't handle them. Some
of them had been taken to Bridewell and to other hospitals
by the police. . . .

I made charts of these gun shots. A great majority of
them were shot from behind. Mel Coughlin, the assistant
state's attorney, asked me, "Can you define the back?" In
the courtroom, I just got up and turned around and said,
"What you're looking at now—that's the back."

The misrepresentation in the newspapers was so great.
There was a picture in the back page of the [Chicago]
Tribune, for instance: a little old guy lying on the prairie
in his white shirt, blood streaming down his face and
Lieutenant Kilroy beating the hell out of him with his
club. The caption said: "Striker Beats Up Police At
Republic Steel Riot." [26]

Paramount Pictures had cameras and soundmen on the
Republic scene, and filmed what the *Times* headlined as
the halting of a steel mob. Paramount then refused to
release the film because it might "incite local riot and
perhaps riotous demonstrations." A Senate subcommittee
under Senator Robert La Follette later investigated the
Memorial Day incident; the committee subpoenaed the
film and screened it before a small group of congressmen
and their staff members. Here is an account of what
they saw:

The first scenes show police drawn up in a long line across
a dirt road which runs diagonally through a large open
field before turning into a street which is parallel to, and
some 200 yards distant from, the high fence surrounding
the Republic mill. The police line extends to 40 or 50
yards on each side of the dirt road. Behind the line, and in
the street beyond, nearer the mill, are several patrol wagons
and numerous reserve squads of police.

Straggling across the field, in a long irregular line, headed
by two men carrying American flags, the demonstrators
are shown approaching. Many carry placards. They appear
to number about 300—approximately the same as the

---

[26] Quoted in Terkel, *Hard Times*, pp. 170–172.

police—although it is known that some 2,000 strike sympathizers were watching the march from a distance.

Marchers Halted by Police

A vivid close-up shows the head of the parade being halted at the police line. The flag-bearers are in front. Behind them the placards are massed. They bear such devices as: "Come on Out—Help Win the Strike"; "Republic vs. the People," and "C.I.O." Between the flag-bearers is the marchers' spokesman, a muscular young man in shirtsleeves, with a C.I.O. button on the band of his felt hat.

He is arguing earnestly with a police officer who appears to be in command. His vigorous gestures indicate that he is insisting on permission to continue through the police line, but in the general din of yelling and talking his words cannot be distinguished. His expression is serious, but no suggestion of threat or violence is apparent. The police officer, whose back is to the camera, makes one impatient gesture of refusal, and says something which cannot be understood.

Then suddenly, without apparent warning, there is a terrific roar of pistol shots, and men in the front ranks of the marchers go down like grass before a scythe. The camera catches approximately a dozen falling simultaneously in a heap. The massive, sustained roar of the police pistols lasts perhaps two or three seconds.

Police Charge with Sticks

Instantly the police charge on the marchers with riot sticks flying. At the same time tear gas grenades are seen sailing into the mass of demonstrators, and clouds of gas rise over them. Most of the crowd is now in flight. The only discernible case of resistance is that of a marcher with a placard on a stick, which he uses in an attempt to fend off a charging policeman. He is successful for only an instant. Then he goes down under a shower of blows.

The scenes which follow are among the most harrowing of the picture. Although the ground is strewn with dead and wounded, and the mass of the marchers are in precipitate flight down the dirt road and across the field,

a number of individuals, either through foolish hardihood,
or because they have not yet realized what grim and deadly
business is in progress around them, have remained behind,
caught in the midst of the charging police.

In a manner which is appallingly businesslike, groups of
policemen close in on these isolated individuals, and go to
work on them with their clubs. In several instances, from
two to four policemen are seen beating one man. One
strikes him horizontally across the face, using his club as
he would wield a baseball bat. Another crashes it down
on top of his head, and still another is whipping him across
the back.

These men try to protect their heads with their arms,
but is only a matter of a second or two until they go down.
In one such scene, directly in the foreground, a policeman
gives the fallen man a final smash on the head, before
moving on to the next job.

In the front line during the parley with the police is a
girl, not more than five feet tall, who can hardly weigh more
than 100 pounds. Under one arm she is carrying a purse
and some newspapers. After the first deafening volley of
shots she turns, to find that her path to flight is blocked
by a heap of fallen men. She stumbles over them,
apparently dazed.

The scene shifts for a moment, then she is seen going
down under a quick blow from a policeman's club, delivered
from behind. She gets up, and staggers around. A few
moments later she is shown being shoved into a patrol
wagon, as blood cascades down her face and spreads over
her clothing.

Straggler's Futile Flight

Preceding this episode, however, is a scene which, for
sheer horror, outdoes the rest. A husky, middle-aged,
bare-headed man has found himself caught far behind the
rear ranks of the fleeing marchers. Between him and the
others, policemen are as thick as flies, but he elects to run
the gantlet. Astonishingly agile for one of his age and
build, he runs like a deer, leaping a ditch, dodging as he
goes. Surprised policemen take hasty swings as he passes

them. Some get him on the back, some on the back of the head, but he keeps his feet, and keeps going.

The scene is bursting with a frightful sort of drama. Will he make it? The suspense is almost intolerable to those who watch. It begins to look as if he will get through. But no! The police in front have turned around now, and are waiting for him. Still trying desperately, he swings to the right. He has put his hands up, and is holding them high above his head as he runs.

It is no use. There are police on the right. He is cornered. He turns, still holding high his hands. Quickly the bluecoats close in, and the night sticks fly—above his head from the sides, from the rear. His upraised arms fall limply under the flailing blows, and he slumps to the ground in a twisting fall, as the clubs continue to rain on him.

C.I.O. officers report that when one of the victims was delivered at an undertaking establishment, it was found that his brains literally had been beaten out, his skull crushed by blows.

Man Paralyzed by Bullet

Ensuing scenes are hardly less poignant. A man shot through the back is paralyzed from the waist. Two policemen try to make him stand up, to get into a patrol wagon, but when they let him go his legs crumple, and he falls with his face in the dirt, almost under the rear step of the wagon. He moves his head and arms, but his legs are limp. He raises his head like a turtle, and claws the ground.

A man over whose white shirt front the blood is spreading, perceptibly, is dragged to the side of the road. Two or three policemen bend over and look at him closely. One of them shakes his head, and slips a newspaper under the wounded man's head. There is plain intimation that he is dying. A man in civilian clothing comes up, feels his pulse a moment then drops the hand, and walks away. Another, in a uniform which might be that of a company policeman, stops an instant, looks at the prostrate figure, and continues on his way.

Loading Wounded in Wagons

The scene shifts to the patrol wagons in the rear. Men with
bloody heads, bloody faces, bloody shirts, are being loaded
in. One who apparently has been shot in the leg, drags
himself painfully into the picture with the aid of two
policemen. An elderly man, bent almost double, holding
one hand on the back of his head, clambers painfully up
the steps and slumps onto the seat, burying his face in both
hands. The shoulders of his white shirt are drenched with
blood.

There is continuous talking, but it is difficult to distinguish
anything with one exception—out of the babble there rises
this clear and distinct ejaculation:

"God Almighty!"

The camera shifts back to the central scene. Here and
there is a body sprawled in what appears to be the grotesque
indifference of death. Far off toward the corner of the
field, whence they had come originally, the routed
marchers are still in flight, with an irregular line of
policemen in close pursuit. It is impossible to discern, at
this distance, whether violence has ended.

A policeman, somewhat disheveled, his coat open, a
scowl on his face, approaches another who is standing in
front of the camera. He is sweaty and tired. He says
something indistinguishable. Then his face breaks into a
sudden grin, he makes a motion of dusting off his hands,
and strides away. The film ends.[27]

In 1941, the National Labor Relations Board was able
to compel Little Steel to recognize and bargain with the
steelworkers' union. But the Memorial Day massacre did
not win labor many sympathizers in 1937; in fact, the
strikers were generally held to be the real troublemakers.
The New Deal was slowly winding down, and a conservative mood was settling over the Congress and perhaps

[27] Quoted in Richard Hofstadter and Michael Wallace, eds.,
American Violence: A Documentary History (New York: Alfred
A. Knopf, 1970), pp. 181–184. Copyright 1970 by Alfred A.
Knopf, Inc.

over the nation as a whole. In any case, the public was weary of sit-downs and labor upheaval generally. President Roosevelt himself concisely expressed this mood of public exasperation. When asked what he thought about the positions taken by labor and management in the Little Steel Strike, Roosevelt said, "A plague on both your houses."

Labor had won great gains in the first half of 1937, but thereafter the drama and the momentum slackened. The emphasis now shifted to the slow and for the most part unnewsworthy work of consolidating these gains in the courts, in congressional hearing rooms, or at the bargaining tables.

There were 4,740 strikes in 1937. In more than a few of them blood was spilled, mostly that of workers, union organizers, or even uninvolved onlookers. But at least some of these strikes had their lighter side, as Murray Kempton observes:

A striker is being led away, bent over with pain after being gassed by company-hired policemen at the Republic steel plant in Monroe, Michigan. Many other strikers also were gassed or clubbed by the police.

BROWN BROTHERS

> The sit-down strike was a civic epidemic [in Detroit]. Myra Wolfgang, just out of Carnegie Tech and the fifteen-dollar-a-week business agent of the AFL Hotel and Restaurant Employees, had been fretting for months over the low temperature of her flock; now, of a sudden, it was swept by high fever.
>
> "You'd be sitting in the office any March day of 1937," she says now, "and the phone would ring and the voice at the other end would say, 'My name is Mary Jones; I'm a soda clerk at Liggett's; we've thrown the manager out and we've got the keys. What do we do now?' And you'd hurry over to the company to negotiate and over there they'd say, 'I think it's the height of irresponsibility to call a strike before you've even asked us for a contract,' and all you could answer was 'You're so right.' " . . .
>
> Waitresses in Stouffer's sat down because their employer lined them up just before duty to inspect their fingernails for the prescribed shade and brand of polish; Negro wet-nurses in Chicago, who did not even have a union, sat down for a higher rate per ounce of milk. Myra Wolfgang herself was on the twenty-third floor of the

Book-Cadillac [Hotel] negotiating a contract when she
heard the voice outside calling, "All chambermaids down
to the eighteenth floor; all bellboys up to the twenty-fourth
floor," and could only wail, "I've been caught too."

Lily Pons, in Detroit for a concert, sat in the lobby of
the Book-Cadillac and wept because she had come all this
distance in pursuit of her art and was trapped in a
"seet-on." When the hotel workers struck the Statler,
[a UAW organizer] swarmed in with 5,000 Chrysler
pickets. The Statler's manager, William Klare, a backslid
member of the Intercollegiate Socialist Society at Ann
Arbor, looked out at them, remembered his forsworn
vision of the advancing proletariat on the day of justice,
and clutched at an old comrade from the hotel union:
"Tell me, Al, tell me, is this *it?*"

But this was, of course, not *it*. The sit-down strikes
defied all the laws of property. Still theirs was only a
fundamental and unconscious challenge. In all matters
of the conscious and the superficial, they were fully aware
of what was theirs and what was the company's. Detroit's
Woolworth strikers sang: "Barbara Hutton's got the
dough, *parlez-vous*/ Where she gets it, sure we know,
parlez-vous." But they faithfully fed the canaries at Miss
Hutton's birdseed counter; and, whenever they needed an
item from the stock, they were careful to leave a dime in
exchange.[28]

Kempton's somewhat tongue-in-cheek point about the
Woolworth workers and the canaries belonging to Barbara
Hutton, the socialite heiress to the Woolworth fortune,
should not be dismissed lightly. In a perceptive essay on
the history of American violence, Professor Richard Hofstadter makes essentially the same observation. Looking
back over the Memorial Day incident, and over the history
of violence in the labor movement generally, Hofstadter
concludes:

No one has ever attempted to take a full toll of the
casualties arising out of industrial violence, nor has anyone

[28] Kempton, *Part of Our Time*, pp. 287–289.

made a close comparative study of violence in American labor disputes and that in other industrial countries. However, I believe no student of labor history is likely to quarrel with the judgment of Philip Taft and Philip Ross: "The United States has had the bloodiest and most violent labor history of any industrial nation in the world." Taft and Ross have identified over 160 instances in which state and federal troops have intervened in labor disputes, and have recorded over 700 deaths and several thousands of serious injuries in labor disputes, but one can only underline their warning that this incomplete tally "grossly understates the casualties." The rate of industrial violence in America is striking in light of the fact that no major American labor organization has ever advocated violence as a policy, that extremely militant class-conflict philosophies have not prevailed here, and that the percentage of the American labor force organized in unions has always been (and is even now) lower than in most advanced industrial countries. With a minimum of ideologically motivated class conflict, the United States has somehow had a maximum of industrial violence. And no doubt the answer to this must be sought more in the ethos of American capitalists than in that of the workers.[29]

[29] Hofstadter, "Reflections on Violence in the United States," in *American Violence*, pp. 19–20. Introduction copyright © 1970 by Richard Hofstadter. Reprinted by permission.

SUGGESTED READINGS

Burns, James MacGregor. *Roosevelt: The Lion and the Fox*. Harcourt Brace Jovanovich, Harvest Books.

Freidel, Frank, ed. *The New Deal and the American People*. Prentice-Hall, Spectrum Books.

Hofstadter, Richard, and Wallace, Michael, eds. *American Violence: A Documentary History*. Random House, Vintage Books.

Leuchtenburg, William E. *Franklin D. Roosevelt and the New Deal, 1932–1940*. Harper & Row, Torchbooks.

Perkins, Dexter. *The New Age of Franklin Roosevelt: 1932–1945*. University of Chicago Press.

Rauch, Basil. *The History of the New Deal, 1933–1938*. G. P. Putnam's Sons, Capricorn Books.

Rozwenc, Edwin C. *The New Deal: Revolution or Evolution?* D. C. Heath.

CHAPTER SIX

THE LEGACY OF FDR

AND THE NEW DEAL

On September 1, 1939, Adolph Hitler's Germany invaded neighboring Poland and thus broke an armistice that had encompassed two decades, the 1920's and 1930's. Two days later and exactly ten years to the day after the prosperity of the 1920's had reached its peak in the stock market, Britain and France declared war on Germany. When World War II began, the Great Depression, the New Deal, and an era in American history came to an end.

The New Deal has been analyzed and debated by historians with many different points of view since the 1930's, and it will continue to be analyzed and debated in the years to come. On a subject so complex, the "last word" will never be written. Working with much the same set of facts, but with sharply different sets of assumptions, perspectives, and commitments, new generations of historians will reach new conclusions about the purposes, methods, and accomplishments of the New Deal. At the present time, however, it is possible to identify three broad clusters of opinion among professional historians; these clusters of opinion may be described as radical, conservative, and liberal.

The radical, conservative, and liberal interpretations of FDR and the New Deal may be characterized in the following way. Radically oriented historians and other commentators argue that the New Deal did not go nearly far enough: namely, that the New Deal did nothing to

The portrait of Franklin Delano Roosevelt, opposite, was made in 1932, before he assumed the office that he was to hold until his death in 1945.

279

A cartoonist's view of FDR's fiscal philosophy.

eliminate the basic social and economic inequities and indeed reinforced and perpetuated them; that the most powerful and least responsible of our social institutions were not forced to serve the needs of the whole society; that at the very least highly public industries like banking, transportation, and public power ought to have been made national property; and that FDR, though simulating a humanitarian approach, was all too willing to perpetrate great injustices or cruelties whenever he thought that traditional political tactics required that a man, a group, or even a whole people be thrown to the wolves.

On the other hand, conservative historians and observers argue that the New Deal went too far: namely, that FDR extended the federal government far too deeply into the private sector, depriving men of the basic natural freedoms to keep and control what was theirs; that he plunged the nation into a condition of financial debt from which it is unlikely ever to recover and did so in order to purchase the gratitude of essentially noncontributing, weak, or unhealthy members of society; that FDR was a demogogue in the classic mold who appealed eagerly to the masses in order to wrest power and wealth from those who had accumulated it, and that he usurped power from the wealthy and talented in order to create a vast dead-handed federal bureaucracy whose ultimate goal was to make over American society into something like the Soviet collectivist state.

The liberal position occupies the remaining territory. In general, liberal historians agree that Roosevelt and the New Deal did approximately the right thing, given the American political tradition and the American social realities: namely, that both FDR and his New Deal successfully brought the nation through one of its most severe crises without harmful change or permanent damage to democratic principles or to the basic individual freedoms; that the New Deal's orderly and pragmatic reforms left the American system healthier, fairer, and more stable than it had ever been before; and that Roosevelt, though operating in the devious or even corrupt atmosphere in which power must necessarily move, was nonetheless essentially motivated by a desire to improve the quality of American life and by a deeply humanitarian vision of and commitment to the well-being of all the nation's people.

Not Far Enough

Radical critics failed to perceive anything *new* in the New Deal; furthermore, they deeply distrusted FDR as a man and deplored the widely held notion that FDR was a great liberal and humanitarian. In the forties, Dwight MacDonald was the publisher and editor of a little radical magazine called *Politics*. In a *Politics* editorial of 1945, MacDonald quoted a letter from a navy ensign mourning FDR's death; in this letter, the ensign spoke of his "deep and terrifying distress" and warned that society, without FDR, would now be "without a soul, without a leader, without life." Commenting on this letter, MacDonald wrote:

> In its sentimentality and its panicky Leader-worship, the Ensign's letter is a naive expression of the liberal reaction to Roosevelt's death. For Roosevelt had become the Father

A mourner plays a final farewell as FDR's funeral train leaves
Warm Springs, Georgia.

especially of the left-of-center section of American society.
This was an unhealthy state of affairs, both politically and
psychologically, and would have been objectionable even
had Roosevelt been a far wiser and more benevolent Father
than he was. Rebellion against paternal authority is the
road to maturity for society as for the individual; in this
sense, while one naturally is sorry to see anyone die, one
must regard Roosevelt's death as a gain. Perhaps the
American labor movement will now grow up—though the
removal of Father by sudden death seems a little too easy
a solution.

The "New Deal" ended in 1937, when three great
turning points occurred: (1) the defeat of the "Little
Steel" strike when the CIO foolishly relied on Roosevelt's
support—and didn't get it—against the terrorism of the
steel companies, a defeat which crippled the union
movement until the outbreak of war caused a labor
shortage; (2) the severe depression which began that fall
and lasted until the war refloated the American economy,
a depression which came about when Roosevelt, yielding
to right-wing pressure, drastically cut down Government
spending earlier in the year; (3) Roosevelt's "Quarantine
the Aggressor" speech a few weeks after the first stock

market break, in which he announced a pro-war, interventionist policy. After 1937, with the exception of the Wages & Hours Act the following year, no more social legislation was enacted. Maneuvering the country into the war (which was, of course, essential for America's national interests under a capitalist system), preparing for war and then fighting the war—these made up the content of Roosevelt's policies in the last eight years of his life. By the time he died, he had emerged as the Commander-in-Chief, the implacable executioner of the Enemy peoples . . . the originator of the appalling "unconditional surrender" policy, which he forced on the reluctant Churchill at Casablanca. He is often compared to Lincoln and Wilson, but there was in him little of that humanity which the former, for all his unscrupulous politicking, often showed, or of the genuine liberal idealism of the latter. In the last few years, he had even grown cynically weary of the pretense of humane and progressive aims, declaring the New Deal was dead, and the Atlantic Charter not to be taken seriously.

Yet when he died, he was mourned as a great humanitarian and the Father of the common people. The myth was still intact. By this, we may measure the deterioration of our politics in the last two generations.[1]

Although not considering himself a "radical" like Mac-Donald, Rexford Guy Tugwell—a member of the early New Deal "Brain Trust" and a close friend and biographer of FDR—is not satisfied that the New Deal really amounted to much, at least in comparison to what might have been done.

While those summer months [of 1932] were passing, we had not fully realized how sharp a bend in history was being rounded. It can be seen now that old wrongs had broken through the concealment of the then establishment, that old mistakes and neglects were demanding their

[1] Dwight MacDonald, *Memoirs of a Revolutionist* (New York: Farrar, Straus and Cudahy, 1957), pp. 286–287. Copyright 1957 by Dwight MacDonald. Reprinted by permission of the author.

consequences, and that the victims of a careless competitive system had reached the full stretch of their tolerance. We talked about this tension. At some moments I thought Roosevelt saw how radical a reconstruction was called for; at others I guessed that he would temporize as the transition was made. I was right in this last. The New Deal was a mild medicine.

In his place another leader, say Bob La Follette or Floyd Olson, might have attempted more than would have been accepted. Being one of this breed, I was always urging more than the elders would swallow. I think now that I was too impetuous. I also think, however, that Roosevelt erred too—on the minimal side. He could have emerged from the orthodox progressive chrysalis and led us into a new world. He chose rather rickety repairs for an old one.

I really believe myself to have been proved right in wanting to reach our known potential more quickly; but that was his responsibility. What he did is still not being assessed at its worth in comparison with what might have been done, because what he did seemed so startling to those who were used to looking backward. He seems heroic to those who measure him by his predecessor, but that is because they cannot accept his amazing resemblance to Hoover—under a contrasting mask. They do not realize that both saw the same light and both followed it. Hoover had wanted—and had said clearly enough that he wanted—nearly all the changes now brought under the New Deal label. Some of them he was unable to achieve because he was obstructed by the Democrats who came into control of the Congress at the mid-term elections in 1930 and behaved in dog-in-the-manger fashion. Others his Republican traditionalist colleagues would not countenance. So not much was done; he was marked for exile, and Roosevelt could carry on. But it *was* a carrying on, not a reconstruction.

If now an observer brings himself to look beyond the year of action and through the haze of hope that so fortunately hid the facts of failure, he must see that the Roosevelt measures were really pitiful patches on agencies he ought to have abandoned forthwith when leadership

was conferred on him in such unstinted measure. I thought
then he could have, and I now think he could have. The
full tragedy of his turning away was measured in later
troubles. Unless I am mistaken, painful reorganizations
are still to be gone through. The compulsion this time is
not cold and hunger; it is a rising revolution of technology,
which demands even more insistently the institutions of
great management. Those institutions ought to have been
perfected in thirty years of experience, instead of being
smothered in the tangles of a system more accurately
called a nonsystem. . . .

The verdict of my own generation, and pretty generally
the verdict of the generations since, is that Roosevelt rose
to the demands of 1932. It seems still to be accepted,
moreover, that he did so magnificently. I grant the
magnificence, because that implies style, *élan*, assurance,
all that sort of thing. I do not grant now, and I did not
then, that this implies adequacy, prescience, all *that* sort
of thing. It had glamour but not substance. It was not
enough.

It is quite clear, in the train of events, that he had
purposes beyond those he disclosed in the campaign and
in communications with the Democratic elders. Certainly
he meant to give the nation a system of security for all;
he meant also to establish an organization for international
government. These were not even mentioned (in public;
they were discussed privately), and this, as will be seen,
seemed to me mistaken. When the party elders took him
for their candidate, there was an understanding. He kept
within their terms of reference. After he became President
he went further, or tried to, but then *he* was frustrated,
and that, I think, was because his campaign had been so
muted at their insistence.

A public that could not be asked to approve Social
Security or an organization for keeping the peace could
not be expected to accept economic discipline and the
substitution of duty for privilege. A later President would
tell Americans that they must ask not what the country
could do for them but what they could do for the country.
Roosevelt told them nothing so impolitic. He kept saying

the country ought to do more for them—make business
better, provide more benefits—but there was no call to
men's creative impulses or to their resources of courage. . . .

Perhaps it was not the time for such urgings; men were
licked, beaten down by a monstrous enemy they could
neither see nor hear. The depression was like Poe's
contracting room. Roosevelt the President was a giant
who hunched his shoulders and pushed the walls outward
again or at least held them motionless. It seemed as much
as any man could do. But he did move; he blocked the
machinery of contraction by assuring men's incomes,
opening sources of credit, conferring rights to bargain,
and so on. The power in men to escape, to break down
walls and build new systems of collective living, had not
been appealed to; and when it was all over, the
establishment was more solidly planted than ever. Its
functions had not been nationalized nor had its elite been
disciplined.[2]

Going Too Far

Conservative critics have failed to see any historical precedents for much of the New Deal legislation. To them,
the New Deal represented a dangerous revolution, and
FDR was its demagogic leader. When the Philadelphia
businessman J. Brooks B. Parker died in 1951, his will
was found to contain a grant of $25,000 for an appraisal
of "the Roosevelt influence . . . before it is too late."
Selected to write this appraisal was Edgar Eugene Robinson, a professor of American history at Stanford University. Robinson's book, *The Roosevelt Leadership,* is
critical both of Roosevelt's methods and of the end-results
of his policies.

In using the methods of the demagogue, Franklin
Roosevelt was doing nothing new. In that sense, his
revolutionary procedures were closely akin to those of a
long line of American radicals. But *his* revolution consisted

[2] Rexford Guy Tugwell, *The Brains Trust* (New York: Viking
Press, 1968), pp. xxi–xxiv. Copyright © 1968 by Rexford Guy Tugwell. Reprinted by permission of the Viking Press, Inc.

in making over the government itself: first, in a tremendous concentration of power in the Executive; second, in building up a vast system of bureaucratic control of private business; and third, by destroying the idea that much could be achieved for the people, by the government as umpire, through a careful adjustment of conflicting economic interests.

It is not possible to get at the heart of the Roosevelt revolution by confining attention to Mr. Roosevelt's wide support by masses of the population. The revolution consisted, rather, in a complete shift of the American view of the *role* of government. Government, and particularly the Executive, was to be all-powerful. . . .

Did the nation emerge from twelve years of Roosevelt leadership economically sound? A national debt approaching three hundred billion dollars must raise a serious question. Two-thirds of this had been incurred for the war and its associated costs. But one-third was a debt incurred in carrying forward policies of relief and reform that placed reliance for the security of the nation in the individual security of the masses of men. Huge government expenditures had saved millions of people, and had won a war, but at a cost of grave concern to all citizens. Could this road lead eventually to anything but national bankruptcy?

Of less importance to national security and national economic well-being were other questions which pressed for answers. Was the Constitution unimpaired? Was the party system productive of real results in self-government? Was the individual citizen enjoying the civil freedoms that he had prior to 1933?[3]

Although not a "conservative," William S. White, a long-time Washington reporter, considers that FDR's immense impulse to do something for the people led him to bruise the feelings of Congress in such a way that lasting repercussions were inevitable.

[3] Edgar E. Robinson, *The Roosevelt Leadership* (Philadelphia: J. B. Lippincott, 1955), pp. 187, 388. Copyright © 1955 by J. B. Lippincott Company. Reprinted by permission of the publishers.

The First Hundred Days of the first Roosevelt New Deal
had seen more than an unexampled Presidential effort to
lift the nation from economic fear and actual want. . . .
A House of Representatives had actually passed major
"bills" which were, in fact, at the time of their passage
only simulated by rolled-up newspapers held aloft by the
floor leaders. There had not been time enough to consider
the issues even to the extent of having those issues put on
paper in recognizable parliamentary language and terms.
Even the Senate of the United States, the storied home
of fierce legislative independence from the White House,
had many times been bent brusquely to the will of a man
who in running a race with disaster had sometimes found
the Constitution to be altogether too slow a companion for
his purposes. . . .

In his contempt for the undoubted weaknesses and
obliquely diffused power of the Congress (which also had
undoubtedly great reserves of useful strength irreplaceable
in the American system) he had wounded the institution
itself. . . .

Roosevelt . . . had consistently treated Congress not as
a respected antagonist in an endless and lawful and
inevitable struggle between the separate and coequal
powers, but often as actually a kind of openly identified
enemy not really worthy of the dignity of office. Toward
the old ultimate symbol of popular government, the
Congress, he had fostered a vast, and on the whole an
uninformed, popular disrespect which was to have many
harmful consequences. He had a hundred times put into
the minds of his followers the implicit notion not simply
that Congress was always slow and "inefficient," as
sometimes in fact it was, but also that Congress had no
real concern for the people's needs and rights. . . .

Roosevelt, in plain truth, had beset the men of Congress
with many aggressions upon their rightful powers and
upon their rightful place and dignity. Aggression invites
counteraggression. . . . So it was that even before [FDR's]
death the forces of Congress had been slowly and
implacably marshaling for a sustained . . . counteroffensive
to recover the lost ground which the Executive had wrested

from the Legislature. He had departed from the Constitution in carrying forward his campaign, often impatiently substituting the cold imperatives of "must" for the warmer and no less effective (if slower) processes of persuasion that end in consent. Now, *they* would depart from the Constitution. He had expended the Presidential power too far; they were now going to cut it back too much. He had acted with purposes that never were evil and always were in pursuit of what he had thought to be the people's higher interests. But he had caused deep injury to Congress, and over this injury Congressional memory would linger long; and it would be resolved in Congress that it must never happen again. Not many years later, for a single illustration, Congress would overwhelmingly submit and the states would overwhelmingly ratify a Constitutional amendment forever forbidding to any President any service beyond two terms.[4]

Approximately the Right Thing

Among liberal historians, the changed role of the federal government in the economic sphere has received generally favorable description. These historians have, however, disagreed about the nature and full extent of this change. Was it an *evolutionary* change—essentially a continuation or culmination of previous historical trends? Or was it a change so deep and so mammoth that it deserves to be called a *revolutionary* one?

Professor Louis Hacker, for example, argues that a revolution was *started* by the New Deal, a revolution in which the attainment of social advances took precedence over the attainment of individual ends. Roosevelt replaced the traditional noninterfering national government with a government that imposed controls and regulations upon the free enterprisers, a government that utilized its vast powers to redistribute wealth and to create income, and

[4] William S. White, *Majesty and Mischief: A Mixed Tribute to F.D.R.* (New York: McGraw-Hill, 1961), pp. 136–143. Copyright © 1961 by William S. White. Used with permission of McGraw-Hill Book Company.

A cartoonist comments on the evolution/revolution debate.

a government that entered into business and openly competed with private corporations. Professor Hacker suggests that the point of all this governmental action—to provide for the welfare and security of the mass of individual citizens—represented a revolutionary shift of emphasis. Furthermore, according to Hacker, this revolutionary interventionist state brought into being a wholly new problem—that of a vast and complex bureaucracy whose many agencies, officers, and multitude of decision-makers operated without popular control and seemingly without responsibility to Congress or the people.

Professor Hacker also notes what seems to him to be a revolutionary change in political power: the New Deal was responsible for shifting political power away from industrialists, bankers, and larger farmers to the small businessmen, the city dwellers, and the working classes in general.

Professors Samuel Eliot Morison and Henry Steele Commager take sharp issue with those historians who interpret the Roosevelt years or the New Deal as revolutionary. Morison and Commager maintain that the New Deal was a culmination of half a century of historical development, that FDR was an instrument of popular will, not the creator or dictator of that will, and that he placed government at the service of the people, as did Jefferson, Lincoln, Theodore Roosevelt, and Woodrow Wilson.

What, then, is the significance of the New Deal in our history, and what are its permanent contributions? First, there is the physical rehabilitation of the country. For generations Americans had been laying waste their natural resources without restoring them. The New Deal attack on this problem was thoroughgoing; it involved an ambitious program of soil conservation, building dams and planting trees to prevent floods, reclaiming the grass lands of the Great Plains and millions of acres of sub-marginal lands, developing water-power resources, and inaugurating vast regional reconstruction enterprises like the TVA and the Columbia river projects. All this changed the face of the country and restored to productive use much of the national domain.

Second, the establishment of the principle that government has responsibility for the health, welfare, and security of all its citizens. The New Deal embraced social security, public health, and housing, and entered the domain of agriculture and labor, and of the arts and sciences. Verbal and ceremonial opposition persisted for the next generation, but in fact the new principle was accepted by the Republican as well as the Democratic party after 1940.

Third, three major developments in the realm of politics and government. One of these was the strengthening of the executive branch and the reassertion of presidential leadership characteristic of every period of progressivism in our history: Roosevelt made clear—as had his forceful predecessors from Jackson through Wilson—that the presidential power was pretty much what the President made it. It was ratified judicially by the reapplication of a "broad construction" to the Constitution where federal authority was involved.

Although the New Deal did more to strengthen than weaken the capitalist economy, the expansion of governmental regulation and functions meant a steady socialization of the economic life of the nation—a socialization going forward under the auspices of private enterprise as well. The immediate impulse to socialization came from practical considerations of the inability of private enterprise to undertake necessary large-scale social and economic programs; its manifestations were chiefly in the economic realm such as government development of hydroelectric power, operation of merchant marine, and partnership in banking. Equally significant was the growing government participation in business activities that came with the depression and the defense program of the late 'thirties. During the early years of the depression the Federal Government had to come to the rescue of banks, railroads, utilities and industries, and inevitably financial aid involved supervision and effective partnership. As the attempt to manage the whole economy was abandoned, regulation of particular departments of the economy became stricter. . . . War brought a vast expansion of governmental activity—the financing and operation of defense industries, construction of low-cost housing, and so forth. States, too, expanded not only their regulatory activities but their participation in economic life, setting up systems of state insurance and employment agencies, while cities took on such diverse activities as transportation, the sale of gas and electricity, the distribution of milk, and radio broadcasting.

Even more significant than the extension of democracy in the domestic realm was the maintenance of a democratic system of government and society in a world swept by confused alarms of struggle and flight. "The only sure bulwark of continuing liberty," Roosevelt had observed, "is a government strong enough to protect the interests of the people, and a people strong enough and well enough informed to maintain its sovereign control over its government." The proof that in the United States it was possible for such a government to exist and such a people to flourish was of fateful significance, and it helped restore the United States to its traditional position as "the hope of the human race." For in the 'thirties it became doubtful

FORD ARCHIVES HENRY FORD MUSEUM DEARBORN, MICHIGAN

Bombers being made on an assembly line at the Ford plant in Willow Run, Michigan, during World War II.

whether liberty or democracy could survive in the modern world, and at the end of that decade totalitarian states felt strong enough to challenge the democracies in a war for survival. It was of utmost importance to the peoples of the world that the American democracy had withstood the buffetings of depression and the vicissitudes of world affairs and emerged strong and courageous; that the American people were refreshed in their faith in the democratic order, prepared to defend it wherever it was threatened.[5]

In his book *Rendezvous with Destiny,* Professor Eric Goldman also credits the New Deal as being within the American reformist tradition. Professor Goldman notes

[5] Samuel Eliot Morison, Henry Steele Commager, and William E. Leuchtenburg, *The Growth of the American Republic* (New York: Oxford University Press, 1969), 2: 523–525. Copyright © 1930, 1937, 1942, 1950, 1962, 1969 by Oxford University Press, Inc. Reprinted by permission.

however that the New Deal attempted to cope for the first time with a general social trend that the Great Depression had finally brought into sharp focus: the loss of economic independence by a majority of citizens. With increased urbanization and mechanization, millions of Americans had come to feel that they were merely cogs in a machine —replaceable cogs. A "specter of insecurity" had been raised by the ever-increasing percentage of Americans who were dependent upon someone else for a job. The decline in numbers of independent farmers, the growing proportion of women who were either supporting themselves or who were contributing a major share of the family income, the gradually advancing average age of the population—all these contributed to a sense of personal insecurity on a national scale. That this feeling of insecurity was justified was amply demonstrated by the Great Depression. Goldman notes that the New Deal attempted to provide for greater security in the form of national *law*. In this respect, the New Deal was responding to a general shift in belief on the part of the people. Although opportunity, competition, and individual initiative were still major pillars of the American "way of life," something else had been added:

> What happened was that millions of Americans were supplementing the credo of opportunity with a demand for laws that would guarantee them greater economic security and more equality in the pursuit of economic and social status. In case—just in case—economic opportunity did not knock, they wanted to be sure that the mailman would be around with a social security check. In case— just in case—the social ladder proved too steep, they wanted laws which would guarantee that they would not be left on too humiliating a rung.[6]

On the other hand, Richard Hofstadter has questioned the extent to which the New Deal may be considered a natural outgrowth of the older reform movements. Al-

[6] Eric Goldman, *Rendezvous with Destiny* (New York: Alfred A. Knopf, 1952), p. 370.

though Hofstadter agrees that the New Deal was in certain respects similar to the populist movement of the 1890's and the progressive era that followed, he emphasizes the differences between these earlier reform movements and the New Deal:

> The New Deal was different from anything that had yet
> happened in the United States: different because its
> central problem was unlike the problems of Progressivism;
> different in its ideas and its spirit and its techniques. Many
> men who had lived through Progressivism and had thought
> of its characteristic proposals as being in the main line of
> American traditions, even as being restoratives of those
> traditions, found in the New Deal an outrageous
> departure from everything they had known and valued,
> and so could interpret it only as an effort at subversion
> or as the result of overpowering alien influences. Their
> opposition was all too often hysterical, but in their sense
> that something new had come into American political and
> economic life they were quite right.[7]

According to Hofstadter, an important difference between New Deal reformism and other reform movements was that for the first time a reform president was faced with the responsibility for curing an economic breakdown. Other reform presidents faced brief economic relapses during their administrations, but they were primarily concerned with distributing a prosperity that already existed to all social classes. Roosevelt, however, was called upon to *create* prosperity. As a result, there was a new source of political protest and political power—the millions of working-class Americans who had been desperately hurt by the breakdown. In other reform movements the goal had been to equalize economic opportunity between the monopolists, on the one hand, and small businessmen, farmers, and professional men on the other hand. The demand had traditionally been to break up privilege and provide opportunity for the men who were on the verge

[7] Richard Hofstadter, *The Age of Reform: From Bryan to F.D.R.* (New York: Random House, Vintage Books, 1955), pp. 301–302.

of financial success. It was this group that had sought equality of competition and had looked to the government only for a minimum of policing or rule-making; they didn't want the government to do anything *for* them, but merely umpire a fair competitive game. But the New Deal, and Roosevelt himself, derived their power not from people who wanted the trusts to be broken up, but rather people who needed and demanded food, jobs, and federal protection against another economic catastrophe.

Hofstadter notes the absence of a consistent *philosophy* in the New Deal; it was flexible, opportunistic, pragmatic. If one idea failed, Roosevelt was quite willing to discard it and try something else. This, according to Hofstadter, helps to account for the new and different *quality* of conservative opposition.

> Classically . . . it has been the strength of conservatives that their appeal to institutional continuities, hard facts, and the limits of possibility is better founded; while it has usually been the strength of reformers that they arouse moral sentiments, denounce injustices, and rally the indignation of the community against intolerable abuses. Such had been the alignment of arguments during the Progressive era. During the New Deal, however, it was the reformers whose appeal to the urgent practical realities was most impressive—to the farmers without markets, to the unemployed without bread or hope, to those concerned over the condition of the banks, the investment market, and the like. It was the conservatives, on the other hand, who represented the greater moral indignation and rallied themselves behind the inspirational literature of American life; and this not merely because the conservatives were now the party of the opposition, but because things were being done of such drastic novelty that they seemed to breach all the inherited rules, not merely of practicality but of morality itself.`

Professor Arthur M. Schlesinger, Jr., emphasizes the middle-of-the-road pragmatism of the New Deal. Schle-

`` Ibid., p. 315.

singer credits FDR and the New Deal with the singular achievement of introducing the United States to the twentieth century. However, this great leap forward was, according to Schlesinger, accomplished not by revolution but by democratic processes, and by long-overdue modifications of the capitalistic system. Roosevelt's own political position was "slightly to the left of center," as Schlesinger calls it. He quotes one of FDR's 1932 campaign statements which he feels comes closest to expressing whatever political or social philosophy Roosevelt might have had:

> Say that civilization is a tree which, as it grows,
> continually produces rot and dead wood. The radical says:
> "Cut it down." The conservative says: "Don't touch it."
> The liberal compromises: "Let's prune, so that we lose
> neither the old trunk nor the new branches." This campaign
> is waged to teach the country to march upon its appointed
> course, the way of change, in an orderly march, avoiding
> alike the revolution of radicalism and the revolution of
> conservatism.[9]

Schlesinger points out that FDR consistently sought out the middle ground; his approach to the problems of the thirties lay somewhere between laissez faire and a thoroughgoing socialism. According to Schlesinger, Roosevelt was not interested in broad theories but rather in the practical questions of government and finance. FDR experimented in piecemeal fashion and frequently resorted to trial and error. But, argues Schlesinger, pragmatism and practical politics were not, in Roosevelt's case, mere empty techniques:

> Without some critical vision, pragmatism could be a
> meaningless technique; the flight from ideology, a form of
> laziness; the middle way, an empty conception. For some
> politicians, such an approach meant nothing more than
> splitting the difference between extremes; the middle of

[9] Quoted in Arthur M. Schlesinger, Jr., *The Age of Roosevelt*, Vol. III: *The Politics of Upheaval* (Boston: Houghton Mifflin, 1960), pp. 648–649. Copyright 1960 by Arthur M. Schlesinger, Jr. Reprinted by permission of the author and William Heinemann, Ltd.

the road was thus determined by the clamor from each side. At times it appeared to mean little more than this to Roosevelt. But at bottom he had a guiding vision with substantive content of its own. The content was not, however, intellectual; and this was where he disappointed more precise and exacting minds around him. It was rather a human content, a sense of the fortune and happiness of people.[10]

In evaluating the New Deal, Professor Schlesinger maintains that it performed its necessary tasks well, that it brought the nation successfully through an economic and moral crisis without resort to revolutionary methods but instead worked within the framework of democratic tradition, and that its accomplishments are now accepted parts of the fabric of American political, social, and economic life.

However Roosevelt and his New Deal may be interpreted, one fact remains inescapable: the size, strength, and role of the federal government had changed. To many people it seemed that something new and good had come into their lives, and that something old and good had gone out. This mixed sense of gain and loss has a certain note of sadness in it, a note subtly reproduced in the following passage by Professor Hofstadter:

Much of America still longs for—indeed, expects again to see—a return of the older individualism and the older isolation, and grows frantic when it finds that even our conservative leaders are unable to restore such conditions. In truth we may well sympathize with the Populists and with those who have shared their need to believe that somewhere in the American past there was a golden age whose life was far better than our own. But actually to live in that world, actually to enjoy its cherished promise and its imagined innocence, is no longer within our power.[11]

[10] Ibid., pp. 651–652.
[11] Hofstadter, *Age of Reform*, p. 326.

SUGGESTED READINGS

Adler, Selig. *The Uncertain Giant: American Foreign Policy between the Wars*. Macmillan.

Goldman, Eric. *Rendezvous with Destiny: A History of Modern American Reform*. Random House, Vintage Books.

Hofstadter, Richard. *The Age of Reform: From Bryan to F.D.R*. Random House, Vintage Books.

Schlesinger, Arthur M., Jr. *The Age of Roosevelt*. Vol. 1, *The Crisis of the Old Order;* Vol. 2, *The Coming of the New Deal;* Vol. 3, *The Politics of Upheaval*. Houghton Mifflin, Sentry Editions.

Tugwell, Rexford Guy. *The Brains Trust*. Viking Press, Compass Books.

Tugwell, Rexford Guy. *The Democratic Roosevelt*. Penguin, Pelican Books.

BIBLIOGRAPHY

Chapter One

Adams, J. T. *Our Business Civilization*. New York: A. & C. Boni, 1929.

Albertson, Dean. *Roosevelt's Farmer: Claude Wickard in the New Deal*. New York: Columbia University Press, 1961.

Allen, Frederick Lewis. *The Big Change: America Transforms Herself, 1900–1950*. New York: Harper & Brothers, 1952.

Allen, Frederick Lewis. *Only Yesterday*. New York: Harper & Row, Perennial Library, 1964.

Barton, Bruce. *The Man Nobody Knows*. New York: Bobbs-Merrill, 1925.

Beard, Charles A. and Mary R. *The Rise of American Civilization*. Rev. ed. New York: Macmillan Co., 1933.

Carver, Thomas Nixon. *The Present Economic Revolution in the United States*. Boston: Little, Brown, 1925.

Chase, Stuart. *Prosperity—Fact or Myth?* New York: A. & C. Boni, 1930.

Gustin, Lawrence R. *Billy Durant: Creator of General Motors*. Grand Rapids, Mich.: Eerdmans Publishing Company, 1973.

Hicks, John D. *Republican Ascendancy: 1921–1933*. New York: Harper & Row, 1960.

Krutch, Joseph Wood. *The Modern Temper: A Study and a Confession*. New York: Harcourt, Brace & World, 1956.

Leighton, Isabel. *The Aspirin Age: 1919–1941*. New York: Simon & Schuster, 1968.

Leuchtenburg, William E. *The Perils of Prosperity: 1914–1932*. Chicago: University of Chicago Press, 1966.

Link, Arthur S. *American Epoch: A History of the United States Since the 1890's*. 3 vols. New York: Alfred A. Knopf, 1967.

Lynd, Robert S. and Helen M. *Middletown: A Study in*

American Culture. New York: Harcourt, Brace, 1929.

Morris, Lloyd. *Not So Long Ago.* New York: Random House, 1949.

Mowry, George E., ed. *The Twenties: Fords, Flappers, and Fanatics.* Englewood Cliffs, N.J.: Prentice-Hall, 1963.

Nevins, Allan, and Hill, Frank E. *Ford.* 3 vols. New York: Charles Scribner's Sons, 1963–1967. See particularly Vol. 2, *Expansion and Challenge, 1915–1933.*

Ripley, W. Z. *Main Street and Wall Street.* Boston: Little, Brown, 1927.

Robinson, Henry M. *Fantastic Interim.* New York: Harcourt, Brace, 1943.

Sprague, Jesse Rainsford. "Confessions of a Ford Dealer." *Harper's Monthly Magazine,* June 1927, pp. 26–35.

Sward, Keith. *The Legend of Henry Ford.* New York: Atheneum, 1968.

Tindall, George. "The Bubble in the Sun." *American Heritage* 16, no. 5 (August 1965). The entire issue is devoted to the 1920's.

Wilson, William H. *Coming of Age: Urban America, 1915–1945.* New York: John Wiley & Sons, 1974.

Chapter Two

Adams, Samuel Hopkins. *Incredible Era: The Life and Times of Warren Gamaliel Harding.* Boston: Houghton Mifflin, 1939.

Allen, Frederick Lewis. *Only Yesterday.* New York: Harper & Row, Perennial Library, 1964.

Bagby, Wesley. "The 'Smoke-filled Room' and the Nomination of Warren G. Harding." *Mississippi Valley Historical Review,* March 1955.

Cox, James M. *Journey Through My Years.* New York: Simon & Schuster, 1946.

Daugherty, Harry, and Dixon, Thomas. *The Inside Story of the Harding Tragedy.* New York: Churchill Co., 1932.

Goldman, Eric. *Rendezvous with Destiny.* New York: Alfred A. Knopf, 1952.

Hicks, John D. *Republican Ascendancy: 1921–1933*. New York: Harper & Row, 1960.

Hoover, Herbert. *The Memoirs of Herbert Hoover*. 3 vols. New York: Macmillan Co., 1952. See particularly Vol. 2, *The Cabinet and the Presidency, 1920–1933*.

Hutchinson, William. *Lowden of Illinois*. 2 vols. Chicago: University of Chicago Press, 1957.

Leuchtenburg, William E. *The Perils of Prosperity: 1914–1932*. Chicago. University of Chicago Press, 1966.

MacKay, Kenneth. *The Progressive Movement of 1924*. New York: Columbia University Press, 1947.

Moos, Malcolm. *The Republicans*. New York: Random House, 1956.

Murray, Robert K. *The Harding Era: Warren G. Harding and His Administration*. Minneapolis: University of Minnesota Press, 1969.

Murray, Robert K. *The Politics of Normalcy: Governmental Theory and Practice in the Harding–Coolidge Era*. New York: W. W. Norton, 1973.

Noggle, Burl. *Into the Twenties: The United States from Armistice to Normalcy*. Urbana: University of Illinois Press, 1974.

Schlesinger, Arthur M., Jr. *The Crisis of the Old Order*. Boston: Houghton Mifflin, 1956.

Schriftgiesser, Karl. *This Was Normalcy*. Boston: Little, Brown, 1948.

Sinclair, Andrew. *The Available Man: The Life Behind the Masks of Warren G. Harding*. New York: Macmillan Co., 1965.

Warren, Sidney. *The President As World Leader*. Philadelphia: J. B. Lippincott, 1967.

White, William Allen. *The Autobiography of William Allen White*. New York: Macmillan Co., 1946.

White, William Allen. *A Puritan in Babylon: The Story of Calvin Coolidge*. New York: G. P. Putnam's Sons, Capricorn Books, 1965.

Chapter Three

Allen, Frederick Lewis. *Only Yesterday*. New York: Harper & Row, Perennial Library, 1964.

Crowe, Charles, ed. *A Documentary History of American Thought.* Boston: Allyn & Bacon, 1965.

Darrow, Clarence. *The Story of My Life.* New York: Charles Scribner's Sons, 1932.

Davis, Ronald L. *Social and Cultural Life in the 1920's.* New York: Holt, Rinehart & Winston, 1972.

Debate on Prohibition. New York: The League for Public Discussion, 1925.

Goodman, Paul, and Gatell, Frank. *America in the Twenties.* New York: Holt, Rinehart & Winston, 1972.

Grebstein, Sheldon. *Monkey Trial.* Boston: Houghton Mifflin, 1960.

Hanson, Ole. *Americanism Versus Bolshevism.* New York: Doubleday, 1920.

Hicks, John D. *Republican Ascendancy: 1921–1933.* New York: Harper & Row, 1960.

Holman, Charles W. "Race Riots in Chicago." *The Outlook,* 13 August 1919.

Koenig, Louis W. *Bryan: A Political Biography of William Jennings Bryan.* New York: G. P. Putnam's Sons, 1971.

Leuchtenburg, William E. *The Perils of Prosperity: 1914–1932.* Chicago: University of Chicago Press, 1966.

Levine, Lawrence W. *Defender of the Faith: William Jennings Bryan, The Last Decade.* New York: Oxford University Press, 1968.

Link, Arthur S. *American Epoch: A History of the United States Since the 1890's.* 3 vols. New York: Alfred A. Knopf, 1967.

Lippmann, Walter. *Men of Destiny.* New York: Macmillan Co., 1927.

McBain, Howard. *Prohibition, Legal and Illegal.* New York, Macmillan Co., 1928.

McCoy, Donald. *Calvin Coolidge: The Quiet President.* New York: Macmillan Co., 1967.

Mencken, H. L. *Prejudices: Fourth Series.* New York: Alfred A. Knopf, 1924.

Mencken, H. L. *Prejudices: A Selection.* New York: Random House, Vintage Books, 1958.

Mowry, George E., ed. *The Twenties: Fords, Flappers,*

and Fanatics. Englewood Cliffs, N.J.: Prentice-Hall, 1963.

Murray, Robert K. *Red Scare: A Study in National Hysteria, 1919–1920.* New York: McGraw-Hill, 1964.

Palmer, A. Mitchell. "The Case Against the Reds." *The Forum,* February 1920.

Sinclair, Andrew. *Prohibition: The Era of Excess.* Boston: Little, Brown, Atlantic Monthly Press, 1962.

Steffens, Lincoln. *The Autobiography of Lincoln Steffens.* 2 vols. New York: Harcourt Brace Jovanovich, Harvest Books, 1968.

Sullivan, Mark. *Our Times: The United States, 1900–1925.* Vol. 6. New York: Charles Scribner's Sons, 1935.

Willing, Joseph K. "The Profession of Bootlegging." *Annals of the American Academy of Political and Social Science,* May 1926.

Chapter Four

Allen, Frederick Lewis. *Since Yesterday.* New York: Harper & Row, 1940.

Bernstein, Irving. *The Lean Years.* Boston: Houghton Mifflin, 1960.

Bird, Caroline. *The Invisible Scar.* New York: David McKay, 1965.

Congdon, Don, ed. *The Thirties: A Time to Remember.* New York: Simon & Schuster, 1962.

Conroy, Jack. *The Disinherited.* New York: Hill & Wang, 1933.

Cowley, Malcolm. "The Flight of the Bonus Army." *The New Republic* 72 (17 August 1932).

Galbraith, John Kenneth. *The Great Crash, 1929.* Boston: Houghton Mifflin, 1954.

Goldstein, Malcolm. *The Political Stage: American Drama and Theater of the Great Depression.* New York: Oxford University Press, 1974.

Greenway, John. *American Folksongs of Protest.* Philadelphia: University of Pennsylvania Press, 1953.

Hofstadter, Richard, ed. *Great Issues in American History.* Vol. 2. New York: Random House, Vintage Books, 1958.

Kennedy, Susan. *The Banking Crisis of 1933*. Lexington: University Press of Kentucky, 1973.

Leighton, George R. "And If the Revolution Comes . . .?" *Harper's Monthly Magazine* 164 (March 1932).

Mitchell, Broadus. *Depression Decade*. New York: Holt, Rinehart & Winston, 1947.

Ostvolenk, Bernhard. "The Farmer's Plight: A Far-reaching Crisis." *New York Times*, 25 September 1932.

Patterson, Robert T. *The Great Boom and Panic*. Chicago: Henry Regnery Co., 1965.

Rauch, Basil. *The History of the New Deal, 1933–1938*. New York: G. P. Putnam's Sons, 1963.

Rothbard, Murray N. *America's Great Depression*. Princeton, N.J.: Van Nostrand, 1963.

Schlesinger, Arthur M., Jr. *The Crisis of the Old Order*. Boston: Houghton Mifflin, 1957.

Shannon, David A., ed. *The Great Depression*. Englewood Cliffs, N.J.: Prentice-Hall, 1960.

Sherwood, Robert E. *Roosevelt and Hopkins*. New York: Grosset & Dunlap, 1948.

Symes, Lillian. "Blunder on the Left." *Harper's Monthly Magazine* 168 (December 1933).

Tugwell, Rexford Guy. *The Brains Trust*. New York: Viking Press, 1968.

Williams, William A. "What This Country Needs. . . ." *The New York Review of Books* 15, no. 8 (5 November 1970).

Wilson, Edmund. *The American Earthquake*. Garden City, N.Y.: Doubleday, 1958.

Chapter Five

Baruch, Bernard. *The Public Years*. New York: Holt, Rinehart & Winston, 1960.

Burns, James MacGregor. *Roosevelt: The Lion and the Fox*. New York: Harcourt, Brace & World, 1956.

Fishel, Leslie H., Jr. "The Negro in the New Deal Era." In *America's Black Past: A Reader in Afro-American History*, edited by Eric Foner. New York: Harper & Row, 1970.

Freidel, Frank, ed. *The New Deal and the American*

People. Englewood Cliffs, N.J.: Prentice-Hall, Spectrum Books, 1964.

Greer, Thomas H. *What Roosevelt Thought: The Social and Political Ideas of Franklin D. Roosevelt*. East Lansing: Michigan State University Press, 1958.

Hofstadter, Richard. *The Age of Reform: From Bryan to F. D. R.* New York: Random House, Vintage Books, 1955.

Hofstadter, Richard, ed. *Great Issues in American History*. Vol. 2. New York: Random House, Vintage Books, 1958.

Hofstadter, Richard, and Wallace, Michael, eds. *American Violence: A Documentary History*. New York: Alfred A. Knopf, 1970.

Johnson, Vance. *Heaven's Tableland: The Dust Bowl Story*. New York: Farrar, Straus & Co., 1947.

Kempton, Murray. *Part of Our Time: Some Ruins and Monuments of the Thirties*. New York: Simon & Schuster, 1955.

Moley, Raymond. *The First New Deal*. New York: Harcourt Brace Jovanovich, 1966.

Perkins, Dexter. *The New Age of Franklin Roosevelt: 1932–1945*. Chicago: University of Chicago Press, 1957.

Phillips, Cabell. *From the Crash to the Blitz, 1929–1939*. London: Macmillan & Co., 1969.

Rauch, Basil. *The History of the New Deal, 1933–1938*. New York: G. P. Putnam's Sons, 1963.

Robinson, Edgar E. *The Roosevelt Leadership*. Philadelphia: J. B. Lippincott, 1955.

Roosevelt, Franklin D. *The Public Papers and Addresses of Franklin D. Roosevelt*. 13 vols. New York: Russell & Russell, 1938–1950.

Rozwenc, Edwin C. *The New Deal: Revolution or Evolution?* Boston: D. C. Heath, 1959.

Schlesinger, Arthur M., Jr. *The Coming of the New Deal*. Boston: Houghton Mifflin, 1958.

Schlesinger, Arthur M., Jr. *The Crisis of the Old Order*. Boston: Houghton Mifflin, 1957.

Schlesinger, Arthur M., Jr. *The Politics of Upheaval*. Boston: Houghton Mifflin, 1960.

Sherwood, Robert E. *Roosevelt and Hopkins.* New York: Grosset & Dunlap, 1948.

Terkel, Studs. *Hard Times: An Oral History of the Depression.* New York: Avon Books, 1970.

Tugwell, Rexford Guy. *The Democratic Roosevelt.* Garden City, N.Y.: Doubleday, 1957.

"TVA I: Work in the Valley." *Fortune,* May 1935.

Chapter Six

Burns, James MacGregor. *Roosevelt: Soldier of Freedom.* New York: Harcourt Brace Jovanovich, 1970.

Davis, Kenneth S. *FDR: The Beckoning of Destiny, 1882–1928.* New York: G. P. Putnam's Sons, 1975.

Freidel, Frank. *Franklin D. Roosevelt: Launching the New Deal.* Boston: Little, Brown, 1973.

Goldman, Eric. *Rendezvous with Destiny.* New York: Alfred A. Knopf, 1952.

Hamby, Alonzo L. *Beyond the New Deal: Harry S. Truman and American Liberalism.* New York: Columbia University Press, 1973.

Hofstadter, Richard. *The Age of Reform: From Bryan to F. D. R.* New York: Random House, Vintage Books, 1955.

MacDonald, Dwight. *Memoirs of a Revolutionist.* New York: Farrar, Straus and Cudahy, 1957.

Morison, Samuel Eliot. *The Oxford History of the American People.* New York: Oxford University Press, 1965.

Morison, Samuel Eliot; Commager, Henry Steele; and Leuchtenburg, William E. *The Growth of the American Republic.* Vol. 2. New York: Oxford University Press, 1969.

Robinson, Edgar E. *The Roosevelt Leadership.* Philadelphia: J. B. Lippincott, 1955.

Schlesinger, Arthur M., Jr. *The Politics of Upheaval.* Boston: Houghton Mifflin, 1960.

Skotheim, Robert A. *The Historian and the Climate of Opinion.* Reading, Mass.: Addison-Wesley, 1969.

Tugwell, Rexford Guy. *The Brains Trust.* New York: Viking Press, 1968.

White, William S. *Majesty and Mischief: A Mixed Tribute to F. D. R.* New York: McGraw-Hill, 1961.

INDEX